Dear Je!

Peace and love
to you and
yours.

Blessings,

GOLDEN STATE MISADVENTURES

By: Han Vance

Golden State Misadventures:
GRIEVANCES, EPIPHANIES

In Eternal Loving Memory of:

Jeff Childers, Jeff Edens, Mark Johnson

Also by Han Vance:

"ATL Fire: New and Selected Poems," 2015
Harriette Austin Poetry Award winner

"Richt Era: 15 Years in Athens," 2016

"Silver Stone Press Presents," 2017

Table of Contents:

Act I: So, Here is Van

Act II: Shine On, You Star (The Road Trip)

Act III: Golden State Genius

Bonus Chapter (Epilogue):

Golden State Misadventures:

AN AUGUST MORNING BACK IN 2005 and I'm way out West, where a pesky fly is tormenting me, buzzing in my face: *"Wake up, wake up...wake up. WAKE UP!"*

My head throbs and as the shot widens to encompass a sunny inner city Los Angeles daytime streetscape, I realize I slept outside on a filthy junk couch left on the sidewalk.

Suddenly, I hate LA. I hate the pretentious Hollywood image lovers and half-brained actors, all of them, even my best friend in the whole wide world, David Weiss. His jeans don't fit me. So, fuck LA. Fuck Los Angeles and its petty materialist fakes.

I am real.

Around a month or so before that special morning, on a middle of nowhere mountain with double glass doors wide open to a bright blue cloudless sky and the world famous Golden State sunshine streaming in, I'm far removed from the looming divorce and my usual Atlanta urban grind. Deep sadness resonates, but I'm already of such better physical and mental health and enjoying a palpably happy vibe in the air amongst the trimmers. Even the usually too-cool-for-school growers have joined in the menial work today.

We've been trimming for days, steadily preparing pounds of green and purple high grade for the streets of San Francisco, Los Angeles and the rest of America. This definitely isn't the dude ranch work I was told I'd be doing, but I've adapted to it. It's becoming a fun summer job.

Play us another loud Dirty South rap track while we bop in our seats and eat health food snacks and whack away at these massive piles of marijuana stacked on the table. The thumping beat seems to get louder, and then I hear a whooshing, whirring sound getting louder and louder. That sound isn't in this beat. What's that sound?

An ominous black helicopter instantly materializes over the mountains. Directly facing us at this close range with the curtains and glass doors open, they can clearly see what is happening.

What am I even doing here? Jail is suddenly a distinct possibility.

3

ACT I: So, Here is Van

RASCAL TRAIN
(-Oakland/-San Francisco)

MAYBE A WEEK BEFORE THE BLACK HELICOPTER appeared atop those picturesque mountains, I was down in the Bay Area where I awoke on a plush couch in a fancy hotel in downtown Oakland. I'd just arrived at SFO the day prior, traveling economically on a holiday.

Instead of my original plan of staying for free at my old University of Georgia college roommate's house in San Jose, a cool wine rep dude I met on the plane let me crash in his suite here across the bay from San Francisco. If I'd stayed in San Jose I'd have been farther from San Francisco, where I need to be later today to meet a ride, heading way up to the top of the state to work at a dude ranch. I couldn't even afford a cheap hotel in The City last night.

Breathtaking as we drove the Bay Bridge from the San Francisco airport to Oakland last night, Fourth of July fireworks bombastically lighting the sky in celebration of American freedom.

Middle of the year, middle of the first decade of the new millennium, middle of my life straight ahead of me as I'm turning 35 end of this summer. I'm out West again looking for friends, diverting away from what I'd made a harsh reality. My good old friend Crispin Jones hooked me up with some roughneck dude ranch manual labor with folks he knows, and I fled the huge mess I'd made in Georgia for California.

I just grabbed two complimentary green apples from a wicker basket in the hotel lobby. The wine rep dude used his expense account to buy beers for us throughout the flight across the country yesterday. My old roomy drove us to the hotel, and wine dude even expensed the full bar tab for the three of us in an Oakland sports bar last night. Since I'm taking the hotel's free shuttle to the BART station, the train to San Francisco will be the first money I've had to spend since leaving Atlanta. For as broke as I'm traveling,

5

things are working out well on this trip.

I notice a picture placard of actor Tom Hanks displayed in the lobby. He worked as a bellhop here and liked to catch a surface glimpse into people's lives, which was helpful acting research.

I thank my new friend after he finishes checking out and give him a T-shirt from my lowbrow fashion label. We walk into the crisp morning breeze gusting off the Pacific and shake hands and wish each other well.

Outside, I wait alone and read Fast Company magazine while crunching an apple. Less than five minutes later the shuttle arrives, and I'm headed to The City. I love the stimulation of a city, especially an American city grand enough to be adoringly called "The City" like New York and San Francisco. I'm stimulated, and stimulation has almost equaled happiness to me for so many years.

I realize I'd be happy now if I hadn't signed for a divorce yesterday. My family is fraying and I have two sons. Next, I'm in the train station on my way to San Francisco. Let's see: How do I purchase a train pass? Different than MARTA in Atlanta, you choose your destination ahead of time. I don't have a predetermined destination other than San Francisco. Meeting someone there I don't know later today, a friend of a friend, for a ride to the work site.

Whirling winds whipping through the station give me a shiver, and I'm confused and starting to feel hung over. Behind me I hear, "You put your money right in that machine and get a pass. Here! Give me your money! I will do it for you."

He sounds so demanding. What the fuck? Oh, he's a crack head.

"No. I can do it," a young blond woman says in response to her pushy "helper."

"But you didn't do it," he says. "Stop reading the signs and put your money in! Give me the money!"

"No, I...don't need help," she says.

"You need help. Some people don't want help, but they too stupid to help they selves."

Knocking him out crosses my mind because he's being a dick and I'm funneling such personal anger, but jail would be a bad way to start a trip. "She'll be okay," I say to him while stepping in between them.

He sizes me up, stares me in the eyes as meanly as he can. I stare back and he backs down. She, meanwhile, has moved over one machine and dropped some of her money on the ground, clearly panicky.

"See, too stupid and don't listen," the crack head says. "I was mainly just trying to help, but you too damn stupid."

He slowly starts to back away, giving me tough looks between glances at the money on the ground. If he reaches for it, I may snap. He is departing, and my adrenaline surge comes back from peak, begins to decline from warrior mode, and I'm just glad nothing bad happened.

"Let me get it for you, you're okay," I say as calmly as I can.

She holds bags in both of her hands, has a big bag over one shoulder and a fresh coffee spill on her right breast highly visible on her designer white T-shirt. She's diminutive, too tiny to be my type, but she's curvy enough and shiny pretty.

"Oh, you let a white boy help you, but you too stupid for me to help," the man says. He is still slowly creeping away, and I decide to keep one eye on him until he's all the way gone to encourage him to move. He is taking an easy out and playing the race card, but the situation was clearly more about him exerting physical intimidation over her to get money from her. I recognized him as a crack smoker immediately, preying on the vulnerable to get another hit.

"Racist motherfucker!" I blurt in his general direction as a parting shot, as he further distances himself from us.

"Thank you very much," she says, her eyes sparkling in the brightest shade of blue.

"You're welcome," I say, intentionally slipping into a slight Southern drawl, trying to sound charming and light. "It's okay. Here you go. Go ahead of me and use this machine. I'm still trying to figure out how to select a destination myself."

I wonder where to get off, maybe Mission. I think that street had some hip boutiques and a bunch of good Mexican restaurants, but I haven't been to San Francisco in over a decade so I can't be sure.

She pays. I pay. We get our passes and board the same train car. I give her my seat and move to the standing area near the door. While she was fussing with all her bags, every seat had filled. She's still flustered.

I feel chivalrous because she loves me. I would've fucked that dude up for her benefit if I absolutely had to, for her to be protected, to be safe.

I need to avoid violence. I almost got into it a few times with hicks at a drunken exurban party the other night and realize I've been ready to rumble the past few days. I'm eager to jump, and that's a dangerous attitude. I've historically been smart enough to avoid fighting much, so I know I'm not myself right now. I better stop that before I hurt someone or get in trouble or get hurt. Only fight if you have to, stay out of trouble.

Speaking of trouble, those white dudes right over there look like a couple of rascals.

"Yeah, I was gone," one rascal is saying to the other. "Fuckin' totally floored, man. I knew that shit was some bomb shit 'cause Leo had tried it, and his ass couldn't fuckin' stand up, and I was fucked the fuck up too last night. It was great! I could barely stand up."

"Ha. I told ya, boyee," the other chimes.

I'm eavesdropping on two white Oakland b-boys on their way to San Francisco. One is overweight and disheveled and clearly sweating out booze. Even from a short distance, I notice that he reeks of cheap vodka or maybe malt liquor. The other one looks like an athlete of some kind, probably an ex-athlete like me. He's carrying a huge backpack and sweating slightly less. They are standing near enough to me that I don't have to strain to hear. They have on backward baseball hats - one Oakland A's and one Oakland Raiders - and, of course, thug jewelry: big chains, big watches. Both have buzzed hair. They stick out talking about drugs pretty loudly on a packed train full of business people, but no one seems to be listening besides me. I always listen.

"Gotta get some work today, but always do, no problem," says the fat one. "I never have no fuckin' problem findin' some shit ta do. We always gonna fine somethin' in The City. ... I hate to work, ha, but you do what you do. I'll go to work at a pizza place or some shit, ha Subway or some shit until I get my shit straight."

"For real," says the ex-athlete.

I can only wonder why he's still holding that big

backpack. I've put my bags down. Clearly struggling, he keeps shifting it from one position to another every couple of minutes. He's at least six-foot-three, but too skinny to comfortably carry a bag that heavy. It must have drugs inside.

And what's my lovely little lady doing? She's relaxing. That's good. I continue listening to the young thuggish rascal homeboys.

"Leo a real pussy," says the ex-athlete. "He tried to fuck me over for that girl. I was like nope, all the bitches in Oakland are mine."

"You mean Monique?" asks the other one.

"Yep, she still loves me. Straight up."

"Leo best not even be playin' that shit with you, ha. I told him, boyee. I was so fucked the fuck up last night for real, but I told him don't fuck with the ladies over there and don't fuck with Big Ray or Monique cause that use ta be his girl, and he's tha deal, fool."

"I'm the real deal, fool, for real. Ha!"

"For real. Hey, where we get off today, Ray?"

"Two stops, nah fuck, next stop, Chubs. Where's 'at pizza joint?"

"Way the fuck downtown, Big Ray. We can go this afternoon or not even go if you don't want to. I don't care."

"You don't care about shit do ya, Chubs?"

"Nah. Them A's and Raiders, I care about when them A's win, and I get pissed as hell when my Raiders always lose."

"Me too, that and the bitches. Well, the bitches, my teams and keepin' my shit flowin'...that too."

"You the deal, Big Ray."

"Me and you the real deal."

I may have played ball most of my life, but these dudes are twice as "black" as I could ever be. Oakland is probably full of white homeboys like them, like Brooklyn was when I visited, like Atlanta is.

The view of downtown Oakland from the train is a nice free throw-in. I guess it's hard to go wrong with buildings on the edge of the water. I'm sure they're trying to fix it up while urban revitalization is the hot national trend and people are fluxing toward city cores.

If things go well for this area, I wouldn't mind

living in Oakland in the future and taking the train to San Francisco regularly, but I wouldn't want to live too near that train station. I could hang out there with my buddy, and we could rob girls of their train fare, or I could get Big Ray's spare chicks and get wasted every day with him and Chubs. Sounds great. Go A's. I could love them A's.

I bet they have some nicer neighborhoods in here somewhere, I think, as the train is swooping around to show me a lot of Oakland. I wouldn't want to live in the last neighborhood we passed, which reminded me of the rougher areas of Newark or the not yet made over part of Jersey City Heights. Urban survival isn't my idea of a good time, but I adore a thriving urbanism and love places that are transforming for the better. I need to transform for the better this summer.

I look back again, and she catches me checking her out this time and smiles warmly. She's suddenly so beautiful, and I see in her eyes that she likes me and appreciated me intervening. I want her admiration too much and start to feel weak and needy. My emotions are wrecked.

As Big Ray and Chubs get off at the next stop I nod to them. They don't notice. I hope they stay out of trouble, but that seems unlikely.

Focus on yourself. Mission is in two stops. I need to sell shirts so I can eat lunch later and quell this hangover. I hope my ride to Humdoldt County wants to leave soon. This'll suck walking around with these bags.

My lady friend gets off at the next stop. Maybe I'd have given her my card if I had cards with current information or my number if I had a cell phone. Things aren't the way they were before my meltdown. No phone, no cards, I quit my job. No real money, either. That's not so bright to be traveling nearly broke. I can't be, say, buying a lady lunch with no money.

She thanked me again when she left the train and beamed at me with those eyes. I needed that, and I didn't want her to think that I was only helping her because I was attracted. She loved me but I didn't want to ruin it by her having to actually know me now. Not on this low. I'm doing me. And I'm ready for a golden San Francisco morning.

Here is my stop. ... Up the escalator, here I go. The majesty of The City...

10

Fuck. This looks like a crack slum now. I may have made a huge miscalculation by getting off here.

I try to remember how far it is to the Haight and wish I'd headed there to sell to those hippie boutiques. I don't have enough money to spare to pay for another train until I sell some shirts or stickers.

What is that little place? The Hippety-Break. A hip-hop clothing store, that's perfect. I bet they buy some shirts, and then I'll be set. In New York the shop owners would pay cash right out of the register for merchandise. Maybe I did choose the right place. Just roll along with it.

I'll sell some gear then grab a nice Mexican food lunch and call my ride. Then, I'll go to the Haight and sell more or just head straight to the safe harbor of my dear friend Cris up in the mountains and get to work, as soon as my ride is ready. That single act of chivalry may have turned the tide for me. Shifting winds keep blowing me in the right direction.

ON A MISSION
(-San Francisco)

"What up, playa?" I say to the store employee behind the counter eating a sandwich. "You the manager, by chance?"

"Nah, her name is Caprice," he answers. "She's the owner actually."

"Is she in today?"

"She won't be in until 3:00. Something I can help you with?"

"I have some products I wanted her to check out, some shirts and stickers from my company, fly-wear. It's based out of Atlanta."

"Cool, ATL. Let me see that shit then."

I open my bag and unfold the shirts, then say, "This is the only design I have with me, and I have it in red and blue. And here are the stickers I have on hand today."

"That's cool, check this out, Peter, some Atlanta shit."

"I like that, do you have triple extra large?" asks Peter from the floor of the store. They are both predictably decked out from head to toe in baggy hip-hop clothing accented with bright colors.

"No, the largest I have is XL, but it is a big XL," I say holding the shirt out so he can see that it would engulf him. He probably weighs under a hundred and fifty pounds, but he likes stupidly huge stuff, like many of the hip-hop music fans I know back home.

"I can't wear anything that small," Peter says, "but she will probably buy that shit."

"Yo, come back at 3:00 and tell her that you talked to Flip," says the counter guy. "She pays cash for shit, straight up, but only she can buy shit. All we do is sell shit."

"I'll try," I say. "Give me a card, and I'll send a catalog if I don't make it through. My name is Van. I'm just passing through on my way up north to Humboldt to work on a dude ranch."

"You gonna be smokin' real good up there, fool," says Peter to me. "That's where all the bomb shit comes from, Flip." He looks back to me, "You, um, need anything today, dude."

"I might," I say, grinning. "I gotta sell some product first."

"Come through," the counter guy says. "One phone call plus a small finder's fee. ... So come through. You obviously ain't no cop."

"I'll try. You want an apple?"

I depart and struggle to make my way with my baggage, even on the flatness of Mission. I gave away my last apple, but I need to eat something different anyway. My big suitcase is on wheels with my purple Adidas gym bag on top, but the gym bag is a bit too wide for the wheeled bag and keeps slipping off. I'm getting frustrated having to stop every ten feet to readjust.

I sell a shirt for only $5 to a big black guy trying to sell me crack on the sidewalk. He puts it on immediately. He loves it and I have trouble judging him too harshly for being a drug dealer since we're all doing what we know how to do to survive. I wish he had better options in America and think of a crack dealer named Black I knew back home in Atlanta. He does that same horrific work. Bad parenting, no father figure, hardly any education, low-paying job market, he played football until there was no ball left to play. Then he started selling hard, preying on people.

The shops aren't what I had in mind at all. They are mostly cheap tourist trap shops, and the owners aren't interested in anything hip or high end. Probably paying too high a rent and selling cheap crap. This isn't fly-wear's market sector. I'm glad to be doing fly-wear again and haven't done anything with it in a couple of years because I was too busy once I started working at Ascot Commercial Realty as a regional manager. I didn't have the time or energy left for anything creative. Instead I recreated dangerously and self-destructively.

I have good parents and an education. I bet I had every advantage over that motherfucker. Yet I'm here just like he is, hustling to eat today. My unquiet mind and soul has brought me down to a filthy street level.

I find one larger shop that has the right type of stuff for sale, and the owner makes me wait for thirty minutes while he finishes his Indian food. He sees my stuff and says he likes it then tries to haggle on the price. Shirts cost

13

more to make than he is willing to pay. He retails shirts for around $30, but he wants to rip me off. Then he asks me if I have anything with SF on it.

"Why would I have something with SF on it? I just told you this is an Atlanta-based shirt company!" I snap.

Every clothing shop on this street has that cheap tourist crap. I thank him for wasting my time, and he scolds me for doing business the wrong way. He is running the shop with his wife, and they are both at work. Do I really want to run a business like he does?

Across the street, in another at first promising store, I meet some professional motorcycle riders that like my stuff but won't wear anything smaller than double extra large. These dresses that people still wear for shirts are so outdated.

They congratulate me on the impending divorce and tell me that it is time for my big come up, saying: "That's what happened to my boy after his divorce, he came up huge."

That makes me feel better, but selling my shirts on this street isn't happening. The store buyer here is based out of San Jose I find out.

Some super poor Mexicans illegals I meet leaving the store have me follow them to talk to their cousins who try to talk me down from the ridiculously low $5 a shirt I ask of them, out of sympathy for their dire poverty. I'm temporarily poor now but five means five.

"This sucks, fuck this," I say aloud to myself when I'm alone. I have to eat something and buy a pastry and some small bananas from a little market since I can't afford a sit down Mexican lunch. I love how there are little markets everywhere in SF and NYC, much more fun than shopping in a big box grocery store. The pastry is pretty tasty and the tiny bananas are out of this world delicious.

I decide to call my ride from the next pay phone that I see, and the first phone that I find doesn't work or give me my change back, and I almost rip it in half. The sign on the phone indicates that no change is returned, but there is a number to call for refunds.

"How are you going to call if this piece of crap doesn't work and they stole your last bit of change?" I yell. "Fuck this place!"

14

I see a woman moving her children away from me. I'm embarrassed. I have anger issues, so I shouldn't be pushing myself.

Yuck. That girl has exposed facial wounds and is walking around this slum begging for money. Crack is not good.

I'm over this. My shoulders are hurting from lugging these bags around, and I'm carrying the purple bag by hand much of the time to keep it from infuriating me by falling off the suitcase.

I finally get through at the next phone I see after getting change, and he doesn't answer. I leave a message indicating that I'm in town and doing fine, but I would like to meet with him, if possible soon, to at least drop my bags, and I'm ready to leave when he is. It took a long time to find another pay phone. They're getting to be relics of the past.

I will call back again soon. I'm almost out of money, and I'm starting to worry that I may not reach my ride and be stranded.

At almost 3:00, I start walking back to The Hippety-Break. The only stores even worthy of my products haven't had their buyers in store today or have been run by idiots. A fucking SF logo on a shirt from Atlanta? He was serious, too. What a myopic fool.

Calm down, fool. I collected a bunch of business cards and can send catalogs, but this has been a bust. I could've walked around the park today instead. Nothing would have worked with me hauling so much heavy luggage. Actually, I could have checked it somewhere.

I think this little smoke shop here said to come back after 2:00. I stop to find that the owner just left, and I buy water and a candy bar from the surly shop worker. Nearly flat broke again, but I was getting dehydrated and the sugar will keep me moving. Dude better pick up his phone soon. Another pay phone, finally. My last bit of change and at least the phone works, but I get the answering machine again. My message is a little more frantic this time, and I indicate that I'm out of change so he should expect a call from a strange number and to please answer it.

I only have one phone number, and he knows he is my ride, and he isn't answering his phone...all day. This is irresponsible. Crispin Jones set me up to get a ride from

15

someone who is straight up abandoning me in this lonely outcast city, and it's getting late in the day. I fear the night.

Finally, back in The Hippety-Break: "Hey, homeboy, did Caprice make it back in yet?"

"She came in early and then left," says the same counter guy. "You sell any shit yet?"

"A little, but I'm mainly just getting cards to send brochures later."

"Straight," he says, nodding.

"Hey, is there any possible way I could use the phone for a quick local call?"

"I'm not really supposed to let you, but okay, what's the number?"

I give him the number and he dials, and my ride does not pick up, so I leave a message asking him to please call back if he gets this because I'm basically stranded.

He calls back right away. I'm so relieved. Thankfully I'm meeting him now, even though he tried to put me off for a bit. I wouldn't let him. He is heading to an art studio right up the street. That is the first truly convenient thing about today since the free shuttle. I give the shop worker a free sticker for letting me use the phone and tell him I may make it back through to get hooked up with some weed. He tells me to come back if I can.

The art studio is a fun place to look around and feels like the lap of luxury just to not be carrying bags and walking in man versus city mode. I'm so physically tired.

The artists are predominantly sculptors and there are also some neat paintings displayed, which is the art medium I enjoy most. The cute, in a plain androgynous-looking way female artist that runs the place is friendly and her stuff is pretty good: cool paintings and great business cards she made. I give her and the other artists free shirts, but she doesn't return the favor and comp me one of the shirts that advertise the place when I inquire about them. She says, "They are $17."

She seems straight and her parents live in Atlanta so I tell her, "Give me a call next time you're in ATL." Why I'd invite her to hang out with me back home is puzzling. She isn't my type, and the connection is minimal. I realize I'm just practicing since I'm in effect newly single.

16

One of the artists is from Texas, like me, and we share a few tidbits about Austin culture and Ft. Worth museums. He is the type of ultra-reserved artist who has good taste and smart opinions about everything but mainly keeps to himself in his studio feeling like a social misfit.

My ride, Rick, seems like a nice enough co-traveler. He's the typically pasty, semi-handsome and semi-fashionable - but please don't notice that I'm trying too hard - artist of The City. He's far more outgoing than the dude from Texas yet still quite reserved compared to me.

Before we can head to our jobs way up in the mountains, Rick needs to ship a sculpture to Manhattan for an art show. My thoughts cross the vast continent to the museums and galleries of NYC, and my emotions rush up toward joy.

I feel as if I'm embarking upon an exciting urban adventure.

BEFORE WE GO:
(-San Francisco)

Rick temporarily double-parked in front of the old warehouse art studio, and we are standing at either side of the car talking over the roof. His sculpture is in a huge box on top of the car and wouldn't fit in his trunk.

"That would have been perfect," I say, gesturing to an El Camino, which is driving away.

"Oh, I know," Rick says. "They wanted $75 to use it, so I passed."

We use some rope to tie the package to the vehicle, but it doesn't seem very secure.

As we get in his car I say, "We can hold the straps down until we get there. How far is it to the UPS?"

"Not far," he says. "I'm just worried about it falling off."

"Just drive slowly. It should be okay."

"Oh, I'm not going over fifteen miles an hour. People can wait."

Talking Heads is on the radio as he and I pull off alone in the art delivery mobile, and David Byrne is singing about experience. I'm enjoying this, feeling like the trip is finally unfolding.

I notice some cool posters and graffiti along the way to the shipping store. I first notice a Mao poster that I like, done up in pink. I'm having a pleasant city moment and smile, thinking that only an hour or so ago I was stranded in a not great part of town, hauling my luggage around cumbersomely and assaulting pay phones. Now I'm pondering political iconography, thinking that pink really is the color this season, listening to art rock, hanging out with artists and taking in architecture.

We drop off the package without a hitch.

Back in the car Rick says, "We can head back to my place real quick and grab my music and stuff, and I'm gonna grab a coffee real quick, and then we are out."

I'm turned down and feeling the fabled mellow California vibe. The man-versus-city streets before were the real California for many; they were the struggle.

Rick says, "I figured you may not want to do all this stuff with me, so that's why I didn't call you back. I didn't realize you were lugging those bags around hating it, dude."

"No problem. Just glad we linked up. Thanks for the ride. I can pay you something when we get there, I'm sure. I'm broke at the minute."

"No, Smoothboy took care of it. He's got you covered, Van. Actually, I'm trying to avoid somebody, and I was afraid it was him calling from those pay phones. That's why I didn't pick up, and you can't call pay phones back in this town. I'm surprised you found one that worked."

"It was a challenge. I was on a mission."

"Why were you on Mission by the way? I'm glad you were because it's next to my place. I live off Mission, but it's the wrong part of town."

"I remembered from when I was last here like twelve years ago that they had a bunch of shirt shops, so I was collecting cards from stores to send them brochures from my shirt company. Mostly way too low end."

"That must have sucked. The Mission is getting cool but...slowly."

Rick's place is similar to the residences I last visited in San Francisco: long, tall, narrow, roommate world, not in great shape. His flamboyantly gay roommate meets me briefly. Rick seems straight.

On the wall, I see a painting that Rick did and like it. We smoke hash that he made, and I'm floored by it, super stoned and can't stop coughing after the smoke from his pipe expands in my lungs. I look at the art again.

He leaves me in the room for an extended period of time while I space out on my surroundings. Very similar indeed to that one apartment where we hung several times in San Francisco in 1993. Crispin and I met with friends in boring old "Sac-Town" Sacramento that trip and used our one friend's place there as a staging area for a month, while visiting SF, Napa, Lake Tahoe and Muir Woods. We were too young to fully enjoy wine, but the vineyards were gorgeous, and Tahoe and Muir were great hikes.

When we went to The City, we basically lived out of Crispin's car for a few days and squatted with various people for a night here, a night there. By day, we wandered around soaking up the eclectic urbanity and the natural beauty of the great park. We spent at least ten nights on the town, partying under the glow of lights.

"San Francisco!" I say, hearing sounds pulse through the window. There's an offbeat exciting edge to The City. It's scenic and vibrant, so densely packed with people, places and energy. Just being here is an edge urban experience. I feel the city pulsing around me. Its architecture and the steep lay of the land creating a sensation of a dream city in the hills. Vertical San Francisco winds around curves and big hills but also somewhat contains a grid of blocks, which means distinctly unique neighborhoods. The people look so urbane and ethnic, yet so melting pot American. This is our second densest city, after New York City, all the housing right over the street. Hear it thronging through every window.

Though NYC is the undeniable world headquarters, no town impacted culture for a stretch of time as much as San Francisco did. It really mattered. Just as the Bay Area is a hub for the modern technology boom that shapes our lives now, it was once a time and a place for the pioneering beatniks and then my parents' generation: the hippies.

SF is modernity incarnate, a modern sad and lovely city, up to the minute and caught up in its past while looking to the future.

I wonder if I will move somewhere eventually? It doesn't have to be pulsing, just cool. My estranged wife would have to agree to live nearby too. I may just move to Athens to work for Ramon's bars if he will have me. I'd also like to manage my friend's band from there, SVA. I'd be back and forth between Marietta and Athens, which I've done well at before.

Maybe I'll work for a small business in Atlanta if Athens doesn't work out. My fly-wear brand could take off with a little investment behind it. I could put it all together and become a mogul.

I could crank out Mafa's business plan, and we could get grant money or investors and make his export business happen in China. Money. Businesses require venture capital and that is what I'm short of right now. I have intellectual value again...now that I'm off blow.

I'll sort things out on this trip.

I will be in my sons' lives and provide and be a role model and good father. I'll be present for them, and God will help get me through these troubling days and heal me.

Good to be off the blow, but I still can't believe I'm getting divorced...soon.

"I will be just another, maybe fifteen minutes. I had to take a shower," Rick says while peeking into the room.

I say. "I'm fine. Just daydreaming, resting up a little."

"This music okay?"

"Fine. I'm in the mood for background noise anyway, just kinda dreaming, thinking. That hash is good."

"Yes it is. I'm gonna change your background noise."

I just need to think right. Many sincere thanks, for those kind words, motocross dudes. It's big come up time. It's time for me to make my big come up. I wonder how it will unfold, this trip...and my life.

"I'm ready," Rick says a few minutes later, breaking my mogul trance. "Before we go, it'd be cool to...get something."

I say, "Well, those guys at the Hippety-Break store were saying that they could hook up."

"We have enough weed."

"I'm stoned as hell."

"But it would be cool to get some...never mind."

"Okay...what?"

"It would be cool to have some coke or something, for the drive."

"I'll go try if you have the money," I say while briefly contemplating the near future high on the freeway. Since I'd already told Rick I was broke, I don't feel cheap. All I feel is pure jones, my addiction, in my mind, in my stomach, a twinge of worry that I'm about to go back down a dark road. I thought I was already free from that crap, but the mere suggestion of using has me strongly craving.

Back in The Hippety-Break: "She come back to work?" I ask the same clerk from earlier.

"You missed her for the day," he answers.

"Fuck it. Hey, y'all still know where to find something?"

"Yeah, some bud."

"How about blow?"

"Nah, the only dude I know that even fucks with blow anymore is the dude you talked to earlier today, but he went home."

"Would you want to call him?"

21

"Okay, hold on."

He dials. "No answer. He ain't pickin' up. These dudes right down the street fuck with blow."

"Oh yeah?"

"Those dudes right up the block, always in a group."

"Crack heads?"

He just shrugs.

Conundrum. I know it's a bad idea. But I go to try to score, and I find a decent-looking guy, not dressed too shabbily. He says he's holding powder when I ask and takes me into the little Mexican restaurant next door to where we are standing on the sidewalk.

He suggests that we get a table and not look like anything is going on. To my chagrin his homeboy has followed us, obviously cracked out, bald, scary expression, eyes glazed over from smoking crack.

I should be more freaked out, but I'm desensitized from buying drugs in Atlanta.

The food is ready at the counter quickly. They begin to eat their burritos and the decent-looking guy tells me to hand him the money.

I repeat, "Are you holding?"

"Nah," he says, "right around the corner. Give me the fucking money. Baldy will stay with you. One second. I'll be right back; that's why I wanted to come in here."

"You said you were holding."

"So you'd listen. Now trust me."

"Come back!" I say a little more desperately than I try to sound.

"I will. I got you."

"I know," I say.

I have no other non-violent option besides running out, which I briefly consider. That may not go well, so I hand him the money.

I sit around the small Mexican street cafe with this guy, Baldy. He has now taken off his shirt to reveal a knife hole in his chest.

"What happened?" I ask.

He says, "The Mafia did this...fucking Italians."

He whips out a cloudy crack straight shooter, known as a stem.

"You wanna hit this?" he says.

"No, not in here," I say. "Is anything in it?

"Look in my eyes, look at my eyes, hell yeah they somethin' in it."

He is high as hell on crack and has enormous, glowing brown irises. I can see that the screen is loaded with white cocaine residue but think better of it and say, "Maybe later."

I realize that the other dude probably isn't coming back, and now I'm jonesing coke hard.

"Is he coming back?" I ask Baldy.

"Yeah," He says. "He should."

"He should?"

"Yeah."

"Is he comin' back or not?"

"Nah. I don't know."

"Fuck it. Later, man."

I get up and walk out and walk over to the crew of people he was with and ask for him, Marcus, in the blue hat. They only want to sell me crack. The money is gone. I hang near them, near the restaurant.

Then I walk away. I don't get far before the jones propels me to turn and walk back. On the way I notice the white girl with open wounds, same nasty, poor girl I saw earlier. Rock bottom.

"Someone say you the police," a chubby, black female crack head says as she approaches me.

"I'm not. I'm waiting for someone."

"You best walk away. We gotta gun. Show him, Rachey."

"I'm out," I say as I turn and walk away. Where the fuck is Rick? I see him across the street acting like he is talking on a pay phone of all things. He sees me and crosses the street.

"Sorry," I say.

"Fuck, no dice?" he asks.

"I got robbed."

"I figured you might. You okay?"

"Yeah. I tried to go back to the group he was with, they had a gun."

"Wow, but you're okay?"

"Yeah, let's just go, I guess."

"No one pulled no gun on him," says a voice behind

23

us. One of the females from the group has followed me. She is somewhat sane looking.

"You know anything?" Rick asks her. "You have anything on you?"

"Yeah," she says. "I have powder."

"On you?"

"Shhh. It's in my pocket."

We walk to the car, and she gets in with us and asks if we are cops. For whatever reason she grabs our groins.

"Let's go," she says.

"Do you have it on you?" Rick asks her.

"No, trust me," she pleads.

"Get the fuck out," Rick says. "Get out of my car."

"Okay, faggots," she says as she gets out.

We stop for coffee, but it turns out that Rick's favorite little local coffeehouse is unexpectedly closed. I'm feeling sorry that Rick lost his money and disappointed in myself for wanting to relapse.

"Sorry about everything," I say.

"Sorry you got robbed," he says.

I realize how vulnerable to addiction I still am and worry. Then I lose myself in the street culture sights knowing my San Francisco experience today is only an aspect of what this place is all about.

We go back to Rick's place again, since he'd forgotten his medical marijuana card.

"That is the last stop," he promises. "It's for our safety."

We finally depart, and I quickly lose myself again in the urban majesty. The way the buildings shimmer boldly against the water as we get to the edge makes me almost forget how stupid and reckless I have been. Almost. That was perhaps one of the lamest San Francisco "vacations" of all time, and it could have been so much worse.

"Beautiful City," I say to Rick as if it were a brand name. "You are lucky to live in such a beautiful place."

"I know," he gloats.

"Sorry again, man."

"Forget it."

And we are off up the continent toward the mountains.

DRIVE 1:
(-Highway 101/-Willits)

I'm out in the vastness of the nation.

Free from an anticipated uncomfortable high full of regret, free from the intensity of urbanity. We head up through what quickly becomes countryside north of the Bay Area on Highway 101, known in California as "The 101."

"Rick, what do you do for money besides art... anything?" I inquire.

"I have to do a few other things, but art is my main thing," he answers. "I have an art studio in Oakland where rent is cheaper - that was actually my friend's studio. That used to be mine, too, but I moved over to Oakland to save money so I could work less. I work at the baseball stadium when the Giants are in town."

"Cool. I have known, and still know, a bunch of people that work at Turner Field when it's baseball season. What do you do there?"

"I sell beer." He sounds slightly embarrassed.

"I would love to get to a game while I'm out here."

"Let me know. You should go when I'm working if you go."

"You work every home game?"

"I've been working most games."

"I wonder when they're playing the Braves."

"In a couple weeks. Atlanta's coming in pretty soon, and I'll work."

"I saw the Braves play in LA. San Fran'd be awesome."

"I also sell weed to the medicinal marijuana clubs."

"Do you get a permit for that making it perfectly legal?"

"We have an arrangement. Weed is never perfectly legal nationally, but I can do it relatively safely. It's not legal for me to drive around with a ton of weed, which I may have to do on the way back, but you won't be around for that."

"They buy the shit from Humboldt?" I half-ask.

"Oh yeah. They love the Humboldt stuff, if it's top of the line. They only buy top of the line weed."

"I'm sure. We are entering Hop-Land according to

25

that sign," I announce.

"This is a cool little town. Too bad it will be dark soon and you will not get to see the area as much as I would like you to. It's a pretty area."

"That's okay. I'll get to see it on the way out. I have to come down from the mountains at some point."

"That's true," he whispers.

Hopland is a wine town, blip on the map that you may blink and miss. They have wine tastings offered at the high school, advertised by a banner. It reminds me of Helen, Georgia or Charleston, South Carolina in that all the buildings are built on a theme, zoned that way. It's tiny, much tinier than those towns, but the same type of tourist cute, only this place is surrounded by row after row of fields of grapes.

We stop for some food in Willits. Willits, California is the home of the pregnant teen from what Rick and I can tell, and it takes forever to get burritos there from these chicks with hickeys on their necks.

I sell two shirts to three nice gay guys from San Francisco while we wait. It takes forty-five minutes total, and Rick gets increasingly pissed as the clock ticks.

After we eat, we stop by to see a friend of Rick's in the country north of there. He loves my stuff and buys four shirts and some stickers, so I pay Rick back for the burrito right away and am flush with cash.

Rick's friend, James, is "just glad to have someone to drink with." He continues, "People get lonely up here. It's not like living in a city."

We chat about my shirts and his life up here and The ATL. He is from Atlanta, and he has met Crispin a few times but knows him only as Cris. I ask if he knows of the ranch where Crispin found me work north of here, but he isn't sure what I'm talking about.

And we are back driving in the vastness of rural America, as the sun begins to set. Talking Heads is on the CD player by my request, and asking me how I got to this point in my life.

I'm blessed with two wonderful sons. I love my sons so much and love being Daddy. I want the best for them in their lives and want to come out of this current low and be a great father.

I have, or had, a smart, sophisticated and pretty wife. Even though there's been an undeniable big chill between us for years and we never communicated well, I still love my wife.

We have a nice enough home on a nice piece of land, surrounded by people that know and love us. Her father gave us the down payment on a house right as our first was about to be born, and we moved home to Marietta, where we grew up outside the Perimeter. We left the city.

Atlanta is the capital of the South and has a strong, dynamic economy, and I worked in-town, had cool friends and a good job. I dressed well. I was hip, educated, talented, a regional real estate manager with an ever-growing skill set.

Then I started to slip. I gradually got more and more addicted to cocaine until it became a really serious problem. I fell down.

Plus, hard drugs took two of my best friends over a six-month span. They were both named Wes, and I got the word about both of their deaths while I was at work in my office. I had the same frame-of-mind both times: middle of a workday, caught up in details, to-do lists and minutiae of the job. The next second you get a phone call, and your breath is taken away.

The first time I broke down openly. But the second time was worse.

I had to act like I hardly knew the guy because how many corporate executives are regularly contacted at their office and informed that a good friend has just died of an overdose or drug-related heart attack? Not very many, I suppose.

Then...that second friend, that fucking time all I could safely get away with saying at work was: "A guy from my neighborhood just died."

Try holding in the emotion of your friend's death in front of a bunch of corporate cogs that only care about pathetic career survival.

I'm a good person that got in too deep, first with drugs. Then with my judgment clouded, I had an extramarital affair. She and I would occasionally smoke marijuana joints with cocaine in them, and we stupidly got somewhat hooked on them.

27

After a few months, I stopped using drugs and broke it off with her. Right after that my wife received an anonymous call informing her that I had cheated.

Yet my wife and I still tried to work it out. Things were actually good between us, until I eventually went back to using powder some.

Then more as I finally became a full-fledged addict: paranoid, skinny, usually broke, using almost daily, addicted, lying by saying I was fine. I ruined my marriage. I fucked up. I fucked up so bad.

I wasn't partying at night on weekends so much as I worked it into my busy schedule. My pattern became this during the workweek: I would wake up, commute to work and work hard and well. Then when I got off I'd head to the trap in south Buckhead. I would use cocaine. I'd do it all at once, and I was doing this almost daily. Then I would stroll back down Peachtree Street to the train high. By the time I took the train to the bus, the high would level off some, and after a long bus ride to the park-and-ride, I'd be comparatively sober. By the time I actually got home, I'd finally be all the way down and just sad and disappointed in myself.

Each day I'd wake up and vow to stay clean, and most afternoons I'd find myself heading toward the drugs after work no matter which way I tried to turn. See, I was trapped in a bad pattern and becoming more and more of a sad addict. A fucking joke of a man is what I was, then.

I got separated from my wife for the first time and stayed with my dad. Less supervised, I used a whole lot while we were separated. I was using almost daily and losing weight and going crazy. I bottomed out and some friends helped send me away to Texas try to clean up. A friend there, another old college friend, he tried to help me out. He did what he could to help.

When I got back to Atlanta, I used in a motel room with some addicts, street people. I told her what was happening the next morning, and we got back together. She took me in to save my life.

I went back to work the following day and left work early and used and then went home and quit my job, because I realized that I couldn't even go back into the city without using.

I was clean for two months. Then I used once, and we got separated again. My addiction was running and ruining my life.

I was worn to a fizzle and moved into my mom's guest room and basically hid to stay clean, but the damage to my marriage was too great to overcome by then. I wasn't working and then suddenly became desperate to escape Georgia for a few months, urgently running from myself. So I called friends around the country for days and asked for them to find me some temporary work. Finally, Crispin did.

So, here is Van. Here I am. In northern California, on my way to work for a friend of a friend in the middle of nowhere, riding in the passenger seat with someone I trust but don't even know, through the dark night, a stranger in a strange land, crying silently to myself.

I became legally separated from my wife yesterday, and I tried to relapse on cocaine...today. I regret so much and have to get better. I must get whole during this trip.

Help me, God. I want to heal and be whole. I want to fully recover and be a better parent and man. I'm better than this. God help me.

TRIM SCENE:
(-Humboldt)

Up many mountain roads we went by car, then up a mountain Rick and I went by foot, breathing heavy in the thin air. Even at night, I could see just enough to understand that this was beautiful country. The air was clean and crisp and sharp, and I could sense a sparseness that was very dissimilar to the thick, thatched pine forests and dense swamps of my beloved South.

I suddenly felt invigorated about working in nature and seeing old friends. The ranch where I would work was near where Crispin had been staying, at one of Smoothboy's houses. We'd all get to hang out.

Last time I had seen Smoothboy in Atlanta he said, "In California, money grows on trees." I would soon find out first hand just how true this was.

Upon arrival, the news that I was a professional weed trimmer that worked for Smoothboy was only slightly disconcerting.

In the kitchen of what I quickly come to realize is just a marijuana shack, I say to Crispin: "We stopped in Willits on the way up for burritos. Met James, too. He said he knows you."

"Yeah," Crispin drawls. "He's cool. I hang with him sometimes just 'cause he's the main person I know up here that throws down huge for Georgia football games religiously. Those burritos are great."

"They took forever to make them," I say.

"I was pissed it took so long," Rick says. "It was almost an hour for a burrito! I would have made them myself faster."

"Holy Sheet" Crispin says in a bad Mexican accent, glancing back and forth at both of us. He is a white boy, but he uses many voices, loves doing impressions and is generally amusing. He looks similar to actor Paul Newman as a young man but of course not quite as pretty.

"You like Willits at all?" he asks me in his Southern accent.

"It was actually pretty cute," I say. "I sold some shirts to tourists there. And I liked James's place out in the

30

woods. I liked him. He loved my fly-wear, bought a bunch. I brought you some too, Cris."

"I didn't know you were still doing fly-wear."

"I'm bringing it back and I want to maybe do a new fashion line before too long. Funny when Rick had just told me Willits was home to the pregnant teen and then they came out of the woodwork. They were everywhere, hitchhiking and wandering around. Even the burrito girls were like sixteen and covered in hickeys."

"I noticed that. That is fucked," Cris agrees.

I say, "Most little towns in California seem to have some charm."

"I figured you'd think so, Van," Cris says. "Where else y'all stop?"

I say, "I would have wanted to stop in Hopland if we had time for wine. We made pretty good time instead."

Cris contemplates: "Hopland. I saw that place too. Maybe we will hit Napa again when you are done with this work."

"I can't believe he did not even know what he was going to be doing," Rick says to Cris while nodding to me.

"Yeah," I say. "I asked him in the car on the way up if he knew exactly what I was going to be doing for work." I chuckle a little.

"Sorry about that," Cris says. "I couldn't um, really say too much on the phone..."

"...Or he might not have come out," Rick says.

I mumble, "Nah, it's fine. It's cool, I guess. Dude, what ranch, you know?"

"Are you cool with it?" asks Cris.

"I better be, right?" I say. "What else am I going to do on this mountain? I don't see any fuckin' cowboy ranch here, dude. Do you?"

"It's not that bad. It's cool work," Rick reassures. "I just think it's funny that you had no idea until you got up here."

"It is...funny," I decide to just agree and go along with it.

I can see a look of trepidation in Crispin's clear blue eyes indicating he'd rather this conversation be over. He closes, "It wouldn't have been prudent to say too much on the phone."

31

The next morning I started, and it did turn out to be pretty cool. In fact, "trimmin'" just may be the only ranch work for me. Though I'm a Georgian by residence, I'm also at least fifth-generation Texan and a big fan of the football team from Dallas, yet I'm far from a real cowboy. This is cushy work I can easily handle.

You sit at a table in a trim shack in the woods with a bunch of other trimmers and use a pair of scissors to cut marijuana buds off of large stems after they have hung up to dry for a few days. Then you clip the leaves and bang parts off of the buds, sculpting them into tight buds that are ready to sell.

Then it is usually sold to a wholesale distributor, and he or she sells it to a more retail-level seller. It is the best weed in the world, and you can smoke as much as you want while you work, talk and listen to music. The actual labor is a bit tedious, sort of like factory work.

Like most jobs, how much you enjoy the people you trim with, who the people are, is tantamount to how much fun you will have performing the work tasks. And my fellow trimmers are pretty cool people.

I first click with a cool chick named Regina as she trims beside me for the first few days. An expert trimmer, she coaches me up on technique. She's a white homegirl and dresses like she is one of the Beastie Boys. She's planning to relocate to Santa Cruz next month and wants to attend Reggae Fest near here soon.

"I was huge into going to reggae shows in high school," I tell her.

Rick and I have continued to get along fine. He trims near but not next to me. He is also considered an expert trimmer and gives me some techniques the first couple of days, even admonishing me for being a messy trimmer. At first, I was not cleaning up the bang, the fluffy leaf that was left behind after I fine trimmed, leaving a messy workstation. He had to tell me to put the trimmed away parts in a paper bag under the table, and he will use them to make bubble hash later.

Paolo is a fashion forward soccer player. He attends Humboldt State and is bisexual. His girlfriend and fellow student, Mika, is also here on the trim scene. I hear from Crispin that they are called the nickname "Mike and

32

Mayo," behind their backs, of course. Paolo is "Mayo," meaning sperm and she "Mike," all-American cute but with tomboyish short hair that contrasts Paolo's cool, long dreads. His dreads are as exceptionally well maintained as those of a model - which his clothing and sculpted face suggests - yet he still looks the part of a weed grower.

A blue-collar American hippie I remember from Athens named Judd is here. He trims part time and seems mostly recovered from what I hear was a serious drinking problem for a few years. He dates Ashley now, Smoothboy's charming big sister. She is also here trimming.

A cute, art school brunette from The City named Debbie is here. This is her first trim scene, too. And I would like to make out with her.

Hippie is here overseeing the trimming operation for Smoothboy. Dude is so unabashedly hippie that he just goes by Hippie. Throughout the first workday, he whacks big stalks for us to trim the buds off of and keep working, keep trimming. Hippie likes good music, for a big old stinkfoot. He and I sing Pixies together and smoke way too powerful hash that hurts my lungs. I've been having trouble breathing.

It's a small house we are all in, in these huge woods, a trim shack existing for the purposes of trimming and housing the growers. The greenhouse has twice the square footage. Only one grower at a time was usually here during the grow cycle, and then the place was full of people during the trim. Once the weed had been harvested and hung to dry, or cured, the place became a trim scene.

I learn a lot from watching Regina and asking questions; she is by far the fastest trimmer. But she has "other stuff to do" and stops coming by after the first three days...days.

It drags for days. Two six-foot tables this way and one six-foot table that way and you crap in the woods and bury it. A toilet paper roll on a shovel is known as "the bathroom."

Smoothboy has gone so far as to provide us with a chef that cooks up a varied and tasty selection of meals and snacks all day and night, all 100% vegetarian, of course. Plenty to eat and too much to smoke and these kids, this crew I am trimmin' with is nice company.

We don't drink alcohol, but we party. There is hot music from a satellite radio and we drink iced coffee and soft drinks and eat and smoke all day. The chef actually serves us, so we never have to stop working. While we work, we talk in small groups or just zone out, and we listen to all sorts of good music.

I start getting fast at it by the middle of the second day. Stoned and overwhelmed, I crash out early each night while my coworkers keep trimming. Then I wake up before the rest of the crew and get started.

Generally, Hippie or Smoothboy or Ashley stocks us up so we can keep trimming. Only they and Crispin are allowed to grab the bud from upstairs in the loft. The thicker plants are easier to trim, and Ashley consistently brings them down since she is also trimming. Smoothboy seems to grab the hardest to trim, as we move from strain to strain. I overhear him tell her to bring any kind she wants down except for the Purps or the Kush. The more seasoned trimmers complain about the looser, fluffier strains, as they are so much harder to trim. They appear to have grown around ten different unique strains of marijuana.

I've taken to calling Smoothboy "Pretty." He and "Mr. Crispy," as I derogatorily call the blue-collar hipster Crispin, are too done, too huge now to have to trim much anymore. They trim when they feel like it, if they feel like it. I spend day after day trimming their pot while Cris and Smoothboy are off doing whatever they need to do. They come and go.

The almost white-haired Smoothboy makes the house light up when he's around. He's full of amped energy, all the time, and it rubs off on me. Now, he's telling me about when a mutual friend, Russ Chris, had pissed himself, in Athens, and was bragging about it. I remember that.

"And he tries to hide the wet spot from this hot girl," Smoothboy is saying.

"He was on a date and that wasted," I interject.

I think about Russ Chris. His mom eventually had to get him out of Athens. He was just nuts, and then a few years later he moved back, like me, went back to school and was normal. He was on my last recreation hoops team at school. We were the scrappy, veteran reserve guards on the squad. We were a bad team, but it was cool to play defense with him. He was good at defense, which is mostly will. Ladies man, still, he lives in East Atlanta, flips houses and I run into him on occasion. On defense, he had a strong will I remember. Defense is all about will.

I have a strong will. I need to find a way to use it to do something good. I could do something great. It's not too late to do something great. Even these off the wall guys here, these societal misfits have created a world for themselves. It's only semi-legal and all about weed, but they are doing pretty well. I could do something great. I want to do something great.

Crispin tells me he almost solely grew this stuff, and this was going to be his first real Humby payday. He had earned money trimming, doing trim scenes and catching a few tile jobs, when those came around out here, but this was what he had waited for all these months. It was huge for him. He had worked hard for this, and it was his big come up.

Crispin Jones had an unusual work history. He seemed to have done a little bit of everything and had done pretty well at most things. He was intelligent and had the traditionally strong Southern work ethic, but he could not take the critical component of being managed, and he was a dreamer, a bit of a drifter really. He was a drifter that did not drift as much as his soul wished to roam. He would feel stuck and just quit. No notice or anything, he would just be gone, sometimes after years of loyal service to an employer, often right before a promotion would have come his way. The key would just be slid under the door.

He worked at a drugstore in Athens after suddenly quitting his job at a tire factory. Some friends of his good friends owned the drugstore. When he quit and moved to Memphis, he slipped the key under the door and was gone without a word. He called me from there, saying he was moving to Roanoke. Memphis was too hot for his dog he said, and he knew it would be cooler. Then he was home briefly in Atlanta again.

His dog, Chauncey Bear, was his anchor. She was what kept him grounded. The only truly stable thing in his life over the years and the thing that kept him on a regular schedule. Cris didn't drift and roam as much as he wanted because he had her. He belonged to his dog. How could he

35

really travel and be free when it was not in the best interest of his girl, Chauncey? She was named after Chauncey Gardener, the gardener and accidental philosopher played by Peter Sellers in the movie, Being There. Cris was an accidental philosopher himself. The fact that his dog was a female only made the name cooler, typical Crispin. He had a complexity of character I'd always found amusing.

Humboldt is breathtaking country, and I felt like I was reconnecting with nature. I stared off into the sky and breathed the clean, pure air. I woke to the sun peeking over the mountain at me.

"Good morning sun," I said each morning after a well-rested night in the open air. It was lovely, and I began to have a sense of restoring health. Bucolic beauty was something that had been missing in my life, and a Southerner should never be far from trees and nature for long.

DUKES OF HUMBOLDT:
(-Humboldt)

At night, there were bodies everywhere. At least four different sleep pads were set up on the porch. I slept out there alone each night, although I would have rather cuddled with art school Debbie. In the middle of these beautiful remote mountains, I was still intoxicated by the city, interested in city girls. Cris slept outside too, cuddling with his girl, Chauncey.

Before falling asleep each night and early each morning, Cris and I caught up on our past few months. Rick and some others slept out on the porch too; it wrapped around and there was enough space for Cris and me to talk without disturbing the others.

I'd had a few great months at work, a good family life post-affair and then my bubble burst. Too much blow, too much Atlanta ego, too much stimulation and I'd made too many bad decisions. My selfishness and inability to be a good husband disgusted me, but it was good to talk about it.

One morning I said to Cris, "I don't want to be my dad." I love my father, but I need a more stable life than he's had. He is not exactly an ideal parenting role model except for the fact that he really loves his kids and is a basically good man, which does mean a lot. He gives good advice and is educated and intelligent and charming and very loving. But he has been married six times and wasn't always constant like my mother. I love my dad, and I don't want to be like him.

My sister was born in Costa Rica where we were visiting, while my dad was probably having an affair. My stepmom came on the scene after my dad had an affair with her when we lived on an island off Louisiana, while I was in junior high. Now I had done it; I had cheated. I reminded Cris of my dad's less than perfect past. For some reason I felt compelled to ask about his blood father even though he was not a father figure. The last girl Cris had dated in Atlanta claimed psychic powers, and she had taken him to see another psychic who told Cris his dad was smuggling drugs somewhere on the border.

Cris thought that sounded pretty cool. I felt sorry for Cris. His stepfather was more parental and helped raise him, but Cris never had the male role model he wanted. When he was growing up, his real dad had been unavailable. They had re-met as men but had fallen out of touch again. He has a wonderful mother, good stepfather, but he has always had such anger in him, and I wonder if it's because of his dad situation. I really know my dad.

Cris was isolated up here, maybe too isolated, but he was more in touch with himself, healthier in mind, body and spirit. He had more of a spiritual calm. I had only seen that in him once before, when he had lived in Roanoke, and I came to visit him. These mountains were great for him, and I was so happy to see him out of the heat and mostly self-made oppression, out of his box.

Each day, we were the only two awake early in the trim shack that was overflowing with folks. It was good to talk with Cris again and to think and breathe and look around and feel nature. I had been so fragmented.

Morning time was also when I got a huge head start on the other trimmers, working without distraction while they slept late. But before I did much, Cris and I would have a nice talk, before the THC carried our brains away to dreamier, less focused worlds. Then he would do what he had to do, and I would focus on my work. Cris had always been somewhat of a morning person who worked a daytime job, and the trimming suited me fine in the mornings as well.

"Did you find God up here?" I ask one morning while we watch a beautiful sunrise, after Cris finished some work in the greenhouse.

"I'm not sure," Cris replies, but I can tell he is pondering that question.

"It's so beautiful, peaceful."

"That it is, ole boy. That it is," he says as he walks off to do something else in the greenhouse.

I'm staring at the mountains as he returns, talking to himself in voices for my amusement. "I don't wanna do a hundred today, boss. You have to, boy. I don't wanna though, boss. You have to. ... I do a hundred pushups a day."

"No wonder you're looking so much better, breathing

good air, exercising, working."

One late afternoon while I'm on a break from trimming, Smoothboy and I sit on the porch and talk about Humboldt.

"The Dukes of Humboldt is my name for you Southern guys out here, you Dirty South East Coasters," I say.

"Crispin told me," he says. "That's funny. We are some good old boys, and we are harder workers than the guys up here from like Colorado and Cali. We play it safer too. We grow mainly in greenhouses, in relative moderation."

"Is it legal?" I ask.

"We all have medical marijuana cards, and it is legal, locally, for us to grow a certain number of plants in California, on our own land. The weight allowed varies from county to county - but that may be changing soon. Regardless, we may have more than is legally allowable at times."

"I'm sure."

"But we do have a legal right as recognized by the State of California to possess and grow marijuana."

"The feds disagree?"

"They mostly honor state law. The West Coast guys feel that growing weed is their birthright. Us Southern guys are small time growers with small time grow sites compared to many of the locals. We pale in comparison to the Mexican Mafia."

"Are they all the way up here, too?" I ask.

Smoothboy shakes his head and says, "More every day. They came up through San Diego and didn't stop until they reached the Emerald Triangle. The Mexicans go anywhere that means major money, I guess."

"Probably true," I say. "I was down in Tijuana and it was totally lawless. The cops would bust you for nothing and you'd have to bribe them to be let go."

"Major busts are happening here now: drugs, weapons, money. Millions worth of weed grows here every year."

"You get spooked much?"

"Nah. We keep it small. If I had to use fifty locations to keep each one small, I would. Plus there is safety in numbers. Virtually everyone in the woods of Mendocino and Humboldt Counties is at least a small time grower. Rest of the folks service the growers in one capacity or another."

"How'd you fall into this?"

"I came here to do this. To become a grower, you usually start out as a trimmer or laborer then move up to basically an indentured worker and finally you get a place of your own. The American Dream."

"So there is a potential chain of professional growth?"

"If that's what you want. Out here, it's all about making your world how you want it. Some of the trimmers are new to the place, or college students at Humboldt State University, or girls, or some combination thereof. Most of the cool growers own the land. Neighbors are actually the ultimate worst. We worry about having stupid neighbors more than the police. If your neighbors want a piece of your action, they may drop some subtle suggestion about being here first. Some neighbors that have been around the longest are like feudal lords, in their minds. They no longer even have to grow in many cases, just collect a small stipend here and there from the working masses or get work from them. Luckily, most of my neighbors are really cool and now all of them are somewhat cool."

"Does the local government ever bust people just for growing too much, Pretty?"

"CAMP is after people that grow on public land in large scale."

Californians Against Marijuana Production, or CAMP, was a collaborative effort between the federal government, which openly despised the growers, and the California state enforcement, which only wanted a level of control. Locally, anyone that was opposed was basically a hypocrite since the primary industry in the county is marijuana. All the shops out in the mountains were there to support the growers. Local enforcement did bust growers on occasion if they violated state law, but they did not seem to eagerly seek busts. Even the county commissioners ran on somewhat pro-marijuana platforms. At the entrance to each property, a combination padlock and no trespassing sign warned off any outsiders and kept authorities out. If you wanted to get busted, you left your gate unlocked or grew outside on public land. That was the local way, just

40

find some land and grow and hope the helicopters don't land, because in parks people got busted more regularly. The worries were generally less about getting busted than they were about dust mites, the generator going out, neighbors or sunshine. In fact, a lack of sun at the wrong time in the growing cycle would cause a widespread depression.

The next morning, I tell Cris I'm planning to write a novel based on my Atlanta lifestyle, when I have the time to work on it.

"I already have an outline and a name and three chapters and the concept for the art for the book cover."

"Am I in it?" he asks, sounding nervous.

"You will be reverentially mentioned in past tense, since you weren't there for the action of the story, which just took place this year. I may combine some characters and just write you in."

"What will my name be?"

"Landon Stone was what I was thinking about using."

I see in his face a sudden mood shift away from incredulousness. His mood is always shifting rapidly based on his impression of what people are saying about him. If he hated the name, he would have been pissed off and may have even thought I was making fun of him.

"Just make me cool in it," he pleads.

"You are cool."

That afternoon, Cris found out about Rick's money getting stolen while I tried to buy blow and verbally lambasted me for it. He was right. I need to take care of myself and avoid dumb shit...like blow. He seemed to be doing so much better overall. I felt better too, but after several days of overcrowded trim shack life the surrounding beauty was not enough for me. I had been on only one visit. I went to see an old chum named DJ once. Cris paid him some money he owed him, and I went along for social reasons. DJ was the coolest of cool, a ladies man that was too cool to have many friends actually, a bit of a recluse that felt above most people. I like him well enough and that was a fine visit, but now I wanted to go to town, any town... or at least to Pete's house. Somewhere. Anywhere cool.

41

Every day I kept working, working, working until my mood was this: I've become a trimming machine. I'm not on a journey or quest right now. I'm a robotic workman. I'm too damn stoned. ... This isn't exactly how I saw my escape, and that's what I'm doing here, escaping. When I was using before, I got to the point that all I could do was pray to get better. I started talking to God more because I was scared, paranoid, addicted. I'm mostly better already. I've put on some pounds and for the first time in months feel like I'm definitely going to be okay. I sort of like this bucolic isolation, this craggy mountain. I love this clean air and being in nature after spending too much time in the city and suburbs. And if I'm doing this, I'm not doing cocaine, not on this pretty little mountain. It has finally been a full month now since I've done any blow at all. I was using almost daily for a few months. Now it has been a few months since I was using regularly and a month since I've used at all. I see light at the end of the tunnel.

Stimulation. I'm bored and need more positive stimulation to keep my mind right. We should go swimming or hiking or something. I tell Crispin that I need to roll with him anywhere, and we go for a ride. This is a big adventure in Humboldt. We drive to the store, which takes an hour, and the ass that runs the place is so rude I almost punch him.

"He hates growers," Cris explains back in the car, through a smirk.

"Fuck that old fuck!" I yell. "I will stick these breath mints up his wrinkly ass. I...A. I am a trimmer, which I'm sure he hates also. And B. Fuck him. I will kick his ass and thirdly, ha, fuck C. Thirdly, all his customers are growers... stupid asshole."

He laughs and says, "Ha. Old Jim got to you. We all hate him. I won't let him say shit to me either. I am like I want to buy this, now, nothing else, keep the change, have a great day...thirdly...Fuck C! I missed you, man."

"I missed you too, Crispin."

"That entertainment enough for you?"

"I did get a charge, but it was not the...um, desired effect. Let's get high. I don't feel like working today. I'm craving positive stimulation."

Cris and I decide to tour Arcata, Eureka and

McKinleyville - the three towns of the Humboldt Bay.

We drive to Eureka and eat snacks at a health food store there. Then, over drinks at a bar overlooking the Humboldt Bay, Crispin and I discuss the area.

I say, "The crescent shape of the bay reminds me of Acapulco."

Cris tells me: "This is the second biggest bay in Cali. It's bigger than Monterrey Bay – which is Santa Cruz and Monterrey and whatnot. Eureka here is an old historic logging town. It has the most people in the county and awesome ornate Victorian houses. Arcata is maybe the coolest with Humboldt State being there. It's a younger vibe."

"What about McKinleyville?" I ask.

"More blue collar," Cris answers. "But some of the houses around there aren't that bad actually. McKinleyville is to the north; Eureka is farthest south. The airport is in Arcata. Arcata is in the middle of the county. It's also the most liberal...probably. Actually it's all pretty liberal. I like all three somewhat. I mostly like Arcata to party, but it's really nice here in Downtown Eureka like this."

"What's south of here?"

"The Lost Coast. Below here is more rugged with deadfall trees and stuff, no major roads."

"What's north of Humboldt? Oregon?"

"Oregon's a little stretch more, through Del Norte County first. It's pretty wild, pretty natural."

"Del Norte?" I ask. "Is that really it or is it North County?"

"No. 'Del Norte.' That's it."

Pretty bay, pretty day and the drinks are good and the health food store dinner from before was even better. Lots of laid-back locals in the health food store and one big stoned guy who was shopping for health food ice cream and loudly discussing playing rock music out at bars reminded me of an old friend from back home. I can go almost anywhere in America and either run into someone I know or someone who reminds me of a friend. The U.S. is more one country than it sometimes seems.

I feel the bay breeze, and then a light numbness from the booze of a second whiskey sour hits me. Emotion washes over me like a wave. It feels good. It hurts to feel

43

good. Everything hurts.

Arcata is up next on our tour, and the quaint old square charms me, as we stop the car and find parking right away. In the square's central park area, Cris and I talk about my recent drug problems. I say, "I was in San Marcos, Texas trying to rehab myself. This square reminds me of San Marcos. It's a nice little college and river town near Austin. Been there?"

"Nah..." Cris says softly. "Austin rules."

"It does. San Marcos is...it's okay."

"You were pretty bad off, I guess."

"Awful. And now it's okay. I'm going to be okay."

"I hope so, buddy," Cris says.

As we drive back to the trim shack I think to myself: I feel much healthier already. What if I had died or slipped so far into addiction that I was lost forever. I'm a father and I want to be a great one. It is a terrifying thought that I may not have made it; I was not okay. I was in a state of desperation, and I prayed my way out. God allowed me to climb out of a deep well of despair, from regular cocaine use. This trip must help me to heal. I'm going to be okay. I'm...okay. Thank God, I'm okay.

KUSH LIFE:
(-Humboldt)

The next day I'm back to my normal trim routine. As usual, Cris and I are the first ones up.

"Maybe you should cut down a little," I say to Cris as he coughs after a mammoth bong hit. "I don't want your lungs to give out on you."

"I might," he answers. "I was thinking about smoking a little less."

"A break can be good," I say, remembering how the clouds can lift.

"I was thinking about that."

"Big party night, tonight, Cris," I say, excited about going out.

"Yeah, I guess so," Cris replies unexcitedly.

"I definitely want to go to Paolo's birthday party. He says the restaurant they are having it at is really good. Gourmet Mexican, that just sounds good."

"Consuelitas. It's...really good. I went for drinks and snacks one time, and it was awesome." He sounds bored.

"Well...we should go."

"Sounds good. Why not?"

"Do you think some of the other people I know from Humboldt will be there, too? JimDawg, or Pete...or even DJ?"

"DJ doesn't hang out with anybody anymore. Thinks he's cool. He really froze everyone out after his last girlfriend got busted."

"What for?"

"Some trimmer left a gate unlocked."

"Ouch. How about Jim?"

"I'm not sure if he even knows it is going down, man."

"We should invite him. ... I want to see him."

"Dude, you can't go inviting people along to people's birthday parties. Paolo and Mika may have a set reservation."

"How could they? How would they know how many people will show up when they are just telling everyone to come?"

"But you can't invite people."

I laugh a little. "You're probably right. I just want to see my friend."

"I didn't realize. I forgot you guys were pretty good friends. I keep forgetting that until you keep bringing him up."

"Jim is cool. We used to hang out a lot, especially after almost everyone left Athens. I hung around him all the time. We were like the last two left."

"Where was I?"

"Roanoke."

"Right. He may not be there tonight, and we will absolutely not invite him, but I will make sure you get to see him. Maybe the three of us will go eat, boys' night out, after I get paid."

"That works. I was wondering when the fruits of all your hard labor since you've been out here were going to blossom."

"Speaking of work, you better get trimming. Today may be the last day to earn. I hope you have trimmed a ton." He sounds a little skeptical.

"I've done quite a bit. I have nothing to compare it to."

He thinks about that for a second then says, "other trimmers."

"About the same as them. I do more in the mornings, and they stay up later."

"I can't sleep late either, ever." Cris explains: "I started always getting up because there was daily work to do, and now I just always wake up early with the sun."

"I'm more of a morning person, too, I guess from my day job still."

"You quit or get fired from your job?"

"I had to quit, just to quit going to Atlanta and then fucking up."

"Rough. But you're okay now?"

"Yeah," I answer tersely. I'm glad he cares about me, but this daily interrogation is starting to get on my nerves almost as much as being bored is. "When can we go somewhere?"

"You want to do Portland or LA, Van? You pick."

"My sister's friend would be a cool hang, in P-Town, but let's head south."

46

"Deal. As soon as I get my money. Today, I have to go get some fuel...again. Smoothboy is picking up his girlfriend from the airport, from Austin right now. He pisses me off. I have been alone on this mountain for months, and now I can leave, and he leaves me doing all the errands."

"He is the boss."

"I hate bosses! The point of moving out here was no bosses."

"It's almost over, Crispin, for both of us. We are about to have some good times. Starting tonight, we let the good times roll."

"Whatever you say, Van. See ya!"

"What about Pete?" I ask right before he walks off too far to hear.

"What about him?" he asks, sounding perturbed.

"Will he be at this party, maybe?"

"He may be in Santa Cruz still. I want to bring you by there...tomorrow."

"Where? Santa Cruz?"

"To Pete's place up here."

"Cool." I'm still standing there, smiling at Cris.

"Well. Get trimming! You're going to need money for the rest of your trip."

Crispin seems healthier but to have lost his sense of excitement from being up here where everything is about the weed production. People here live somewhat mundane, nondescript lives that don't call attention. Cris was always a bit overly negative about life's inconveniences, but now he doesn't seem to get positively charged about anything. There's nothing culturally for him in Humboldt County, except the weed money. He needs to get out of here and have some fun.

By contrast, Smoothboy always seems excited about life. But he's rich now and travels and has a hot girlfriend coming to see him. Cris has been stationary for too long, working on the weed ranch. I'll show him a good time in LA.

Semi-stationary at the trim table later while having a latte that chef served me, I'm quietly contemplating myself again. My anger is subsiding, but my sadness resonates. I'm healing. Am I healing?

Then I get to work. It's amazing how slow I was at

47

this a few days ago. By comparison, I'm a trim machine now. The "Purps," the coveted purple weed has finally been brought down. This is nothing more than weed, super kind, dank marijuana that happens to be purple. Because it is purple, it sells for more, has higher demand. Its relative value is based on the novelty of the color, a marketing device. It is no stronger than the rest of the weed grown in Humboldt. In LA and San Francisco, the Purps is all the show-offs want, Rick tells me. The true connoisseur wants potency, high notes, aroma and taste even. But the look-how-trendy-I-am smoker, the hipster pothead, the Big City Dankster wants the Purps.

The Purps have made it to Atlanta now, too. Some black dudes that I know back home have started getting the Purps on occasion and charging $25 for $15 worth of it, enough to roll a single blunt.

The growers love purple weed because it sells. All of this weed will eventually sell, even though some of it has Chauncey Girl's hair intertwined throughout it. The pickiest of users are probably the medicinal marijuana clubs in San Francisco. Rick sells to them, and he has legitimate complaints about dog hair, too much bang, fluffiness, etc. Otherwise, this weed will sell. It is commercially viable, and Cris and Smoothboy know it, and I can sense them getting more and more excited about the impending pay. Maybe Cris is just anxious.

Before long, Smoothboy shows back up with a tall, pretty, athletic-looking blonde, his Austin girlfriend. Texas, Texas, Yee-Haw, I think. That was the cheer, when I went to a University of Texas football game in Austin, The City that spawned The Van. Austin is a great little city. Texas, Texas, Yee-Haw. I was born in Austin and retain certain Texas qualities, but would Vincent Van Treese really have become The Van without Atlanta...Athens, Marietta? No. The Van is an ATL original. I'm pure A-T-L, yet I'm a native Texan. I've been such a character.

They are some hotties, those Austin girls. She looks a bit like a Dallas Cowboys Cheerleader. Except here she wears Diesel Jeans, an art T-shirt and old-school suede Converse sneakers. She dresses hip and is sweet and fine. Smoothboy is King. Good to be king.

I've enjoyed this crew of kids I'm trimming with,

and the core group of actual trimmers were all new people to me. It'd be cool to see them outside of this trim shack. We have been working together for quite a few days now harmoniously, and we know the work is drawing to a close. I'm happy enough to be doing this, but it's hard work. I'm growing a little tired of concentrating at this, so I'm greatly relieved it will be over soon.

I'm happy today, and everyone feels the same: no bad moods. It's jovial mood trim day, with the curtains wide open and the glass doors open with California sunshine streaming in and a little mountain breeze. It's not that we were glum before, but today everyone seems full of glee.

Nothing brings down my mood, even the fact that I can't find my Rockstar hat. I know I had that hat here, because I remember someone commenting on it.

Smoothboy just announced that this will be the last day of the trim scene. Some pulsing, deep with bass, dance music is on the satellite radio, and we are all working on the weed as it melts away. We sit in a world of stem and leaf and resin and trim it down to the most perfectly sculpted little Christmas trees of buds, practically ornate in their beauty. This is an art. Sculpting buds is an art form, and I picked up how to do it. Just today have I truly learned to sculpt beautifully.

The current bright green stuff is floral smelling and has more crystals. Much of the THC potency comes from the crystal. It's so much easier to cut through than the last looser stuff.

This is the "Kush" I have heard about, the stuff that amazingly retails for twice as much. If the Kush has twice the strength of the stuff we have been smoking...that would seem impossible. I guess it's exponential. It can't be twice as strong though, can it? This stuff I'm smoking today is better than almost any weed I ever smoked back home. It's at least as strong. I haven't tried the Kush, but the Purps was no stronger a strain than the rest of this stuff, just purple and good. They say the Kush is twice the strength. I've been smoking way too much pot the past few days; that's for sure. But it does make the time go by faster while I work. I'll smoke less when the trim is done, then quit before heading home. I'm still having trouble breathing, because that hash really did in my lungs.

The satellite radio is switched from dub to the alternative college station, and the Pixies are on again, my favorite band from the late eighties/early nineties, from when I went to college as a traditional age student. No wonder I love them. Everyone, and by everyone I mean anyone that went to college and really loved something musically, something that was just then happening, during those most fun college years, a part of it stayed with them. I don't care if it was the Beach Boys, or the Beastie Boys, or the Beatles, or T-Rex, or REM, or the Pixies or Nirvana. Your youth was burnt into you. It was you, in this case positively. It was something positive to retain from growing up, the love of a band or two from college, from high school. I loved being a Pixies fan when they were cresting, having been a fan for a few years when I first saw them live in Athens, watching them grow.

I'm enjoying singing this, screaming along with Frank Black when he was still Black Francis, and my dude Hippie, again, at the top of my lungs as he and I face each other. I really like that Hippie likes the Pixies; that's cool that he isn't a jam-bands-only-idiot like many modern day so-called hippies.

Smoothboy is actually doing some trimming today. He is leading the troops while making sweet eyes with his girl. Even the chef is trimming with us today. We are working while everyone chats in small groups of two or three.

"I know you aren't supposed to do this, but I love trimming outside," chef says to me from the porch. I'm seated where only I can hear him clearly. "I'm just trimming this for fun since it's Kush."

"Turn it in for money," I say to him.

"I'm getting paid to cook, so that's okay."

I look to Smoothboy, who isn't listening, a few seats down with his girl. He's in love...lust, at least. Maybe love.

"Well, I think you should get paid if you want to trim some," I say.

"Thanks," Chef says. "The next trim scene I'm doing is all topless, so I'm looking forward to that."

"Sounds fun. Thanks for cooking and feeding me."

"You're welcome," he says, then he raises his voice, saying, "Hey, you guys, who wants ice tea?"

A few quiet yeses later, he steps in from the porch

and makes us all red zinger ice teas with fresh lemon slices. It has been beyond nice to have someone preparing food and serving us the past few days. I can't remember ever being waited on at this level. It must be bizarre to always have people serve you.

A Ramones song ends, and the Replacements are starting up. They were a good band.

What a beautiful day in California, I think, as I look out the curtains at the sun-kissed mountains.

No! A black helicopter has just appeared over the top of mountains, out of nowhere. It is hovering, looking at us.

"Smoothboy, look," I say, immediately contemplating police.

"Fuck!" He shouts as he jumps up and closes the curtains.

They are facing us, a table of about ten people, with a mound of weed on it, trimming, and they probably saw us before the curtains were closed.

I used to worry about cops when I was high on blow, and now it's like the old fear is back and more real.

My heart races. This could be what I feared most about this ranch expedition! ...And they fly off. They just disappear back over the mountain ridge.

"You see how quickly it can get uncool out here," Smoothboy immediately says to me, quickly calming down.

As I also settle down, I think to myself: Because I'm a Georgia citizen, I would not have the same protection of rights guaranteed by state as a Californian would. It's possible that I could've been arrested and extradited back to Georgia and tried there just for being here. I'm pretty sure Smoothboy and Crispin are over the maximum allowable weight regardless of how many people are here with medicinal cards, because there is a whole fuck load of weed here.

STEP UP TO THE GOLD:
(-Humboldt)

I wake up and remember: Party...Helicopter!
Scary that there was a helicopter hovering yesterday, then
end trim, then we went to the birthday party, good food:
crab enchiladas and margaritas, cute chicks even, fun
crowd. And Charlie's after party, toasts, that dude called
Cracker, Smoothboy's girl was so hot. Georgia folks, Florida
folks, dancing,

"Say It and Do It!"

I made that shit up. That dance. "Say it and do it."
Did I make that up or have I seen that somewhere? I think
I saw it before. What is the difference? Then, I did one line
of coke and was lightly spaced out. Then that Super Hottie
showed up, and...rejection...well, mild rejection, and then
we slept here. That's all I remember about last night, in that
order. And this is where exactly?

No idea what little town we are in, Eureka or Arcata?
I think this is Arcata. Smoothboy's sister's place definitely,
I vaguely remember that. Seems that no one is here except
Crispin and I.

"You up, dude?" I ask in a creaky morning voice.

"Just getting up. ... How do you feel after last night,
ole boy?" Cris asks, so chipper.

He has been cheery in the mornings; I have to give
him that. I was definitely questioning his level of overall
chipper, but he has been even more of a morning guy than
I have since I've been here.

"Did you like the party, Cris?" I ask in a told-you-so
voice.

"It was great. I thought it was great. The fun has
just started, Van. Just wait until I get paid."

I decide that Cris is way too on for me now and
remain quiet a few more minutes, feeling hung over.
I ask, "What town are we in? Arcata?"

"McKinleyville," Cris answers, sounding amused.
My sweatshirt is missing, my smooth gray and white Polo
hoodie. I have had it forever, and it is the only jacket of any
sort that I have with me, and it gets cool here every night.

"Can we go back by the restaurant? I ask. "I may

have left my hoodie there."

"Yeah," Cris answers. "I want to go by the Harley shop anyway, get some shades or a shirt or something, and I will bring you by there before we go out to Pete's."

"We're going to Pete's today, that's right." I'm excited for something different to do.

"Yeah, hopefully he has more work for you."

"Great...more work," I say in a bored sounding voice.

In a chipper voice Crispin says, "Work is good; it's good work."

"Like I said: Great."

We leave and I half-sleep until Cris stops in the Harley shop. We enter and the girls working are not too bad looking, so I strike up a conversation with one named Lisa while trying on shades. I buy a pair with clear lenses and bondage studs circling the black frames for $12.

"These are suggestive," I say to her.

"Totally. Sexy and shatterproof," Lisa says.

"That will be good for skating," I joke.

"Something told me you didn't ride, cutie."

"Do you ride?" I ask her.

"Oh, I like to ride."

"What kind of motorcycles, Harley?"

"I didn't say a thing about motorcycles."

"But you like to ride."

"I love it. You aren't a local are you?"

"Just visiting from Atlanta. How about you?"

"I just moved back here from San Francisco. I was doing my art in The City: I paint. But I had a bad boyfriend situation, so I felt like coming back home for a bit. Calm here."

"Calm can be good. I'll be heading to The Bay soon, LA too, just traveling a bit." I'm trying to sound like cool surrounds me.

"Sounds good." She may be buying cool.

"Sorry about your boyfriend thing. ... I just signed for a divorce."

"I'm sorry, too. You're going to be okay I'm sure."

"I know. Say, can I call you when I get back from LA?"

"Sure. I'd love to hang out with you. Here is the shop

card and number, and I will write my home number on the back."

When we leave, Crispin says, "You still got it."
I'm pleasantly surprised I got her number. I've been with the same woman for ten years, with the exception of the affair.

"I guess," I say. "This all just seems strange."

"You just need some strange...like me."

"Maybe so. What did you think of her? She had a few small acne scars, a little rough around the edges."

"For Humboldt, she's fucking hot. Big tits, you love that, and she wasn't unattractive."

"I may call her. I may have just been practicing."

"For what? You will call her."

"Getting divorced is weird and sad."

"I know, man. In a way, it's perfect. You're going to see your kids."

"That's what matters most, but being divorced ain't perfect."

"But it is in a way, Van."

My hoodie is gone permanently, I guess. The restaurant doesn't have it, and I don't think it made it to the after party.

When I get back in the car from the restaurant, Crispin tells me we are heading back to the Harley shop. He has broken his $200 shades while I was inside. He fumes the whole way there, calling Lisa an ugly bitch for selling him these stupid shades that broke. It's pathetic.

I tell him they will replace them, and he says, "They should but they probably won't so stop saying that."

He walks inside and they do replace them. He had not purchased the adjustable model, yet he was adjusting them as if he had, based on the brochure. He had one model in his hand and a picture of another in a brochure in the other and was trying to take the padding out as illustrated in the picture and snapped them. I didn't even go in the store.

They gave him the adjustable model this time. Lisa made sure he was taken care of, even though it was pure negligence on his part.

Back in the car together he tells me, "Lisa is pretty hot after all." We have a laugh about the whole thing and are off to Pete's. Shit like that always happens to Crispin, and sometimes it's really annoying, but usually it's just something to laugh about and move on. It happens too regularly for me to get very worked up about it with him.

Cris stops by a friend of Pete's house to pick up a large vacuum cleaner for Pete. Pete's friend meets us in the drive, and I suddenly feel really sick and spit up a little nasty bile on the side of his driveway. I'm embarrassed, but my stomach is relieved.

"So sorry about that," I say.

"He gets motion sickness, and we got hammered last night," Cris explains to the guy.

I feel much better and go inside and meet the blonde live-in girlfriend. I'm attracted to her and wonder why. I'm always horny for some odd reason when I'm hungover - it's incongruous.

We leave their place without further incident and continue our roll around the three little towns of the bay. This is home for Cris now, and he runs a few more errands, buys a few things.

The Humboldt Bay itself is lovely from the car, shining in a crescent under the sun. The sight of the ocean always pleases me, and these are cute enough little towns. Considering the nature element, the proximity to water and the towns, this area is kind of nice. I kind of like Humboldt, it's just way up here, too far up in these weedy mountains.

"Who all lives there again?" I ask Cris, as we finally pull up to Pete's later that day.

"Billie and this guy named Steve," he answers. "Silent Steve because he don't say shit and is a comic book geek who loves Jay and Silent Bob movies. I think Pete owns the place, but he actually lives in Santa Cruz. And Silent Steve is aka the Fall Guy because he was busted at a trim."

Billie (the Goat) and Steve are sitting on a couch together watching television in a stinky room. It smells of weed, body odor and general stale musty uncleanness, like a locker room or an apartment with too many pets and too little ventilation.

"Hey man, I haven't seen you in a long time," the notably scrawny Billie says to me in a super high-pitched nasal drawl. He talks like a prepubescent boy or gruff-voiced girl, not a man.

Only slightly more solid in build, Steve has a pleasant demeanor, mainly facial expressions. His expressions let you know he is with you.

These two lads don't seem to give much of a fuck about anything other than their hobbies. They spend their time getting high, reading comics, watching English Premiere League Soccer on satellite, eating junk food, complaining and generally disengaging. They, like the rest of the Humboldt residents that I have met, have checked out from a society they resented. They have their reasons to resent mainstream, mom and pop, apple pie suburban America. It isn't for everyone and wasn't for them; it only stupefied, suppressed and suffocated them.

Billy tells me they only leave the house if they must. Steve leaves very rarely, but the Goat has to leave daily because he owns a records and comic books store in Arcata. The Goat says, "We sell mostly vinyl 1980's punk records, reggae and beats of any kind: rap, trance, fuckin' break beat. But man I only listen to punk on vinyl and select rap. I sell anything that goes with the stoner vibe up here and lots of stuff that's obscure."

I have only a vague recollection of Steve as a familiar face from Athens, probably because he was so quiet when he was around. The Goat is not quiet...ever. He has not only a goat-like voice but a goat-like beard. He may even smell like a goat. I never knew him well in Athens, but he is definitely memorable from the times I did see him around.

It isn't really a living room where they live. The living room is sparse, unused, mostly a pass through room. They hang out perpetually in Billie's room, his bedroom. Billie had the big TV, so his room was essentially the "living" room. He did not put his TV in the traditional living room because that was common space.

I say to Billie: "I got into blow and had an affair, which were some pretty huge screw ups. I have two great kids, but I'm getting divorced after what I did. I just quit my corporate job recently, and I'm trimming out here now, before we travel. I'm trying to get my head right."

"Good," Billie says. "I ain't trimmin' shit."

"More work for me," I say. "Oh yeah. I'm planning to

56

write a book about Atlanta when I get back there. First, Cris and I will be going down to LA via San Fran to party, in a couple of days. Then we're going to drive across the country together to Atlanta."

"Wow, you guys are doing it up, for sure," Billie says. "Then what?"

"Home to look for work as quickly as I can find something cool."

He grins and says, "And you even hung out with DJ, I heard."

I reply, "Yeah, briefly. He's cool. It was good to see him."

"He is so cool, man. I used to want to be him. He had all the girls, sold drugs. I was like, 'When I grow up, I want to be him.' He had all the cool clothes and things."

"Don't forget his hair," I add.

"Yeah, man! He had awesome hair and all the ladies were always all over him."

"You know him, too, Steve?" I ask, trying to coax words from him.

"He knows him...well," Billie answers for him. "He was trimming with his last girlfriend when they both got busted."

That could happen to me, I worry, remembering the helicopter. Getting busted and shipped back to Georgia to face a harsh judge could happen. What luck that would be, to be on a little visit and get busted for trimming weed. That would suck. I didn't even ask to do this.

It probably won't happen, but I am engaging in somewhat illegal activity at best, because I have no medicinal card. At this point in my life, I want to get away from situations were I'm worrying about going to jail.

I don't want to think like I did on blow. I wasn't controlling my thoughts when I was high. I was controlled by the drug.

There were still moments of light. Not all of my ideas were bad at the time. But that was the darkest of several somewhat dark periods of my life. And I want to come into and remain in the light.

Survive another session, and I will have some money. And I have a friend to travel with, and a friend to see in LA.

I think all of this while Crispin checks out the vinyl collection and Steve reads a comic book, in silence and Billie talks and talks...

"I remember when Ruzick used to drink...when he used to fight. Do you, Cris?"

Billie is telling one of his many back-in-the-day stories. He's funny no matter what the subject of the story because his voice hits such high notes, so Southern. He gets so excited. "...And he would kick everyone's ass. Hmm. Hmm. I would act like I was invincible if he was around. He was a badass."

"Still is, just calmer," Cris states.

"He literally crushed a mean dude for messing with me once, " Billie boasts.

"Yuck," I say. "I'm glad he doesn't fight anymore."
Before long, Pete and his girlfriend, Jena, arrive. We all leave the play room and hang around the island in the kitchen drinking wine and smoking bong hits. The boys, as I think of Steve and Billie, have cokes that I brought because I will need caffeine and sugar daily to work, and we have no chef this time and are far from any stores.

Pete is the landlord of this place, and they treat him almost like a parent. Pete is positive and driven, a Type-A weed smoker. Crispin had told me Pete was an entrepreneur making money selling hydroponics grow systems all over the country now. Pete's company, Grow Star, had started to take off this year. That was Humboldt for him: making money, doing it his own way and developing a version of an American dream.

I'm stoned and dreamy. Too stoned all the time and not enjoying it, but I guess that's the point of Humboldt County: get as stoned as possible on the best weed in the world. I just wanted to get away, but this place is a big waste of my time. This is a bit too like being in college.

I notice that the boys have faded into the background. The rest of us – the grownups – share a nice bottle of wine from Napa, and I feel fine. We eat some healthy food then open another bottle. Pete and I were friends in Athens and enjoy catching up. Jena is friendly and seems interested enough in our conversations, although she doesn't say much.

The second bottle of wine is even nicer and is not too

far from local; lots of wine produced near here. Humboldt has fertile mountains and valleys. The air is fresh, hot and dry, and the weather is nice. But marijuana, as a produced good, is really what this place is known for, not so much the livability.

This area north of the wine country is similar to Napa in that it is renowned for its production. Weed is similar to wine. It's grown. It's harvested. There is a refinement process. It's an intoxicant, an expensive specialized intoxicant. The growers out here constantly try to refine it.

Although Pete still grows weed, I begin to realize his new focus is definitely his startup company that sells growing systems. We talk a lot of business; I give him business advice while Jena begins to warm up and interjects and nods and listens.

Crispin listens, tries not to listen, and grows more and more annoyed, bored, feeling not included. I may do some real consulting for Pete, help him refine his company's branding, some image work.

He says, "Here's my magazine ad for High Times and Maximum Yield. What do you think, honestly?"

"It's only okay," I reply. "I'd change it to having a slogan near the top. You have Grow Star, a good name. Add 'Step up to the gold,' to the top of it."

"Okay. I like that!"

"In the finer print, where you have the description that says you will be growing gold, that's good. A catchy marketing phrase will reinforce your sales message, which is, you will help your customers get rich, by using your product."

"Yes! I love that."

"And it says that without being too explicit. You can have that as a free consult. I could really help your business. We could workshop it up and see what all I can do to help you. I have the marketing savvy to help you grow your business the right way. That's what I was doing before this, helping people grow companies."

We babble on about his business model as his company reaches critical mass. Pete tells me his business is finally on the cusp of providing him with the financial freedom to stop growing weed commercially if he chooses.

"I may only grow my head stash real soon," he

says. "But I have much more than just a head stash in the greenhouse out back. It's full and ready to be cut down, tomorrow."

When I wake the next morning, Pete is smiling at me saying, "You were manic in your sleep last night. It was wild. I listened. You were going places, doing things."

I remember we smoked some hash...and I don't remember much else, I apparently passed out on the floor, on the rug, and they partied while I slept. The place is trashed, the kitchen. I'm disoriented and slow to reply.

"I was?" I ask.

"Yeah. I was worried at first, for a minute."

"I was so baked and out of it from trimming, traveling."

"Do you need some time to just rest?"

"No. I feel fine. I'm ready to trim. I was waking up and starting right away each day at Smoothboy's. I'm a get up and go to work type."

"Good. I have a whole greenhouse for you. I think you'll probably like greenhouse work a lot better. It's less confined; you get to move around more. It's going to be hot this afternoon though, like a hundred, so we should get a jump if you are up for it?"

"Let's work now, boss."

"I know that. What is that?"

"That's from Cool Hand Luke."

We have a quick cup of organic gourmet coffee, while he and I silently look over his yard from the back deck. Then we walk out to the greenhouse, where an entirely different type of trim scene begins. This is outdoor trimming, and the heat of the California sunshine pours down on us as I chop down hundreds of tall, beautiful green weed plants.

BIG COME UP DINNER:
(-Humboldt)

Sprawled again on the living room floor eight hours later, I feel like I've put in a day working construction. It's consistently harder to work at Weed World than I'd imagined but way better to work in the greenhouse.

Crispin has just recently returned and says to me, "I need to go by Target to get some bullshit. Anything you need there?"

I contemplate then say, "I could use a sleeping bag, or at least a blanket of some kind, a pillow, something comfortable. I need to replace my hoodie too with a light jacket of some kind."

"Are you okay on money until I get paid?" Cris asks, sounding parental.

"I guess. Pete gave me some money. I need to send Madeline money as soon as possible. When do you get paid by the way? You have not been paid for your stuff yet?"

"No. Smoothboy sells it and then pays. That's how it works."

"Let me know."

"You'll know. I'm going to help you with the money for Madeline. I'll loan that to you. You just worry about spending money for the trip."

"That is way cool of you, my brother!"

"Don't sweat it, Van. You always paid bar tabs for us in the day or bought me a slice if I was hungry. After we shop, then we can come back here and chill, crash here, and you can get back to work in the morning. Unless they are working again tonight."

"What about JimDawg? We going out with him soon?"

"Oh yeah. I almost forgot. Shit. I'm supposed to call him. It may end up being tomorrow."

A little perturbed and bored I say, "Okay. When we leaving for LA?"

Cris says: "As soon as we get paid and Pete is out of work. Are you guys trimming tonight?"

"No. Start back in the morning. I'm really enjoying the outdoor trim, but I was thinking about maybe missing the indoor trim. We should...I'm anxious to jet. I can't wait for LA."

"I know I'd never want to live in LA, but I can't wait either. Have you called Dave to tell him we're coming?"

"I left him a message, but it was kind of ambiguous since I have no idea when we're leaving Humby or how long we'll spend getting down there. Plus, he can't really call us back and actually get us on the phone with the cell reception."

"You mean the no cell reception."

"Exactly."

"He can call me back and leave a message, but I guess that wouldn't do us any good."

"What would it say? I'm in LA, come on, see you sometime."

"I want to make sure he knows we're coming."

"He does. Dave knows that I definitely plan to come down there, and I don't know when exactly. He will be there. He's a GM of a restaurant, so they need him all the time, and he's always going to auditions, looking for his big break. He rarely, rarely leaves the city."

"Do they call LA that too: The City?"

"I don't think that I've heard that much for LA actually, only San Fran and New York...San Fran! We will be back in San Fran. That will be so cool to do that with you again."

"We'll do San Fran on the way back up, maybe hit the wine country."

"Have you seen Sideways, Cris?"

"Yeah...funny shit. Funny shit, he repeats in a voice I don't immediately recognize.

"What is that?" I ask.

"Gary Cooper: Shay wats da big idea. Shay... dats shum funny shit...funny shit."

"That is some funny shit."

"Shum funny shit?"

"Definitely."

"I want to get some music."

"Me too...maybe."

"A few new things out that I want to get right now, and of course, some older things too."

"I want to get the new Aimee Mann album."

"Are you kidding me? I'm talking about Rock and Roll!"

"I didn't say that you wanted to buy it. I told you what I wanted to buy. She's one of the best songwriters in music right now."

"Touchy. Touchy. I wanted to get the new White Stripes, Van."

"By all means," I say.

At Target, I find a blanket set on sale. One side is dark brown and the other side is pink. I have been wearing a lot of dark brown lately, brown and baby blue. Pink goes good with brown. I also find a white button down with pink checks for $10. This is for LA. Bam. This shirt says bam.

I guess pink is my new color. Pink was electric, androgynous, eccentric, preppy, but lately it has taken on a sort of punk rock expressiveness, too. It's like stating: "look at me." I've always dressed with that statement in mind. Brown and blue was just my job attire.

My look could best be described as "peacock." I dress with flare, to impress or even startle, often in bright plumage, and I love a flashy, yet still classic look.

Oh yeah, my hoodie replacement. I find an Italia soccer jacket, wine colored with a blue logo and wonder how it will look with the new pink shirt. It may be too hot to find out anytime soon. It's pretty hot today, and it will be hot in LA, but I needed a jacket for nighttime. Even in SoCal it can get cool at night. LA is essentially a desert, and even way down in San Diego it's always breezy. I wish we could make it to Diego and the border.

When we go to check out, the cashier asks if we are going on a trip. She can tell from Crispin's items. He tells her we are heading down to LA, and she warns us not to pull out a wad of cash in LA like he just did, to avoid getting robbed. She sees growers with wads of cash everyday I bet, and like many small town folks she fears the big city.

"They are a bunch of complainers," Cris is explaining about his fellow growers, back in the car. "It's either the sunshine or the dust mites or the hired help. They always complain about something. It's a culture of complainers, whiners. I mean, no sunshine for a few days, and the people are dejected because that's fucking up their plants. They have a right to complain if they're losing money. I bitch, too, but some of the shit that the people up here bitch about…"

"It's just to bitch," I interject. "You don't seem to be as in love with living here as I first thought, homeboy."

"I'm not entirely. I'm not going to settle here on the permanent. Maybe I'll just work up here and live at the beach somewhere. Maybe near Santa Cruz. I haven't decided, but it won't be here. I won't live here permanently."

"Country or city?" I ask.

"I don't even know. Maybe as country as I can really get with a big beach town nearby."

"Sounds kinda sweet."

As we stare into the vast horizon of craggy wilderness, I ask, "How far is Mendocino County from San Fran?"

"Pretty far but not a full day's drive. I could go to the beach more often if I lived there. The beach up here is not very…inhabitable. People go out on it, but you know, in wet suits for the water. I'm used to the Gulf or at least the Atlantic."

"Not exactly Destin?"

"Not quite. But then again, no Southern rednecks, only Cali ones."

"Plenty of them?" I ask.

Cris says, "Enough for me not to be out there all the time. I'm not into being heroically obnoxious."

"Right. What color is the sand?"

"Black or close enough to it for me not to be out there all the time."

"Wow. I'd like to see that."

"We may have time before we leave. You know what though, fuck Humboldt. I live here because I have to right now, and I want to travel. I'd rather be in Sonoma smelling the lavender with you, but I need my dinero first. I wouldn't have had you come out here if we weren't going to drive across the country together. I would've told you it was too boring. It's too boring for me, so I knew it'd be way too boring for you."

"It's kind of neat here actually. I love the nature around here, and it's okay for me to not be too into anything for a bit. I just want to check it out a little more. We will see plenty of real beaches down south."

"Damn skippy, ole boy."

"You just need to get away for a while, Cris, like I

did. I had to get away, and this is fine. It could be more exciting."

"That's the thing about Humboldt folks; they may not do much here, but they go on vacations. Smoothboy went to Cannabis Cup in Amsterdam and hung out with the judges. I can't wait to travel like that, man. I want to go to Italy...just to eat. Your new jacket reminded me of that. I keep remembering things I want to do with money."

I say, "I remember Dave never wanting to leave LA because he never knew when his big break was going to come, when that special audition would lead to that special part."

Crispin says, "I've been trapped where I work."

"Most Americans are. I can't stand that we get the least paid vacation time in the civilized world. What's the point in overworking, when it has been proven to only lead to a lack of true productivity?

"Here we can't leave because of the crops, but when the crop comes, when it's harvest time for the crop, we get paid and can do whatever we want, go anywhere in the world."

I ask: "Eventually folks here get like Smoothboy and have people under them and get to travel more?"

"Exactly, that's the progression of things: trimmer first or assisting, then grower working for someone, then you get your own place, then you get someone under you and have multiple places."

"The sky is the limit...unless you get busted," I say.

Cris frowns at me for my rebuttal, saying, "Even then, the laws out here are geared to growing. You fucking lose a bunch of money, maybe everything, but your people... everyone helps out. If someone gets popped, people rally around them and help them get back up. They take care of the people that helped them out when they were down or could help them out if they got down. That's how it works, ole boy."

"What if something happened to the weed before Smoothboy paid you?"

"Like what?"

"I don't know."

"Then we don't get paid. Then no one gets paid. Don't be talking about busts and shit."

"Cris, I'm just asking."

"But I don't like the shit you're asking about."

We are quiet for about fifteen minutes then stop by a stereo store in Eureka, and Cris selects a Memphis Bleak brand speaker set and a new satellite radio for the road trip. "Mempho, bitches," he chants.

The speaker model he picks ends up being out of stock, and he agrees to come back for it. I'm relieved to not wait for installation. We leave and he gets all pissed off trying to get the satellite radio to work in the parking lot out front. Eventually it does, and we listen to a variety of good music on the way back to Pete's, as I enjoy the views. Exposed rocks and old trees, sparsely decorating the terrain as the road twists through and around mountains.

I like the energy of the Golden State. Each unique place I have been in the state still has that same Cali vibe, that sensation of being out in the big world and doing and seeing things. I'm beginning to feel fully alive again. I have to get on with my life sooner or later, and it may as well be now. Although I tried to relapse hard, I didn't. I haven't used much coke in a little while for the first time in a long time. And it feels good to not feel so bad. I must take control of my life again. I'm heartbroken about splitting up with my wife and about the damage I did to the marriage and my family. When I bottomed out with the drugs, I prayed. I prayed my way out of some rough situations, and I'm in a rough situation now, about to be divorced. It's just setting in.

Breathe the clean air. Keep praying. I'm amongst friends and everything is going to be okay. Well, it's going to be as good as it can be. At least, I will get better during this trip and come home and find work...and live on my own and make the best of my torn life. It will be so sad living alone.

"You gonna be okay?" Cris says, feeling my anguish.

"I'm sad," I say.

"That's understandable. I think you are going to be okay, buddy."

"Thanks...buddy."

We are quiet for five minutes and then Cris says, "Gate coming."

"Huh?" I say.

66

"Time to shine, ole boy. Time to shine, gunner."

I chuckle and say, "I got it. I mean allow me, ole boy." I hop out of the car to open the combo lock.

"That's more like it," Cris shouts out the window to me.

I get back in the car and he says, "You are in on the ole boy thing. I hope I don't start saying gunner all the time."

We drop our stuff and clean up and change. Only Silent Steve is around, so I thankfully won't be doing any more trimming this evening. Instead, we get Jim on the phone and decide to head out to dinner. Thank God, something fun.

"You're gonna love this place, Van," Cris says at Jim's house in Eureka.

"Yeah, yeah...it's good," Jim chimes in.

JimDawg, Crispin and I are ready for an early dinner, with liquid libations. We leave and smoke two bowls in the car, first some of Crispin's "Kong" on the drive and then JimDawg's "Trainwreck" in the parking lot before heading inside.

We are super ripped, and I feel like we are walking through a cloud as we enter the restaurant. I'm going with the flow of Humboldt life.

We are seated and Cris says, "We start with champagne."

After it arrives Jim says, "Here's to Crispin's big come up."

"Here, here," I chime.

Chink, chink, the glasses chime.

"You've come a long way," I add.

"Good work, Cris. Great job." Jim continues the verbal rubdown.

'Thanks, boys, here's to friends." Cris looks so proud and gracious as he hoists his glass.

"Here. Here," I say.

Chink, chink

"That's some good stuff you grew, Crispin," Jim says.

"Thank you...that means something coming from you."

I wonder if that is a fade on me as a weed judge, since I don't live here. It's true that I don't know on the level they know; these guys know weed.

"I'm Nanette by the way, guys," the server says. "Hope you are enjoying the champagne."

"We are." Cris and I say in unison.

"Yeah. Yeah," Jim says through a chuckle.

"Should I give you time or tell you about the specials?"

"Specials," Cris answers.

"Okay. Great! The specials tonight are all-you-can-eat king crab legs with one side dish of your choosing or a rack of lamb in a port reduction with a creamy shallot risotto and asparagus. Our special salad is a pear salad. It is a bed of organic mixed greens with an Anjou pear, spiced and candied walnuts, dried cranberries and red wine cherry vinaigrette dressing. The appetizer special is sourdough topped with organic beef tenderloin in a spicy mustard sauce, Humboldt Fog cheese and organic tomatoes. And finally, we have Kumamoto oysters on the half shell, deep, thick, creamy, from just north of here."

"Two dozen of those...and one more bottle of champagne before we switch to Maker's Mark," Cris says.

"Great," says Nanette, departing.

"She's pretty cool," I say.

"Indeed," Cris says. "Jim, you like Maker's? I know Van loves it."

"Yeah, yeah...Maker's," Jim says. "Do you guys mix it with coke?"

"Ginger for me," I answer. "Cris likes it with soda water."

"Maker's-soda. Maker's-ginger. They both sound good," Jim says.

"I don't drink much bourbon when it's not football season anymore, Cris," I say. "Maker's sounds good now, actually, it's almost pre-season."

"Here's to Athens' friends," Jim says.

Chink, chink

"Jim, I was telling Cris how much you and I hung out after he left. We were like the last two."

"Yeah. Yeah. The last of the Mohicans."

We are quiet for a minute while I eavesdrop on the

servers chatting at the server station, Nanette and her coworker.

He rambles, "I'm used to havin' so little...that I got too much. I'm thinking I might need a coffee, dude." He's commenting to her on his plight: He got too much sleep.

"Go get a coffee then, Fred," she says.

I wonder if that is his real name or a nickname, lots of nicknames and funny personalities in the restaurant business.

"Okay, dude." He keeps calling her dude? I wonder if she's gay, or if he's just a joker. She looks like she could be a wee bit butch. Then again, most of the chicks in Humboldt are not very frilly. They are the opposite of the LA princesses, I suppose.

"Here's to you, JimDawg. I miss you man," I say. "To California and to my friend, Crispin, for kicking ass...and for buying dinner."

Chink, chink

GENIUS BECOMES YOU ("pOp 102"): (-Humboldt)

The next day Crispin, Pete and I are standing outside Pete's greenhouse under the blazing heat of the California sun.

"Has anyone gone over what to do if police do come?" Pete asks me.

"I can hear that again," Crispin answers for me.

"First off, run! Run and you very well may get away. If they cannot detain you onsite it is hard for them to come back and say it was you. Even if they catch you up the street, just say you were out for a jog. Second, do not tell them anything. Don't say anything to them at all. Let them figure it out. Don't admit anything.

"Thanks for that, Pete," Cris says.

Cris trims with me then departs to go do something after an hour or so, leaving me to labor in the greenhouse. He's not into trimming. Trimmers are like stoop laborers or factory workers. Growers own the land and means to production in this nearly feudal scene in Humboldt.

Pete directs me what to chop down, and now it's just Jena and he and I, as it was much of yesterday. She helps him feed the machine and gather the ready plants. I'm working hard and fast, creating piles of ready plants, as I move section by section through the greenhouse. It is another nice California day, pretty hot and getting hotter as we work and the sun beats down. I'm mumbling to myself and singing along with the jam box. Thinking things through.

We break for water and to smoke. The weed of choice is a Pete creation known as "Genius." It's lighter in color and taste and way more up in sensation than any weed I've tried. It immediately has my mind racing.

We commence trimming again, and I make comments out loud as my brain zooms.

"I can't really hear you over the engine you know?" Pete says.

"I know," I answer. "I'm talking to myself, really, anyway."

"Okay, as long as you don't think that I'm ignoring you. I can hear that you're saying something. I just can't tell what you're saying."

"I figured that out when you didn't answer the first couple of questions that I asked. I am. ... We are shredding through this quickly."

"Yeah, you're doing great, and my new toy here's great." He's standing next to a weed fan trimmer and dragging the plants through the fan blades over a grill that protects them from going too deep.

"It helps?" I ask.

"Yeah!" he says through a great Pete smile. He smiles a lot. I love Pete's energy, his vibe and demeanor. He is a perfect Californian; it was made for him, and now that he found it he may never leave. Georgia was too conservative to be his permanent home, I guess. California is home.

"Genius," I yell as he has moved back away from me closer to the trimmer. I was trying to make a play-on-words: He is genius; his new toy is genius; we are high on Genius.

"What?" he yells, while shrugging and grinning.

I realize that I'm talking to myself again, so I give him a thumbs-up and grin and keep working.

Pete is a Grow Star, like the name of his company. That's what his company image should become, him, his personality. He may be done growing soon if his company really takes off, and it's on the cusp. I wonder if he would ever stop growing though? You can't be as out-front as I'm envisioning him in his promotions and still grow. But he just loves weed more than anyone else I've ever met. He's like a vineyard owner that just adores wine and wine making, the grapes, the soil. Sure the vineyard turns a handsome profit, but he's in it for the love.

Silent Steve joins the trim for an hour or so, then says to me, "It's just too fuckin' hot; I might be back." Longest sentence he ever said to me. He's probably going to read the comics the rest of the day. I don't expect him back.

I'm plowing through this greenhouse. I've developed technique for outdoor trimming quickly, as this is so much easier than indoor trimming. Yesterday, I was picking it up, and today I'm really refining my methods and working increasingly faster.

I take my sheers and power through the bottom of a big stalk in two motions: crunch, crunch-snap. I hold the plant next to me, the stalk right next to my body. I've removed my #5 Georgia Bulldogs red basketball jersey. I'm wearing only shorts, cut off tan dress pants, golf pants, actually, but

71

I wore them to work back when I had a day job. These are my work clothes now, I think, remembering my sartorial expressionism of the past. A several shades of brown and blue Nautica checked tie and a brown Ralph Lauren suit, a baby blue Brooks Brothers shirt, tan Steve Madden shoes, with socks nearly the same shade as the suit. That's what I would've worn to the office today and looked great. That outfit versus these ragged shorts and no shirt.

"I'm dressed for work...ha, ha. This is really fun."

The plant limbs almost become my limbs as I get inside and trim the big leaves away. I started off holding the stalks way out in front of me, but that was too cumbersome and tired my arms out, so I invented this technique. I'm like a violinist with his instrument, one with the plant. I'm flying at this.

Pete and Jena do all the middle trimming with the new fan trimmer. I only do the large weed trimming, and someone, maybe me, will do the fine trimming later. I love this. It's physical and positively stimulating and has a beautiful nature element, and that weed I smoked has my mind and body surging.

The Clash roars in the background. I'm a big fan of punk rock, even this layered political stuff. My mind is racing while I trim...California Dreamin'...vast LA...dense San Fran...Beach...Sunshine...Nature. This is so much better work than trimming at a table. The greenhouse is disappearing before our very eyes. Pete must be pleased with my efforts.

Thinking while I'm working: I could get to work on my book idea soon. pOp 101: Prince of Peachtree has potential to be a quintessential Atlanta story. Maybe I should write my friend Mafa's business plan first. I'm not up for writing a business plan yet, so I should just write a book. That'll be a big project, something to do: a good book. It'll be a good book, actual literary art, not more boring business writing. No matter how well crafted, business writing is plain and boring. Art is fun and can be genius. Paintings are fun. They're fun to admire. Wish I were a painter, like Basquiat or even Robert Harold or Andy Lee or Rizz or Madison.

Books can be fun, too. Writing a book will be fun. I'm sure it'll be hard work, but it'll be fun work, art. Movies are fun. I love a great movie.

Actually, this is like a movie. This would make a cool scene in a movie. This trip would make a good book, too. Writing about being in the greenhouse trimming like a violinist, the trimmers that I met, the growers, all of this. Humboldt should be in a book, and I'm getting to see it firsthand as almost an insider.

Maybe? Yes. This is a book, now. I will write a book about this trip. Humboldt and the growers and the trimmers, and we're going to LA. LA is good book. We are going to see my actor buddy Dave in LA, and he's a character, and this is a book. I'm a character, too.

After LA with Dave, we are going to do The City scene, have a little urban adventure. And we're going to drive across the country, which has been done too, of course. It could be an adventure, a friend story, a weed story, a city story, an LA actor profile and a modern day "On the Road" and me knowing this is a book may shape the outcome of the story.

It's like reality TV except only I see the camera. I'm the camera. Action. Now. This is my story about now. This'll be a book about the now that I'm experiencing while I'm on this summer trip to Cali. This is a book! I guess this could be my second book, after pOp 101.

I've wanted to do a book about Athens in the 1990s for a long while, maybe, someday. Three books: That could be a career. Am I a writer now? Now was when I became a writer because I'm a writer now. That's like a math problem. Reminds me of that class I took with all those denial statements. I am a writer. With two or three good books, there would be no denying that.

I say, "Pete...Pete! I need to go write something down. ... Clock me out, boss. I am taking a break, boss."

"You need a break already?" He asks. "I told you it was hot."

"I just have to write something down."

I picture myself from before, as if this were a movie. Here I am covered from head-to-toe in resin, weed all over me, only wearing cut-off khaki shorts, nothing else, and I'm in a weed greenhouse on a beautifully natural and sunny mountain in Northern California, and I drop my shears and say, "Pete. ... I need to go inside to write something down. ... Clock me out. I'm taking a break."

That'd be a cool scene in a movie. I may see this

73

scene on a movie silver screen someday and think, yep, that was then. That was the now that started it all.

I walk inside the house and write:

1. pOp 101: Prince of Peachtree
2. Now
3. ATHENS, GA

Am I just way too stoned? Maybe that will be my new job. I've wanted to do something hip, something smart and fun. Even if I just write pOp 101 and this, pOp 102, or whatever, the sequel to pOp 101, that would give me two books. I'm clocking back in. I walk back outside.

"Clock me back in, boss," I say.

"That was short," Pete says, a sense of puzzlement on his face.

"Just had to jot down some great ideas."

"We should be done in another hour or so the way you are totally cranking it today. It's a record pace for one person."

"I want to talk to you when we get done!" I yell to Pete as he walks away, back to the trim machine.

He comes closer to me and says, "What? Okay."

"When we get done I want to tell you what I wrote down."

"Won't be long."

"Genius," I mumble to myself. "pOp 102: California Genius."

Half an hour later Cris shows back up, saying, "You guys are almost finished. I can't believe it."

I babble quickly: "Yeah, we smoked Genius first, you have to smoke this shit. It makes your mind race, good for working hard, and I've been thinking the whole time, and I decided to write another book, a book about this, about California now."

"What about Atlanta and pOp 101?"

"Of course, that too, this will be my second book. pOp 102 or whatever it ends up being called is about now."

"Whatever. ... I got paid, so when you finish up we're heading out."

The Van is ready to roll. LA here we come. This is a book. Action.

ACT II: Shine On, You Star (The Road Trip)

HOPLAND, AGAIN (DRIVE 2):
(-Highway 101/-Ukiah)

So we went out riding on a brand new butterfly called California. Chauncey Bear, Cris Jones and I and a satellite radio. We burst out of our cocoon, zoom through rays of sunshine as the White Stripes blare and the man banter ensues.

"They're a heavy band that deserved to make it and did," I say.

"Definitely," says Cris to me, then to the dog, "Be, be good, Chauncey. Be a good girl."
Chauncey is whistling a little through her nose, whining.

"Many of the famous aren't as talented as them," Cris says. "Just glad to get away."

"I'm sure you are," I answer. "California's beautiful, man. Look at these rolling hills that we are rolling by."

Way out West and in motion again with miles of highway before us and this weedy area and its sort of remote crankiness behind us. Los Angeles and the Southern California sunny lifestyle awaits. We quiet for a few minutes as initial road trip excitement quells. It dawns on me that I'll have to reflect on self again with so much car time. Just leaving the Humboldt Bay area and thinking: neat place and I'm not down on it or especially down with it. We will probably be back before we roll out for Atlanta, for home, before the end of this adventure.

"Will we definitely be back to Humboldt before we leave?" I ask.

"Nothing's definite, but I'm sure we'll stop in," Cris says. "We could leave from San Fran...or Portland. But if we left from Portland, I'm sure we'd stop in Humby first. You left some stuff at the trim shack."

"Fuck, I thought so. Nothing I need. I know the

south route some. New Orleans. Texas. Just glad we'll be driving across the country."

"Me too. I can't believe you haven't done that yet. Glad to give you a ride back home after we have some fun, Van. The VAN is back."

"Thank you! But no...he isn't. We really should go to Portland to see my sister's friend there, if we have time. She's ready to show us around. I wouldn't mind taking her for a tumble, either."

"Sounds fun. We have plenty of time now, to do whatever we want. This is what I've been waiting for... temporarily endless summer. Freedom. Yes! Gettin' the fuck out."

"Later, Humby," I surfer drawl.

"We'll still be in Humboldt County for a stretch...big counties."

"Right. I should get a map of California"

"Oh, I've got one in here. You'll have to navigate, anyway."

"Sorry I can't drive."

"That does suck. I wish you could drive part of the way. We are gonna be on the road a lot it looks like, the next few weeks at least, maybe the next few months."

"Sorry about that, about the license thing."

"Ah, it's just the way it is."

"Thanks, man. I'll probably only want to travel for about five weeks total. Otherwise, I wouldn't mind considering Yosemite National Park or further into the Redwoods or even the Salton Sea. I have to get home to my kids. I just needed to get away and sort some things out. I'll be back home soon, wherever that ends up being exactly... home. I wouldn't want to miss my divorce."

"I've heard they can go long. No stopping it now?"

"It could be stopped, I guess, if she wanted, if we both wanted."

"She done?"

"Yeah...and then I finally considered it done, too once she made me sign those papers. I knew it was done in my mind if not my heart. How far is Portland from here? I know LA is far."

"Portland's not all that bad. Not exactly sure how many hours it takes to drive there from Humboldt...but not too many. Never been. Heading north, so it's cooler at least. Long, hot haul down to LA."

I open the map and say, "Just looking at Cali, this is gonna be a really cool ride, seeing all of this."
He says, "We're gonna miss most of the sights, driving at night."

"Is that for safety because you have weed?"

"The car overheats sometimes. I hope, maybe, Johnny can help me with that a little if he has time to work on her. Be good until then, ole girl." He pats the dash. I chuckle about him talking to inanimate objects.

We sit in silence for five minutes before I ask, "Be dark soon?"

"Yeah, pretty soon. How long will it take to finalize your divorce?"

"I have no idea. I guess it will be over soon...well, pretty soon." My voice cracked a little, saying that last "soon."

We are quietly contemplative for a long while. I cry on the inside until the real tears roll, but I don't make a sound. I don't look over to see if Cris notices but I can feel him feeling the pain in me, so it doesn't really matter if he sees me cry or not. I'm in no way crying for him.

I stop crying on the outside eventually.

Driving through Willits later, we see a pregnant teen right away, and Cris just nods to me.

"We could've stopped at your buddy's place outside of town here, the one who bought all those shirts from me," I say.

"I figured maybe we would on the way back up," Cris says. "Did you go by the little skate shop?"

"They were closed when I came through. I wrote down their info off the door for fly-wear. By the way, I'm thinking about changing the name of the shirts. I'm thinking of coming out with a new line actually."

"What type of clothes?"

"The same. T-shirts with local art, hats, stickers, hoodies...maybe move on to jeans, shorts and khakis."

"What are you gonna do about getting money up to front a business?"

"I haven't decided yet. I may obviously need an

investor or two."

"Just ask if you need anything with that once it's all formula-ized."

I wouldn't want to be in business with Cris, so I change the subject: "What about you? What are you gonna do? Just keep at it up on that mountain? Get your own place eventually?"

"I'm thinking about settling down below Santa Cruz or just north of there. It's too lame here for me to want to be here permanently."

"Santa Cruz would be good. Would you 'work' up here?"

"Maybe I wouldn't have to even go this far up to work. I'd like to actually live at the beach or very near the beach, and I don't mind commuting for work in California."

We meander the state, going down, descending. My mood is settling. We talk. We think. We topic shift. We stare at our surroundings. We get in the frame of mind of people that travel, when they travel. This is the trip.

We stop in Ukiah to have a snack and a beer. This is a little hippie dippy tourist town, an on your way to and/or from the mountains respite more than a destination. It's somewhat fun to be around a few locals and tourists to get a flavor of the place. Nothing too special, but it's cute in that touristy, slightly cheesy way. Hippie mixed with commercial always comes across way too contrived. Commerce is, by its nature, contrived, but hippie commerce is contrived and conflicted.

The snacks are good: turkey sandwiches with refreshing crisp sprouts. We each drink only one hearty local beer.

"I have lost all desire to drink 'good' beer," I tell Cris on the way out of the café, air-quoting the word "good."
"Too much flavor?" he asks.

"Way too much...food was great, though, thanks."

I feel a little better after the stop, after the food. Outside the car, I buy what I'm told is a healing artifact for $10 from a young guy trying to get money to rent a motel room for his girlfriend. Wood with silver and green stones, it somehow makes me feel better.

Back in the car after some time has passed, I come out of an almost sleep and immediately see the Hopland sign.

"There is Hopland, again," I say. "We should've stopped there."

"You stop there on the way up?" Cris asks.

"Nah...cute little place, though."

TOSTADAS IN THE CITY:
(-Highway 101/-San Francisco)

Down we go, down the state, down the country. The physical enormity and mostly sparseness of America can be felt in most of this country's states, including California. Though there are millions of people in this state, and much of it has been developed in one way or another, most of it remains seemingly untouched land.

Land. America is a country of vast land, with many developed areas connected by highways. Otherwise, much of the land in this country is undeveloped or barely developed. We tend to forget how huge America is when we never leave the city or the suburb where we live or when we travel from one city to another by plane.

We're descending, losing ourselves in the length of California. We're out on the freeway, finding ourselves in the middle of nowhere California. In the middle of this marijuana haze-of-a-dream, and in, or rapidly approaching at least, the middle years of our lives, we find ourselves. Two long-time friends together on an adventure again.

I say, "You know Mexico declared independence from Spain, and then later the United States took California from Mexico."

Crispin says, "I recall learning that."

"Texas joined the USA of our own free will; Texas could legally secede still."

"Y'all still talking about forming your own country again?"

"I almost feel as Georgian as I do Texan after all these years, but it's an interesting concept. Outside of Austin, the Nation of Texas would be way too right wing for me if it ever did leave, and it won't."

Changing subjects Crispin says, "Speaking of leaving, you remember that talk we had on the way to the funeral?"

"I do," I somberly say.

When my second friend named Wes died, I was hanging out with Crispin the night before the funeral. I spent the night so we could ride together the next morning. We weren't okay. We didn't deal with it well.

On the way to the funeral, I'd asked Cris if he could think of any of our good friends that we grew up with that were more likely to die than Wes and Wes. And he said no. But who was next most likely to abuse drugs, to use too much of a drug and go? There was some debate about the rankings. Cris had liked to dabble with heroin. I had a penchant for binge drinking and was using cocaine somewhat regularly. We couldn't clearly define number three and number four, because it was too close to call. But both of the contestants for third were in the car.

We had pledged to get better, to be more careful, and Cris left Atlanta before long. He got better.

I got worse. It stopped being recreation or escape and became full on addiction. I clearly claimed third, and number one and number two had floated away. And Cris was gone too, so I was number one with a bullet, with a gun to my head.

Here in the middle of Northern California we speak of home, and Cris tells me that he's glad that I didn't pull the trigger.

I openly cry, saying: "I have to live and get strong because I am a father, and I want to be a great one. I didn't mean for things to get out of control with the drugs. They just did. Then I had the affair. Then the drugs got worse, after the first trial separation or whatever they call it."

Then I get quiet for a half-hour or so and pray for myself and my soon to be ex-wife and my children...and for Cris.

We are like half-golden geniuses in a way. We had always been a little flawed but had so many good ideas and were so generally gregarious and good-hearted and cool that it somewhat compensated for our shortcomings. That was something we had in common.

Chauncey whines to snap me out of it. She is a sweet and loving dog, and she is flawed too. Paranoid like I had become on cocaine, she visibly worries. She has abandonment issues like her daddy, I guess.

"Good girl," Cris says. "Be okay, girl."

Be okay, I think to myself. Be okay.

We space out and almost miss the turn for San Francisco and Cris snaps at me. Then we zoom into the counterculture capital with our senses up. San Francisco has deep meaning to us as friends and friends of the counterculture. We are not just average cookie cutter Americans.

I say: "Cris, this reminds me of when we first pulled up to San Francisco, the last time we were here together. … This gas station could be the very same gas station. Actually, I think it is."

"How do you remember that?" Cris asks.

"Those phone booths. Remember, as soon as we pulled up to The City for the first time, ten years ago, or whatever, it was to a gas station like this with phone booths on the edge of it, like those, and there was a guy shooting up in one of them. He was singing, 'Shoot it up, Little Darling,' to the tune of "Stir It Up" by Bob Marley. He was a white guy with dreads, roughly our age, and I remember having a sensation that I was about to really experience urban life for the first time."

"I do remember that come to think of it. Good memory, Van. Let me go ask these guys in here where a good restaurant is around here."

While Cris is inside, memories of that trip flood my brain like they did when I was at Rick's apartment. Travel allows reflection.

That was the first vacation where I was a true urban explorer on a long trip. Before that it had always been the beach or the mountains or a friend's place for a week. That was five weeks exploring Northern California with friends as a young man, and part of it was Cris and I having a good time searching for the essence of this city.

San Francisco is scenic bridges and densely-populated urban hills and street life. It's the lushness of Golden Gate Park and the immigrant experience of melting pot America. It's the glowing Palace of Fine Art and the twinkling buildings at night, done up in light. It's the history of the Haight: what R. Crumb drew, all that counterculture, the Grateful Deadheads, the hippies, the flower children, the beatniks, Kerouac.

I think of mass transit: electric buses and trolleys, lots of trains.

"Those guys fuckin' suck," Cris says as he re-enters the vehicle. "We will find a restaurant on our own. Fuck them."

Thirty minutes later we are lost in The City, looking for a place to park near a place to eat. The one-way streets are not helping. Driving in circles now and San Fran always has me spinning. I'm trying to enjoy the paradisical pastel sights of vertical Victorian homes mixed with restaurants and shops, while reassuring Crispin that we will find a spot. Eventually, we do. We have tostadas at a little Mexican hole in the wall not too far from what seems to be the only open parking space in the whole town. The food is delicious, and we overhear someone talking about running into HANK III here, "the other day."

"You got drunk with him in Athens, right?" I ask Cris.

"He was there not saying much," he answers. "I was there. We were drinking next to each other...so, yeah. I got drunk with HANK III. God bless his grandpa's soul in heaven."

"Hank Sr. rules. Should we have a drink in The City tonight?"

"I don't want the hassle because of the parking drama. If I saw a cool bar right there I would say yes. I don't need to be drinking much behind the wheel anyway, so let's just get back on the road to Santa Cruz to bunk down for the night."

"Cool. It just seems sort of unlike us to pass through San Fran and not at least have a couple of pops."

"It is unlike us under normal conditions. I guess I'll tell you now since we are here: I talked to my mom on the phone earlier today, and she is coming out to visit soon. She was telling me how she was reading about the California Gold Rush and how Napa and the other original wine areas in Sonoma and whatnot were formed to produce wine for the fools looking for gold, the workers. So I decided then that I am taking the two of you to Napa. I was going to surprise you...so, surprise. We'll do Napa, after I take all of us out in San Fran to do it up huge."

"That's awesome," I say. "We were too young for Napa when we went that time before. Remember, after Napa we decided to go to The City to go out that night...for like the tenth time on that trip? Remember when we stayed with that Candace girl near the park, my friend from Athens, and we all slept in the same bed?"

"Oh yeah," Cris answers. "Why didn't we bang her again?"

"You two were rubbing around a bit, but she was just my friend. I had a girlfriend back in Athens. I do remember thinking at the time that we all sort of wanted to screw, especially you two. It was after that big party we went to, and everyone was all charged up and...jokey."

"A regular laugh riot, it was."

"That was my best vacation probably to that point," I realize aloud.

Cris says, "That was my best of all time until my dumbass big brother and I got in that fight for like two hours."

"That's right...day after I left. It's like you two were just waiting for me to leave so you could rumble without a ref. Sorry that happened."

"Thank you," Crispin says earnestly. He chuckles then says, "At least I finally kicked his old ass like he deserved all those years."

I laugh and shake my head. "Speaking of beats," I say through a knowing smirk, "should we get back on the road?"

"Yeah, good brother. Let's kick it."

SKATE SANTA CRUZ:
(-Santa Cruz)

The temperature drops about twenty degrees on a dark and suddenly foggy night. It's getting late and the visibility is poor. We finally reach the Monterrey Bay and are relieved when we arrive at our friend J.C.'s place outside Santa Cruz safely to crash for the night.

At the door J.C., aka Johnny says, "It's been a long time, Van. Come in and make yourselves at home. Van, you can put your bags...let's see...the porn room is good, I guess. I'm trying to think, yeah, if you don't mind too much put your bags back there in the porn room."

"I'll be good out here, J.C. Too," Crispin says while gesturing to the couch, clearly disgusted at the concept of his bags in a porn room.

We have entered the lair of Jonathon Carter II, lawyer and pornographer extraordinaire. Sometimes known as JC Too because of "his too much personality," Johnny grew up in Marietta as an honor student and heavy metal music fan who loved to restore and drive fast American muscle cars - ugly seventies power machines. He is a pure and undeniable headbanger, who has a few hippie tendencies as well, primarily relating to his absolute devotion to drug cultures of all kinds.

Like me, Johnny generally achieved on a level - handled his business on a level - which made it hard to criticize him too much, since he was always working toward a goal. Clearly hyper-intelligent, his mind and mouth move way too fast, and he is just too far left of center and creepy to be normal. Though disgusting, domineering and a bit white trash, Johnny is actually a nice guy. He just talks too much and it's always been obvious to me that he was yearning for some lame recognition or notoriety; he loved the attention.

Plus, he has always been obsessed with his drunken, and now deceased, mother. He is always loudly imitating her horrible voice: "Johnny Boy!, Who's with you?" But otherwise, he's okay.

Johnny ended up here after finally meeting his match in meth. He became a crystal methamphetamine user, then abuser and addict, while living in Seattle. There he got very obsessed with making his own porno movies and lost his law firm job and just sold drugs and collected unemployment. Eventually, he hit rock bottom and escaped to the relative safety of suburban Santa Cruz.

He's glad to see us, having been alone most of the time since he left Seattle, just a man and his dog - a huge boxer named Cynda. The dog is also fired up for visitors and crawls all over us every chance she gets, while we stay up late listening to stories of Johnny's sordid past and the ultimate demise of his amateur porn empire. He would make porn with the neighbor couple or his girlfriend or whomever else was interested.

He even subjects us to part of some of his films. "Sorry I'm so ugly," he says to us as he appears on camera. In the scene, he is hairy except he has ridiculously shaven himself bald from right above his navel to his mid-thighs.

"It was for the shoots," he says.

We drink California table wine from Napa and Canadian whiskey and listen to old metal, after begging him to stop showing us his films. He tries to blame his problems in Seattle on the craziness of his girlfriend, which is truly insane. He mixes stories of how everything started to go wrong with brags of his sexual exploits and gross humor and mom impersonations.

I get bored listening to him go on and on, so I try to change the subject by telling him about my Atlanta book, pOp 101. I give up after a few interrupted broad descriptions. I am annoyed yet still somehow genuinely glad to spend time with him.

Plus he has good piney weed and breaks out cases of whip-its, a.k.a. hippie crack. We take turns doing bong hits and inhaling the nitrous through a balloon, the burning brain cells causing brief but intense aural hallucinations, sounds bouncing around the room.

I don't remember the end of the night, but when I wake up the next day and walk to the living room the Braves are on TV playing the LA Dodgers, so we settle in and watch the game. Probably the only entire baseball game that I will watch on TV this year. I'm more of a fan of the culture of the ballpark, hot dogs and beers, rooting for the home team, the Americana of it all. The passion and rivalry of college football actually matter to me; this is just whiling away another summer day.

"Baseball's so much better live," I say.

After the game Johnny says, "We should head to the beach."

We agree and start to get ready while the constant bantering continues. We talk about the long streak of Braves' playoff appearances being in jeopardy, and it feels wholesome to be discussing sports since we've recently discussed all of Johnny's favorite subjects: meth, porn and anal sex.

Crispin and I next steer the conversation farther off course, to his mom coming to The Bay. We haven't had to resort to the discussion of apple pie, yet, but I fear we might. I laugh about that to myself a little without sharing it with them: moms, baseball and apple pie versus meth, porn and anal sex...and, of course, Johnny's weird mom complex.

Cris says, "Let's eat first."

"I know a cool diner that's not too far," Johnny says. "Then we can head straight to the beach. We have a beach nearby there." He switches to mom voice: "Shtay out of the water, Johnny!"

In the diner, we seat ourselves in a big booth and peruse the menu. The place reminds me of every classic Californian diner I have seen in movies. Under a James Dean poster, I think of icons: too many dead young icons. Dying helped make them icons, of course, and many of them are immortalized here in these posters. James Dean could express so much emotion with so few words. I love the way he dressed and looked...that wave he did in Giant. I think it was in Giant. He only made a few movies. Marilyn over there, the female James Dean. Marilyn, Elvis, James Dean, is everyone in here a young dead icon? They could change the name of this place to Dead Icon Diner.

Wait, the Vegas Rat Pack...they aren't even all dead yet, so I won't suggest the name change. Lots of pictures of acting icons: very LA, very Southern California.

I say to Johnny, "I was wondering where the line of demarcation is between North and South California,"

"SoCal and NoCal," Johnny says.

"Or NorCal," I say.

"I haven't heard that. Is it "NorCal" now?"

"Crispin, you want this one?" I ask.

"Yeah," Cris says, including himself in the discussion. "They had a fuckin' contest or whatever way up north to decide if they wanted to call it NoCal or NorCal, apparently it is NorCal now. ... What's good here?"

"I always get that second breakfast," Johnny answers.

"What are you getting, Van?" Crispin asks.

"Huevos rancheros," I say. "I was raised on my Nanny's huevos."

"Nice," Crispin says. "I think I will get number two, like JC. He of course gets number two because all he cares about is number two."

"You guys. Just because I do girls in their tight, pretty butts, that doesn't mean I am fixated on shit...or does it?" He is chuckling.

The waitress is approaching from across the restaurant. "Ask her about the poo poo platter, JC?" I say quietly. We are all cracking up as she comes all the way over. We order and she leaves.

"Sorry I did not have enough food at the house," Johnny says.

"You are a good host," I say. "We did all your whip-its and drank most of your booze last night."

"Really. Thanks so dang much, JC," Crispin says.

"You guys don't have to thank me. I'm just glad to have someone to hang with. I'm all alone in Santa Cruz, and tomorrow's my birthday."

"Should we stay?," I ask, glancing to Crispin. "You wanna go ahead and hang with JC on his day?"

"Maybe so," Cris says.

"Is this SoCal?" I ask Johnny.

"Good question," he says. "There's The Bay: San Fran, Oakland, Berkeley. San Jose is still the Bay Area, but Santa Cruz isn't The Bay anymore; it's the Monterrey Bay or the Central Coast. From south of right around here down is Southern California, I guess. Monterrery's rugged NorCal and then Santa Cruz feels sunny SoCal, but they are actually in the same bay."

"What beaches are around here?" I ask.

Johnny answers: "There's the Santa Cruz beach by the boardwalk and Twin Lakes to the south. We'll go to Sunset Beach, which is really more Watsonville than Santa Cruz. We're like fifteen miles south of S.C."

When we hit the beach, for the first time on this trip I feel like I'm in the California that I anticipated. There would be no "California" without beautiful beaches, as that lifestyle is all about nice weather and golden sunshine. The valued real estate is on or near the coast.

On an almost empty beach, I stand next to the edge and contemplate the vastness of the ocean, the expansive shimmering horizon, rough and raw, yet a peaceful energy. To think most of the earth is water and many of us only see the edge occasionally. I've been landlocked for too long. I want to see the world again and feel free.

Johnny and I are running and throwing the frisbee, playing keep away from his dog while Crispin walks Chauncey. I'm a former football wide receiver, and Johnny has a nice arm. He is getting it almost high enough for me to be at the peak of my jump as I snag it.

"Higher. Throw it higher!" I shout through the wind, glad to be exercising in the open breeze of the ocean sky.

"Okay!" Johnny shouts back.

"That was too high. Almost that high next time!"

We start to connect at the point I want, above ten feet and I yell, "Snag....Touchdown!" I feel exhultant in the ocean air, the water at my feet as I land. My juices are flowing. I realize I haven't played in too long.

A half hour later we tire and decide to break from sport. I stand at the edge of the ocean and feel its vastness again and my relative smallness in the world. The world is so big. You are so big, God.

Eventually, we head back to Johnny's to shower up. There I start to tell Johnny about my book ideas again, but he quickly interrupts saying, "I'm writing a book about a lawyer turned cosmic detective. It's loosely, very loosely based on me."

"I'm writing about me too," I say softly. "Is your genre mystery?"

"Kind of cosmic and karmic in a way, but sci-fi," he

says.

"You always liked sci-fi, so that figures."

"I love sci-fi. You can do anything."

I think sci-fi is often lame. I'm bored and say, "Let's go out."

Johnny says. "There are a few rock bars in town. Maybe we can find some girls to make a movie."

"I don't think Cris wants to be in any of your, um, films?"

"How about you, Van?"

"Maybe...with the right co-stars I'd at least consider it, I guess."

We check the exterior of a few places in the little Santa Cruz downtown before settling on a rocker bar called The Axis. It's a garden-variety dark cave with a jukebox, stiff drinks and a few girls in black. I'm wearing my new white and pink shirt, looking radiant with a fresh day's sun. I don't exactly fit in tonight with the trying to look dark and sort of jaded crowd. This is Crispin's scene, but he is shy, and Johnny's scene, but he is not very cute.

We never really connect with any girls which is a slight letdown, but we still have a pretty good time just being out. We talk and listen to rock and get tipsy and head home way too early for my liking. Johnny is understandably worried about driving drunk, my license is suspended and Cris definitely needs a night off from driving.

When we get home, Johnny takes the dogs out. I'm fairly bummed we didn't have much fun.

Crispin says, "You gotta promise me not to dress so pretty next time we go to a rock bar. Those chicks were actually digging my look...but I needed you to talk to them, to break the ice, and you were not their type, I'm sure."

Half-joking, I say: "I should be every girl's type. Why are you shy?"

"I don't know. Promise me you won't wear a pink oxford to the rock bars in LA."

"Are we really going to hang around rock bars the whole time on this trip? You go to the same bar no matter what city you are in. I like watering holes sometimes too, but we could mix it up. Besides, pink is punk now, not just preppy like it used to be, and you giving me fashion advice.

That is a huge joke, and you know it."

"Fashion is a huge joke."

"I liked that place; I just don't want to hang at the Highlander."

"Bullshit. You used to love the Highlander."

"For a change of pace in Atlanta," I explain. "I was much more of a Stein Club guy until they shut her down. It was way more eclectic."

"I just like you to be the icebreaker, Van. I'm no good at that."

"Because you never even try. ... JC was trying. We just left too early. That chick in the red was into y'all and could have been a big star."

"Johnny ain't filming my white ass, Van."

"Me neither, Cris."

"If the girls were hot enough, you would do it."

"So would you, asshole. Good night."

"Good night, buddy. I guess we are staying for JC's b-day?"

"You are my ride, so whatever you say."

"Let's stay then."

"Fine. I wanted to hit a skate shop anyway before we leave."

We wake. It's Johnny's birthday. We go to the same diner again for brunch and then stop by the liquor store on our way to the beach. This time we go to the actual Santa Cruz beach and do shots in the car.

We're right under the boardwalk, near the famous amusement park ferris wheel. Lots of people are out.

There is a beautiful blonde woman with huge boobs barely contained in a white bathing suit. I sit us down on one of the few empty spots near her and her husband.

"Gorgeous," I whisper to Cris.

"SHH, I know. I knew why you chose this spot."

I watch the waves roll and try not to glance at her more than every thirty seconds. She catches me looking and pouts her lips and sits up straight, sticking her chest out further.

It's a beautiful day to be at the beach, but we get sunburned quickly on beach day two and soon decide we have to leave.

Departing, we see two very hot young women, maybe age twenty, stacked on top of each other in what looks like a yoga pose, back to back.

"I want one of those," Cris says to me, loud enough for them to hear. A guy standing by them holding a frisbee smiles at us and his luck.

I say, "Reminds me of something from that Heironymous Bosch painting, The Garden of Earthly Delights."

Back in the car, Johnny is getting hammered, alternating shots of peppermint schnapps and tequila. The more he drinks, the louder and more he talks. Elated to be celebrating, he keeps shouting from the backseat: "It's my birthday!"

We all end up taking a few shots, while Johnny blabs: "Everyone we grew up with has a freak flag. You guys know it's true. I just sail mine a little higher than most. Does that make me bad? Am I a bad guy if I do crazy sexual things with girls? They let me. ... They love it!"

Back at Johnny's, we shower up and relax for a few hours then head to town to shop.

"I have to buy my son a purple skateboard with yellow wheels and a Spiderman sticker," I say. "That is specifically what he asked for."

I'm on a quest, and I had called the local Humboldt skate shop, and they didn't have one. Santa Cruz must have one, somewhere, since Santa Cruz is the skate capital of the USA. It's the place we knew about in Georgia when I skated, twenty years ago. The good skate videos came from here, and I had a red and yellow "Santa Cruz" sticker on my skateboard back when I was fifteen years old.

Santa Cruz is far cuter and has more locals than most tourist traps back Southeast, with way hipper shops than redneck haunts like Myrtle Beach, Panama City, and Gatlinburg. In essence though, all tourist shopping is roughly the same, in a word, lame. Lame Americana: that could be the name of some of these shops. Is Cali a tourist trap?

Walking alone and I need to enjoy this trip. I'll probably travel less after this. I'll have to rebuild my life. It's possible.

Starting over from scratch: no money, no house, no job, no car, no license, no wife, not much of a "life," yet. I have two sons to take care of, so I'll have to re-establish my life brick-by-brick.

God, help me to become the man and father I want to be. I can do this. I have to. Now that I'm off the sauce I can begin to think about that. I couldn't even help myself before.

I eventually find a cool shop called Skate World; the font of the store logo is a knock-off of Star Wars. They have an Alien Invasion brand board in a nice lavender and purple with a jester on the bottom.

They carry Vans, too, and have my size in stock, unlike the shoe shop I first tried. I'm still separated from Johnny and Crispin, but I will find them eventually. I decide to buy all black Vans slip-ons that remind me of Bruce Lee. As soon as I pay for them, Cris shows up wearing the same all black Vans that I have, with the exception that his have a small burgundy section. The clerks give the skateboard to me without ringing it up and go on to the next customer, and I realize these are cool guys that I'd never steal from and pay them before leaving. Independent entrepreneurs have always been the lifeblood of America. They're relieved I was honest and give me free stickers, but I still need a Spidey sticker.

Out in front of the skate shop Johnny says, "I want to relapse, badly." We get in the car and start to leave. He asks me to try to score some hard drugs, and the temptation is back. Cris wants no part of it. I should want no part of it, but the powerful addiction takes over.

I try to buy cocaine outside a liquor store from a handsome young black guy obviously posturing as a dealer of something. I'm not naïve enough to try for powder again and ask for hard. Instead, I end up with a $20 peanut in a small black bag. I'm not amused, but I do have a sense of relief mixed with a nauseating adrenaline surge. JC asks if I want to try again, and we settle on just a drink at The Axis. I'm suddenly so over being here, so ultimately bored. I want to get on the road. Johnny has to be right about everything, and his drunken overbearing attitude is starting to grate on me, which is not his fault. I'm agitated: I tried to buy drugs, started jonesing, failed to score.

Back at the house, JC goes into a long rant about how Mayor "Guliano" ruined New York City by closing all the sex shops in Manhattan. I eventually snap, "It is Guiliani, not Guliano. You don't even know how to pronounce it, and yet you are the ultimate authority on it. You don't know shit. Have you ever even been to New York? I have, recently, a bunch. It's far from ruined. Manhattan is fun. That Mayor's name is Guiliani. He's far right wing and I'd never vote for him, but do you have to be right?"

"I'm just saying," Johnny begins his honed defense, "without all the peep shows New York is lame. The East Coast is lame."

I'm further annoyed and say, "Fuck that. East Coast!"

"If you lived in Seattle or Cali you'd know the West is the Best."

"I've been to Seattle and wasn't all that impressed. I much prefer New York. Capital of the World, not just a regional headquarters. Seattle isn't better than Atlanta. It's just more politically liberal and rainy. I like real cities. You can't even buy a liquor drink in Seattle unless it is in a hotel bar. What's so progressive about that? I had trouble seeing the allure. ... It was pretty and all."

"If you lived out here in the West you'd understand."

"Maybe." I'm fuming. I'm disproportionately angry. I don't want to discuss anything, and you can't convince Johnny of anything.

"I really think it is Guiliano."

"Well, it fucking isn't!" I snap. "I'm positive. Do you have internet?"

"Yeah."

"Look it up."

"I'll pass. I would but it takes a long time to connect."

"Better to believe you are right?" I say while leaving the room, laughing to myself about JC using a dial-up connection. I get too upset about trivial conversation sometimes and realize it's just symptomatic, a byproduct of addiction. I'm unhappy and bored and bullshit pisses me off to give me something to do.

Johnny and I talk nice the rest of the day. Cris goes to bed earlier than Johnny and I, and we stay up watching porn together and drinking amicably until I retire to the porn room for a few hours sleep. We have smoked most of his pot while we have been here, done all of his nitrous, drank his liquor. I feel bad about snapping at such a gracious host.

I go to bed and when I wake up the next morning, "Darryl" is fixing Crispin's car. "Darryl" is one of Johnny's semi-fake personas, the redneck mechanic. His overalls even have a "Darryl" name patch. I had forgotten about Darryl. Johnny is such a freak.

"He is always too much," I say in the car as we depart.

Cris says, "That is good. I'm glad he grossed you out. You used to talk about sex a lot."

"Have I talked about sex much this trip? I'm abstinent right now, not even masturbating. When I was high on blow, I guess I had to fixate."

"Well, it was gross. When we get to LA, let's don't fixate on girls."

"We will see if you don't start talking about girls while you look around LA. Let's just get there, then we can worry about my problems."

"I lent Johnny a bunch of money before we left. I was carrying way too much cash, and I'm grateful he fixed my car and is watching my dog so we won't have to worry about her."

"Y'all are like your own banks up here."

"That's just part of what we do, and we really aren't up here anymore. This is almost SoCal, remember?"

DOWN THE 101 (DRIVE 3):
(-Highway 101/-Santa Barbara)

Again, Crispin and I meander the state in a common ritual of wanderlust. We feel like better friends when we are in action or motion, and this feels like a road trip adventure again once we hit the highway.

California has the largest economy and the highest total population of any state in the country, yet is so remote feeling at times. The 101, as Highway 101 is referenced, is long stretches of wide-open countryside between developed areas. Just to think how huge and relatively uninhabited the eastern side of the state is gives me some sort of scope of America: This young country is giant, diverse and still developing. California is giant, diverse and still developing. Each pushes the other.

Riding in the car through a mostly uninhabited stretch of American country, I ask myself: Is California emblematic and representative of America?

It represents so much of the US in economy, land and population, not to mention the cultural contributions of Hollywood and of other Californian artists, and what California means to Americans.

When the rest of the world thinks of America, they may think of New York City first, because NYC represents the whole wide world. But then they think of California: Los Angeles, San Francisco...Texas, the Deep South, Chicago, D.C., Vegas, Florida.

California is America's top mascot. When the world thinks of what the United States is, they actually think of Hollywood - the America that they see on the silver screen or picture tube. Hollywood wins in the end. Confirming California's importance in Crispin's car I say, "Great state. I've been to a lot of different cities on this journey now: Arcata, Eureka, McKinleyville, Willits, Ukiah, San Fran, Oakland, Santa Cruz, Watsonville. How many is that? Nine."

Crispin says, "That's fun; you know this is my first trip to LA?"

"I know," I say. "Santa Barbara is down here, too – I haven't been there yet. Nor San Jose, where we can stop on the way up to see Pook."

We grind up some weed and roll a joint and get stoned. The SoCal band Sublime is on the satellite radio, so we rock out without speaking for a song.

Then I say: "Did you know Santa Cruz is the home of the University of California at Santa Cruz Banana Slugs."

"Really? I saw those shirts and thought that was a joke."

"I heard they let the student body vote on a mascot, and apparently the slugs are everywhere because of the weather and all the farming. That's some radical California for ya."

"Totally rad. Who could play football with a name like that?"

"How many trips to California have I been on, I was wondering?"

"How would I know?" Crispin snaps, sounding perturbed.

"I'll count silently."

Count the trips. This is one. 1993 is one, making two. In between, I went to two comic book conventions in Diego to work, that makes four. LA last year, and LA and Orange County and Diego on my honeymoon. I actually went to LA twice on my honeymoon, but since the honeymoon was all one long trip it makes more sense to think of it as once. I've been to California six times.

"Six," I announce. "I've been to California six times so far and out West seven times. I went to Vancouver once and took the train down to Seattle and back. Vancouver is probably my favorite city. The views of ocean and mountains and sky alone are so out of this world; it's unfathomably gorgeous. And they have great transit and people walk like San Francisco or New York. It's big dense city North America. They have a cool city park that's a rainforest, Stanley Park."

"Hash bars?" Crispin asks.

"Not really hash bars but there is a place called Cannibas Café..."

"I remember Cannibas Café from an issue of High Times."

"Right, right. I found that place. They let you bring herb from outside and smoke there; they can't sell it. It's sold right on the street."

"But you really love it there in Vancouver that much? Maybe we should have gone there."

"I thought about doing that, but I don't have a valid passport right now. You only needed a license for Tijuana or Vancouver before 9-11. Not sure about that anymore, but I'd love to go to Mex and Diego. Diego's a perfect blend of breeze and sun, and the people there are fun. Everyone moves there, like Atlanta, and it's fun to be that close to Mexico, where you can walk right in, and you're not far from the action of LA, without actually having to deal with living in the megalopolis of LA."

I'm internal for a stretch of time, while I mentally add to my total list of California towns I have visited: Sacramento from 1993, Napa. Part of Lake Tahoe is Cal. El Segundo once to get gas. Huntington Beach to visit my cousins, such a great beach town. And I've seen Hopland. This is all new to me now, this stretch of pretty highway. First time north of LA and south of Sacramento and the Bay Area. The Golden State and we are zooming under the radiant California sunshine.

I say, "I can speak on California from experience after having been here so many times."

Crispin adds, "You're just getting used to the golden Cali lifestyle."

Hollywood dreamin' as we continue our descent. I see palm trees and everything seems like a dream, like in Hollywood, like the cameras are rolling. The people of LA are so used to a camera rolling, cameras clicking. We will be there soon. This is SoCal, so I put my shades on.

"Check this out," I say. "The back of this sticker says, '30 years of California sole;' they've been making shoes a long time. You love yours?"

Cris says, "Except for the fact that we bought almost the same pair, yeah."

I'm a little hurt but cover it by saying, "We are a bit like frat brothers, with almost the same shoes on."

"Exactly. Frat boys."

"You want to stop anywhere in particular along the way?"

"You pick it, Van."

"Santa Barbara sounds good enough to me. Only

place the mountains aren't parallel to the sea. It finished first in this "Hottest Girls in America" article I read in some magazine at Lazy B's. All the usual suspects: New York, Austin, LA, Diego, Atlanta, Miami...Dallas. Athens made it, which gave the article more credibility in my eyes. Charleston was robbed, but it seemed fairly accurate."

"Santa Barbara was number one?"

"With a bullet."

"Fuck. Let me catch this call. It's ole homegirl from Atlanta again."

"Hey, I understand. It's home. Home is Top Ten."

I'm still a little miffed that Cris yelled at me outside San Francisco a few days ago. This morning before we left I told him that I don't navigate well on the fly from a lack of practice, while checking the map ahead of time. Glancing at it again now, it looks like finding LA should be pretty easy. And then Dave will be easy enough to find from Bicco, which is on the strip. He's probably working this weekend.

When Crispin hangs up I say, "I called Dave and left him a message before we left. He hasn't picked up at all, but I'm sure we are fine. He hardly ever answers."

"We better be fine," Cris says.

I slip back into quiet thought. Now we get to rock LA. I get to write about LA. And I'm being so LA with this project. I've always been a bit Hollywood. What, besides a movie or LA-based reality show, could be more LA than this experiment? Maybe a whole book on LA, that'd be pretty LA. Can't wait to be back in pretty LA.

I need to get a hand-held recorder. I need to physically write some of this down. I will remember most of this, but I should get a notepad. I need a journal. I'm really stoned.

"What kind of herb is this," I ask.

"Just some of the early stuff y'all trimmed. It's "Diesel." I actually don't have that much of my own stuff, which is fucked because I was supposedly meeting Smoothboy again, and then he just kinda flaked."

"I'll be cool if we run out," I say. "I'm totally self-medicating."

He says: "Legal out here since 1996 - big Olympic year back home."

I need Kava Kava every couple of days to keep me

even right now but don't really need weed. I think about coming home to Georgia stone sober before long and about being a responsible adult when this is done.

It's not so I say, "Cris, I've got a candy tin full of like eight types of weed. I bought some of it and worked for some of it. It's not much in weight, but it's pretty neat to have so many different kinds, so whenever you want just ask. We should smoke some of Pete's Genius next, maybe. We're almost to Santa Barbara by the way. American Riviera."

"I was thinking that," Cris says. "It's getting more tropical."

As we drive through it, earthy and airy Santa Barbara is charming houses with brick red, Spanish-tiled roofs, it is palm trees and ocean breeze. I could definitely live here. Very affluent SoCal, nice like Orange County. Almost suburban Los Angeles when you consider LA's largeness, yet more than far enough away to be a city with a completely separate identity from Los Angeles. It cascades postcard-perfectly down the hillside to the ocean, almost Mediterranean.

I say, "Beautiful. They call this the American Riviera. I read that in some travel magazine."

"It's gorgeous," Cris agrees. "You can see how they make pretty babies here. I'm so glad to be out of the land of the hairy legs and armpits. Too many of the girls up north are beasts. Beasts I tell ya."

"You don't love that now?"

"Never did. I ain't no stinkey hippie. I like 'em shiny clean."

"Speaking of beautiful, I'm feeling a bit bloated for SoCal. Maybe we should have something healthy and light for lunch."

"Yeah. I was thinking either health food or sushi."

We find health food first, and inside a bright and fancy health food store in Santa Barbara Cris asks, "What sups are you taking again?"

"Kava Kava for the prolonged detox." I answer. "You don't want to feel all tweaked on blow so bad when you feel great on Kava. There is a partial ban on it. They aren't selling it everywhere anymore because it's bad to mix with alcohol for the health of your kidneys. You can share what I have left whenever we aren't drinking. You buying all those supplements?"

"Yeah, Van. I want to feel really good."

"That's so LA, money. Feeling good is so LA. Almost as LA as looking good."

"These women in here are...healthy," Cris says through a smile.

"I noticed. I thought we weren't gonna talk about girls in SoCal."

"Something tells me they might come up, Van. We can talk without being gross, right?"

"Whatever you say."

"Dude, are you trying to start with me?" Cris says, sounding hurt.

"No, I mean it," I assure. "Don't be so sensitive all the time."

"You can't tell me not to be too sensitive. You know how I am! It helps me fully appreciate...when I do appreciate something."

"You lost me with all the negatives and double uses, but yeah. I know you, dude. You could definitely use some good Kava."

"Of course it would work for me, so they make it illegal."

"It's not illegal, dude." Glancing to the food counter I say, "I think that's your order. Ready to eat?"

Crispin says, "Sprouts and things here I come. What did you get?"

"Same. I loved the name and it sounds soooo good. Actually atomic tofu drop was a pretty good name too, but tofu has to be just right or I don't love it. I guess I'm a tofu snob from growing up vegetarian."

As we migrate toward the register with our trays Cris says, "Well let me buy you lunch, snobby one, and then let's get back on the road. It's a hot one today, and I want to get to stupid LA."

"You already hate LA? We could've headed to Portland."

"Nah. Get it off my list."

We sit and eat, and the fresh carrot juice I'm drinking gives me a charge. The bread is hearty, the sprouts are refreshingly crisp and moist, and the way the avocado mixes with the ginger dressing is so savory.

We stare out the window at the ubiquitous palm trees and sunshine. "Even the parking lots are pretty," I say. "Thanks very much."

"For what?" Cris asks.

"For lunch, this is so good…and sincerely, Cris, just for being a friend, man."

"You're welcome."

"I want to come back here and spend more time someday."

Back on the highway with the satellite radio blaring T-Rex, I'm full of anticipation. The land is not so developed at all for a stretch, and then we hit some lame suburbs, next replaced by less lame suburbs.

As we get closer to Hollywood, I look at myself in the rearview in these clear lenses. These glasses are emblematic of this experience. They are ornamental yet I'm slightly different with them on. I'm putting on a personality. But a clear lens is symbolic. I have eyes wide open on this journey. They are the camera I'm looking through, the lenses, my eyes.

"This book is these glasses," I tell Cris.

He says: "Dude, are you gonna spend this whole trip talking about your book? I don't wanna do that."

"I'll just get all jacked instead and talk about big tits."

"Great, Van. You do realize we will probably use in LA."

"I knew it was a possibility." The thought makes my stomach swirl and knot up. "I really shouldn't…but it's up to you."

"You think you can use and be okay?"

"I haven't had much luck with that. Look, bro."

"I can't. I'm driving. What?"

"A Vans outlet. No way."

"A little late for that."

"I'd love to go there, but I guess we're all stocked up on Vans."

"I would say so."

CITY OF ANGELS:
(-Los Angeles)

The view from a car of the palm tree-lined and sundrenched streets is the shot you always see of Los Angeles in movies and on television. We see it now and have finally arrived. This is LA. We are surging.

Where to go? What to do? Dave. Must find Dave, of course, King Dave, but we should do something else first - get a taste.

We turn onto the Strip and see teenagers of all races trying to look hip, many of them succeeding at it. Thirty-something affluents with shopping bags in their hands and thousands of dollars of casual wear on their thin, trim frames. I say, "Wanna stop first place I see that is cool?"

"Everything's cool," Crispin says.

"Right. Prepare to stop the car at the first place that has age-appropriate hot babes, then."

Model hottie actressettes are having a laugh, eating on the patio of a spot called Sushi Shop. "A little snack if you will," I say to Crispin in a dad from a 1960's sitcom voice as I point out a street space and we park. "We'll eat dinner at King Dave's place."

We get a patio table next to an actor dude in a hand-stitched Ed Hardy trucker hat with a dragon on it. He's having a big bowl of soup; I wonder if he eats only liquids this time of day. He's almost awkwardly good-looking: tall, chiseled face, pretty eyes, super fit, overly fashionable in an LA - I'm trying to be casual - way. He seems frustrated or anxious for some reason and keeps glancing at the time on his blackberry.

We order sushi and beers. Crispin and I have always enjoyed eating out together and have done sushi a few hundred times together, so there isn't much need for discussion regarding what to order. We are hot from having been in the car so long and having been in NorCal which is cooler. It's warmer here so I try imagining the air back home today, and being from the Southeast the lack of humidity is palpable.

Actor dude checks his messages, then finishes and grimaces at his fancy phone.

103

"Can I ask you a question," an indigent man passing by asks him.

I amuse myself, thinking: Actually, he already did ask a question.

"No you may not ask me a question," actor dude says bluntly.

"We're broke," I quickly say as he glances to us, before he speaks. Crispin may have been meaner, more personal. He dislikes blatherskites.

"You know," actor dude says to us. "I wonder what that question would have been. It's like, fuck, I'm eating soup, about to hurry out of town to bust my ass working. I mean, I'm eating, just having my soup."

"Oh, I know," Cris agrees.

I laugh a little under my breath. I'm no huge fan of panhandlers either, but I don't have any interest in this conversation. I'd much rather stare at girls and drink beers than complain about the impoverished.

Hot, tall woman sitting down there is yummy; I bet she models.

"He should be asking for an application to wash dishes," actor boy continues.

"Exactly, that's what I would be doing if I was him."

Cris is not lying. He has done worse jobs, but they would hire Cris and wouldn't hire our now departed bum friend. The reality of the situation is that once you are too far gone, it isn't easy to find any work, even the lowest menial labor. No one wants to give you a chance, and maybe you don't deserve a chance after a certain point. Could I have become that bad off?

Now actor dude is on a rant. "Not while I'm eating, you know. I sometimes help people out."

"Of course," Crispin chimes.

"I really have."

"Not while you're fucking eating."

"Exactly!"

I'm wondering if these two should sit together. It would be funny to tell them to get a room. Since I feel the need to show them I completely disapprove of this super lame discussion, I lose myself in the room, staring at my surroundings. My A.D.H.D. mind can just race thoughts in a stimulating environment, and I don't have to speak here to have fun.

The women in here are so hot. That was why I'd said, "Stop the car." It's the strip in LA, so there are pretty girls everywhere, but I do have a thing for beautiful black women, and I saw a bunch of black model types in here. It was the first place we saw on the strip that was packed with lots of girls. We wanted to stop at the first good place we saw, and I specifically saw a huge pair of perfect black, not brown, black breasts virtually busting out of a small top. There she is, so dark and lovely. I wish she would look over here.

"Stare much?" Crispin is back to me. He always monitors my behavior, which is ridiculous and pathetic on two fronts: one, he is not extremely well behaved, and two, I can be worse than he is at times.

"Who can blame him," actor boy says. "The way they dress."

"I want her to see me check her out...this ain't Humboldt. These chicks live to be checked out. It's what they do." I want to continue on about it being their jobs, but I'm sure it is what our new friend here does and don't want to somehow insult him.

He says, "They aren't very shy in LA. ... You guys from Humboldt?"

"He is," I answer. "I'm from Atlanta."

"I'm from Atlanta too," Cris responds defensively.

"He just lives in Humboldt," I quickly clarify, embarrassed I misspoke. Cris is from ATL too and didn't give that away when he moved.

"Bet you smoke some good herb," actor dude says.

We all laugh without saying anything else on the subject. The sushi arrives, and not much is said outside of commentary on the food, which is fresh and enjoyable. We quickly finish the meal and say our farewells to actor boy, as he tells us he's on his way to New York.

We leave and decide to look around a few overpriced clothing stores, mainly just checking women the whole time. Is that what we need to do? See a ton of hot ladies. I'm enjoying being on vacation; this feels like a vacation suddenly.

As we walk back to our car, I realize that I'm single and on vacation at the same time for the first time in maybe ten or twelve years. Did I even go on a trip while single between my two very long-term relationships? I can't think of any. Carolina Beach that time I got in a huge argument with Dad, but that was after Madeline and I hooked up.

It has actually been fifteen or sixteen years since I was single and on vacation. No wonder this is so unfamiliar to me.

I can't only look, but I can touch, too. Of course, I touched some in the past when I shouldn't have, and I got caught. Now I could touch, and it would be okay.

I'm so low and lonely even on a high, like now. I hope this visit to LA cheers me up some.

"Ready to roll?" Crispin asks.

"Sure," I lie, trying to sound chipper. We get in the car.

I would rather be at home - I have no home - with my wife and kids. I have no wife. Thank God I have wonderful kids I love dearly, but I have no wife anymore, so I may as well make the most of it.

It's a time to grieve, actually. I'm in mourning for my marriage and shouldn't even be here like this, maybe. I am here though, and it will be fun. This should not have happened, but it did. I did this, and I'm stuck with this, so make the most of it.

I need to be comforted and distracted by this wild place, though I know all that glitters is not gold. Be blessed to be here in beautiful Los Angeles, the City of Angels. Or as Jim Morrison from the Doors called it: Fantastic LA.

The sun is setting now and the lights are shining brighter up ahead. Los Angeles an intoxicating expanse of lights at night; the glowing downtown skyline only a small part of the wide swath of vast life, illuminated in light. It'll be an exciting drive on The Strip, so I hide the fact that I actually just feel like crying...again.

"Let's go find Dave," I say, trying not to sound too sad. "I wonder what he's been up to?"

THE STRIP:
(-Los Angeles)

The lights, the Strip, the girls, LA. All of it. A city done up in pinks-reds-flash-bling-glow-pretty. There's an easily recognizable shine to the main street of most major cities, and this is main street LA-style: palm trees, neon, modern businesses, and hot people in cars. Los Angeles is a vast ocean of lights, cameras, action, and we're rolling the world famous Sunset Strip, Sunset Boulevard. The Strip. We are surging.

We eventually see Bicco, every inch of it in yellow. We find parking in back and charge to the scene. And by the time that Mr. Crispy and The VAN arrive at King Dave's restaurant, after having driven through a glowing river of lights, we are in full character. This is our LA vacation, our Hollywood movie, and we are holding court.

And The VAN says, "Game on," as I fluidly slink down on a barstool and glance to my costar. "This is the sporting life now, chap."

"Indeed I concur," he says.

Cool, Frank is bartending tonight.

"Lo and behold," I say. "I know the bartender." To him: "Good to see you."

"What can I get you?" Frank says flatly.

"Two Stellas and menus," I answer.

He is married to Joan, my first of two serious college girlfriends. She is an executive at Capitol Records now. After freshman year we stayed friends, sort of, and most of Joan's exes over the next few years became pretty good friends of mine. She dated cool people and married even cooler. Frank is from Austin, which automatically gives him some cred in my eyes. He is hip and smart, yet very unassuming and easy to be around. Dave hires only cool people, and he worked for Dave before at a restaurant that had a flower shop in the same common space, both businesses flowed into each other. He was the server there on my honeymoon, when Maddy and I bookended Acapulco with LA. We also saw him at a show at the end of that trip, at the Whiskey. I miss Maddy.

On my last trip to Cali, Dave and I stopped by the

old place of business to see Frank for coffee. Dave had moved on to this place by then. I remember Denise Richards happened to be dining at the old restaurant once when I was in there. I tell myself not to forget to namedrop...even just in my mind, because This is LA.

Atlanta has become a bit of a star scene because of the music industry, so most modern Atlantans, like me, get the LA thing. LA is the star scene. Anywhere you go in LA, a star might be shining, but the closest thing to a star that cool Cris and I see tonight is a room full of the hip and well-attired, many of which are gorgeous young women.

Frank didn't talk much with me at all. I guess he's just too busy, but he acted weird. Great that he works here at Bicco now, because he is someone I'd like to get to know better. I think he acts in a few television commercials and maybe does music.

I'm just quietly enjoying this, shining here in character: wearing the clear-lens, Harley Shop glasses with perfect jeans – the California classic: Levi's. My personally designed T-shirt is bright red and in brand new condition, with a colorful street print popping. Plus, Van's new Vans shoes almost match my dude's shoes, so we're surely a team. My hair is sort of spiked up and semi-messy with pomade, where I styled it in the car. And I suddenly feel amazing tonight. Though Cris's wardrobe consists of mainly Hawaiian shirts, he obviously picked out his nicest light blue one and his coolest jeans for this event. We look and feel on.

Cris is busy studying the menu and the scenery. I'm sort of headbobbing to the music, just feeling the cool vibe of the place.

"Van?" Frank says. "I didn't recognize you before. I'm a little embarrassed I didn't. Heard you were coming to town."

I say, "It's these glasses. I almost forgot I had them on."

We order more beers and pizza by the yard and settle in, and then I see Dave and say hello. He is helping with the door and being the general manager. That's the way busy weekends in the restaurant business go. Every table in here is full and people are flowing in and out. I'm just glad they are doing good business, which a place with high overhead based on location must.

I show Frank the tin I have packed full of eight different kinds of bud from Humboldt. The middle section is bright purple, and each type is distinguishable by look.

"It's unbelievable," Frank says.

So I wow him further by giving him a free purple bud. I tell him it's part of his tip. He asks how my trip is going, and I tell him a bit about trimming in Humboldt. I ask him about Joan, who is doing great.

When he walks off to pour a draft beer, I have a moment to silently admire my surroundings. This whole place is yellow, shades of yellow. Lots of neat original LA art and good up-tempo music. I've been here before and need to feel it here now. Wrapped in colored glass, wrapped in yellow, wrapped in ass at Dave's house of commerce. Now this isn't so bad after all.

He should own this place, of course, but owning a restaurant is not the dream. Dave is an actor. He does own a little piece of it actually, and he could have a restaurant of his own by now if that was what he really wanted. He generally gets what he wants, and instead he wants to act. And he does "act:" He gets national television advertising campaigns regularly, which is better than ninety percent of actors in Los Angeles who are unemployed by virtue of not having worked in the past year.

He seemed a little anxious about something when we briefly spoke, maybe just that it's so busy. But I'm sure he must be used to that. I hope everything is okay.

An attractive, slightly older woman sits to my right. She notices me noticing her and immediately starts to flirt. She is the mother of an employee here, Warren, who looks like an eighteen-year-old James Dean. She introduced herself as "Janet from Georgia" when she heard us mention Atlanta. She lives in Florida now, one of the many Florida boat ladies who only date dudes with boats. Interesting to immediately run into a fellow Georgian.

A beautiful young woman named Judi shows up next, grabbing the last bar seat beside Cris. She soon decides to go out back with us to smoke, so he and I get her high and feel her up a bit, caressing her exposed back and shoulders. She is like velvet, a Persian actress and former soccer star with muscles covered in the softest flesh, wearing a ribbon dress that shows so much skin it would be illegal in some states. Her long jet black hair is exquisite and her necklace is a miniature brass knuckles. She is buff, tough and outgoing and has dark, mysterious eyes and a gorgeously smooth face.

"Oh yeah, feel free to touch me," she says. "I love to be touched."

This is LA and I'm on vacation, so I do touch her a little more while we finish up the joint. I hear LA throng around me as I caress her silken skin while she moans and coos a little under her breath.

Back inside, we eat, drink, talk to the ladies. We are in regal moods tonight, and Bicco, like LA as a whole, is so chock full of the beauties that move here because of the magnetic draw of Hollywood. Plus, it's the energy of the weekend on The Strip; that still has meaning.

I wonder if I'm ready to hook up with someone. If I do, I want to make sure there is a real connection.

I notice that Cris and Judi are deep in conversation about Humboldt. And suddenly Janet and I really start to connect. She makes it known that she wants to hang out with me, but she is not sure how her son will take it. He is young, nineteen she tells me. She is over forty, but very attractive.

Her eyes smile at me and her hand is on my leg a few times as we talk about the beauty of Georgia, her boat and ocean life in Florida and the glitz of Los Angeles. She is a charming Southern woman.

Judi's friends eventually show up and call her from the patio, so she heads out front to meet them. I realize the evening is winding down, so I get Janet's number. I'm not too sure if we will connect. I liked Warren right away and don't want to freak him out by seducing his mother, but I may at least call her. My attraction toward her grew as we spoke.

Dave stops by and tells me his brother-in-law is in town and staying at his apartment. Unfortunately we will need to get a motel. That was the anxiety I sensed. Surprise, Dave won't be able to host us.

Dave says Frank will help us find a room. Then Frank comes back to us and tells me he will get us all set up. They know a good place.

Cris gives me the word to score and we arrange for Frank to find us some blow after work. He is getting off very soon. I go along with it, even knowing it's a bad idea.

Janet leaves with Warren, who is getting off work, after he briefly tells me about the acting school he attends. She basically ignored me while he was near, which makes me way less likely to hook up with her.

Dave is obviously flirting with a young Bettie Page-type brunette customer seated at a table beneath us. I can see from her eyes and posture that she is clearly enamored with him. I wonder if the guy she is seated with is her date. He sort of seems to be. That isn't stopping Dave.

Crispin and I decide to drink one more beer each. We watch Dave run game then discuss the local art on display. I comment how various pieces remind me of famous artists, and we agree that we especially like all of the bright colors against the yellow backdrop.

Soon Frank gets off and heads to the back of the restaurant to turn in his cash drawer, so Cris and I say bye to all the girls out front on the patio before strolling around toward the back to wait.

"Judi's friends are way calmer and less sexy than she is." I say. Judi is as overtly sexual as any woman I've ever met; she literally drips sexiness, and I wish I'd kissed her neck. Her friends seemed more like traditional nice girls, and for some reason I'm a little disappointed. But we did make vague plans to see Judi again, and I got her number.

Walking near the car, Cris says, "I want to have a relapse of titanic proportions."

I laugh and worry and say nothing and jones. Frank comes out through the back entrance, and the three of us leave together. Dave will be here late closing business for the day.

In the car, I try not to think about getting blow. Instead, I think of the history of my friendship with Dave. He has always been a leader. People gravitate to him.

I first met him the final week of high school. We went to neighboring schools and were both members of the class of 1989, both king of the world seniors when we met. The '80s were about to be over and high school was drawing to a close, and I wanted to majorly celebrate graduation. I

111

had spent much of my childhood fantasizing about high school, watching anecdotal John Hughes' movies and Risky Business and stupid sitcoms about high school. It had finally almost reached an end, and I was amazed and a little alarmed that it would be over so soon. We'd almost be grown ups, I'd then thought.

I met Dave that very last week of school. Right away we were two of a kind, and with my younger classmate Rich we stole the admittedly lame nickname the three amigos. When I had the largest graduation party in the history of the county, an epic event my friend entitled Vanfest, we earned rock star status for the summer as the organizers. We clicked with everyone we met that summer. It was a blast, spent in Buckhead drinking underage on the deck of a reggae bar that served us, in houses where parents were permissive or at work, with Dave meeting our friends and Rich and I meeting Dave's friends.

I remember Dave's old piece of crap Mustang. He called it Thunder Dome because he would crank music so loud in there, with alternative rock playing through a bad stereo. Throughout that golden summer of fleeting youth that old bomber hauled us to concerts, parties and nights out in the city. We all had a bullshit door-to-door sales job together, just hung out for three solid months. And there were always hot girls around.

Vanfest cemented my legacy as a legend of Cobb County, and Dave was already legendary amongst his peers by then because he had charisma to spare.

In retrospect, when Dave left for college in Florida that fall the fun was diminished. We still went out in Buckhead. In fact, I went out way more once Dave procured me a good fake I.D. and mailed it to me from school, but it began to change for us. People started getting in trouble: fights and arrests. We started using ecstasy and blow, just wasting a year, clubbing and barhopping four to five nights a week.

That was my whole first year out of high school. Nothing much good came of it, and thankfully I moved east to Athens for school at UGA the next year. Meanwhile, the charisma king was hanging out with actor River Phoenix and all the other cool kids he was meeting in Gainesville. Something terrible came of it. Some of them got into speed, and eventually Dave got in too deep and got arrested surrounding a friend's overdose and went away for a while.

He resurfaced my third year out of high school and moved in with us in Athens and attended UGA and managed restaurants. Eventually, he followed a beautiful classmate to Atlanta. A year later, they moved to Los Angeles where he worked in restaurant management while she worked in production and acted. Not much later, Dave tried out for a Nike commercial and got it and got his union card and became an actor.

OUR FREAK OUT:
(-Los Angeles)

Dave won't be hanging with us late night, but he will join us for a few beers at Steeplechasers. I've been before, and it's a real bar. For such a large city, not too many real bars in LA. In fact, not much in Los Angeles is real.

I have done relatively little blow over the past few months, and I am jonesing, hard. We are in the car leaving the Los Feliz area after scoring. I go second after Frank and do a giant key bump. The paranoia starts right away.

The lights and house and cars blur by. My sensory perception is too turned up. That was too much, or it's really good or something. My nose is running and I sniffle twice.

"Is that a cop car behind us?" I ask.

"No," Frank answers. "You okay?"

"He did too much," Cris says. "That key bump was remarkable in its hugeness."

We reach the strip and find a parking place in the neighborhood behind the bar and walk. Dave is right outside waiting for us. I look high. I'm too obviously wired and can't stop my mouth from twitching, and my nose is still running.

I see cops. There are cops. A cop car is passing, I hope it's passing. And those two cops are right outside on their bikes, and I'm visibly geeking, my mouth and eyes twitching. I know I look fucked up, and I'm scared out of my mind.

"Get me in the bar, fast," I say to Dave, who is standing in front of the bar on the sidewalk. He was out to greet me like a champion of LA, which he is. I am no champion. I'm having a bad time.

I'm panicky as I show my I.D. to the doorman and Dave ushers me into the bar. I know I should be okay, I'll be okay if I can just calm down. I'm amongst friends inside a dark tavern. Dave is guiding me down.

"I see from your eyes," Dave says.

"I know," I say.

"Calm down, Van."

"I'm trying. I don't like this."

114

"You want me to get you out of here pretty soon?"

"Yeah, dude. I'm sorry. I just can't...handle it anymore. I'm sorry."

"Don't worry about that right now. Relax. I'll get you out of here before too long. You are fine."

"Okay."

Crispin likes the place. He and Frank play rock songs on the jukebox and buy drinks. Dave has me sort of partitioned off from the crowd and my friends.

Dave tells me to catch my breath, and I do, I try. I feel better, not good, still shaken, just better. It's so relieving to come back from a paranoid state, like I was in.

Why do I do this to myself still? Addiction. I thought I shook it. I must completely stop using

I'm sweaty and get some beverage napkins and dab my face, especially my leaky forehead. Thank God for bev naps, I think.

"Beer and a shot, beer and a shot," I hear from someone in the crowd. It's a beer and a shot type of bar.

I should be cool now, but I'm not completely. I see from Dave's eyes that he knows I'm tripping still. I try to fixate on the few hot girls in here, just to think of something. I can't shake it.

Yet I am a suddenly bit better. I didn't do that much in the big scheme of things, just quite a little, all at once, like old times. I'm starting to come down. I'll be okay.

This place is packed, mostly with young men pounding beers and doing shots while the jukebox blares out a good selection of loud music, mostly heavy 1990's rock. I like this Kurt Cobain stuff still.

I wish I could shake out of it because these people are what I came to see. This is the slice of America that I came to see. I came down here to see LA, and they are LA, these men and women trying to get down on Sunset Strip, trying to relive a famous time or to help make now a famous time, to do it on The Strip. Everyone is some sort of mover and shaker in this place, even me. And the strip itself is a famous character. This should be cool. I'm not that high anymore. Why am I still tripping?

I'm not really. I'm okay now.

Frank gets my attention and says, "Have you noticed the inadvertent raping?" to describe the sensation of men that are passing by him in this crowded, shotgun-style, narrow, long, packed bar. He continues, "Straight men are rubbing their cocks up against me, and they really don't want to, but there is no other way to get through."

It is funny stuff, and I chuckle, but I am just... shaken, and it is too packed in here. I want to puss out as soon as possible.

A little later, Dave arranges for Crispin and I to leave at the same time as Frank without me having to say anything. Frank takes us to a dive motel after the first place - where they knew people - was booked up. We are right in the heart of things, activity. Nighttime Los Angeles on the weekend is honking and pealing out and playing loud music, loud voices.

All locked in, in the room, I am relieved. Crispin and Frank and I use more. I am so thankful not to be in public anymore that I feel okay. I'm high in relative safety now and have a pleasurable endorphin surge.

My usage pattern has become contemplation, followed by the realization that I will be using, followed by and accompanying a quick spike in adrenaline. That surge makes me almost nauseous in my stomach and excites me to the point of frenzy. Then I actually use and the first rush to the brain is good, soothing. Then I either have already used too much or I proceed to use too much, quickly. I freak out. Then I come down a wee bit, half the edge comes off.

Then, I can't stop and I use more and more and more until it is gone. If it's mine, I bang back the whole bag all at once if I can and get it over with. I can't carry without totally freaking out. If it's someone else's stuff, I get it and do as much of it as I can as fast as I can until I have had too much. Only too much is enough. Tonight I did as absolutely much as I could in one big snort. In Atlanta, I was hooving down half grams all the time, in one hard whiff.

In the motel Cris says to me, "I didn't know a little blow was going to do that to you, buddy. You okay?"

"Now I am," I blurt. "I really should never do blow in public."

"Did you see how much he did that first go round?" Cris asks Frank.

"Yeah. I was amazed." Frank says to me, "You did

too much to start out. You should start with a smaller amount and do more later if you want."

"I know," I say. "Bad habit. It's like I don't really even want to have fun using it anymore. That's why I need to quit completely, keep trying to quit. I make it bad, fast."

Frank hangs out until he gets a few lines in him. Cris is with him in conversation, but I don't say much else. Cris gives me another line at my request.

Frank doesn't stay much longer after I break out the new porn mags, just to have something to fixate on. He says he has stuff to do tomorrow and leaves. I'm immediately embarrassed I looked at porn in front of him, but looking at it helped me take my mind off almost melting down.

And a new meltdown is unfolding. Cris is beginning to audibly worry about all the money he is carrying, thousands. And the guy at the check-in may have seen it in his bag, when he had to get a second form of identification out. He fears that the guy may be planning to have us robbed. I'm fixating on Crispin's drama now, and it's my fault because I started the paranoia.

He freaks hard. He thinks that he may be having a heart attack. I'm worried again. This place is a total dive. This sucks.

He goes to the bathroom to beat off to some of the porn. I lay there listening to the sounds outside the room, scared.

I get really worried that Cris may have had an actual heart attack in there, and I eventually go to the door and disturb him. I say through the door, "You okay?"

It's embarrassing. Better to know he is okay, but we should be, and are, embarrassed. Bad first night.

I get back in bed and pull the covers way up and clutch my pillow, hiding from the sounds outside. It is getting late, so the engine and tire sounds are more sporadic. A car alarm starts then stops. It's almost quiet for ten minutes, just a faint buzz. I start to drift off. Then strong desert winds howl through the motel courtyard, while I listen.

PERRR-FECT!:
(-Los Angeles)

When we wake we are just glad nothing too bad happened. We admire the owner's 1957 Chevy out front before departing.

Two cars are honking at each other at a traffic light as we pull out. "Honkeys!" Crispin shouts at them.

I laugh, remembering this as an old joke of his. "We need to do something fun today," I say to him. "Last night may actually be a good story, but it sure wasn't fun."

"Not really," he says.

"Any blow left?"

"You just said it was no fun, and now you ask if we have any left?"

"That motel madness was obviously no fun, dude, but I am still addicted. I did not say we should do any...yet." Cris shakes his head and says, "I may give you some, much later."

"Whatever, I guess I had to ask...still addicted."

"Yeah. Me too, I guess. You gonna write about last night?"

"Yeah."

"How will you remember what to write about?"

"I have that type of memory for detail as you know, and if something is interesting to me I'm making a mental note to write about it later. I will get a notepad pretty soon and start jotting down notes for later, but I just want to have fun today after the ordeal of late last night. That evening started so good."

"At least no one got hurt," says Cris, referencing his heart scare.

"Thank God, and it was still no fun. I was worried about you."

"Me too, homeboy. Turn that up a little."

"Head that way," I say. "It's a really nice day."

"It'll be hot soon enough," Crispin says pessimistically.

A fifteen-minute drive and a phone call later, I'm thinking that daytime Los Angeles is happening for us. We drove around a bit, then I got Dave on the phone and got clear directions to his place.

"I had us heading in the right general direction," I say to Crispin.

Passing the big Fred Segal store on the way I say, "That is a great place to buy a hundred dollar T-shirt."

"Yeah? I'll pass," Cris says.

"Me too, but I would love to be selling like that."

"What do you need to do it right?"

"Really just a website, a brochure and a new business license. I let mine expire. I was just way too busy with work to do fashion stuff once I changed day jobs. Then I got too busy with bad stuff."

"You should put some new gear out there."

"I plan too, eventually. I should really be collecting store business cards when I have the chance, so that I can send brochures."

"I'm not stopping now, but I will stop for you if you ask."

"Cool," I mutter, realizing I will never ask him to stop for a card.

We take in the sights of iconic LA imagery along the Miracle Mile: the empty diner from Pulp Fiction, the hip city restaurants, the specialty boutiques, the museum and an advertising onslaught of billboards and signs.

"Finally, something fun," Crispin says as the White Stripes stop pounding and he turns the stereo down; hot women are streaming by.

"No doubt," I say. "You haven't had some fun?"

"A little."

I ramble: "Well, yeah, I mean, we have pretty much been driving around in this car the whole time, at Bicco, or in a ratty motel freaking out, so I guess I have to agree that that is not all that fun really."

"Today is!"

"Exactly. Dave is gonna drive down to Venice Beach in the Bronco. He always drives, so you don't have to worry about driving."

"Perfect," Cris says."

"Perrrr-fect," I improve it on repeat. "That reminded me of my old boss, my mentor at Ascot Realty, Steve Cloudsmith. He would always say perfect like that. Perrrr-fect...perrr-fect. I was always giving him these little status reports, and after each item on my agenda, point of business, he would say perfect. For business, it was…perrr-fect."

"Missing your old job, home skillet?"

"No, just the people. I was joking about it being perfect. That guy took me under his wing though and helped me to develop some professionally…and I thanked him for it. I really don't miss that crap."

"Dude, you are thinking about your old job…now."

"But I'm thinking that I don't have to work there anymore, which is actually good considering how tired I was getting of doing it most days."

"Exactly!"

"It was a decent job. I was not good, eventually.

"Oh, I know. If anyone knows, Van, I know."

"I was good at it."

"Of course. You were you. You have been good at every job you have ever had probably, Van. You are talent. You're good at work. You actually like it."

"Sometimes I do. I like to use my brain…and my strong personality to get things done. Let's just have some fun today. That's La Brea tarpits up here by the way."

"What's that all about?"

"Dinosaurs preserved forever in tar. Woolly mammoths or something. The street is right near here."

"What street is it?"

"Cochran. I see now. It's right back over there actually, but we may have to turn around. His apartment is right there. I remember now. No big deal."

"Nothing's a big deal when you aren't driving."
We turn around and turn down Cochran, and I see Dave's Bronco on the left, directly in front of his house. There is nowhere to park.

"Just go inside and get him. I'll find someplace to park," Cris says.

"If you don't, just come back and you can take his space."

"Are you sure? I don't want to assume."

"If you can't find a space, drive back here. He always drives."

"See ya!" he yells as I exit.

That was the farewell salutation the servers used to say to each other at the restaurant where I tended bar

120

in Atlanta way back in the day. I like how slang migrates around a group and from group to group, especially if I know how it started. I remember Dave's funny expressions from college.

"Sweet-ner," I say into Dave's open window. That was his phrase for all that was good. He is on the ground floor, the corner apartment. I've stayed with him in LA twice in the past, once at this apartment.

I hear: "Van. Is that you?"

I joke: "No, Davener. It is not me."

I walk up the sidewalk and the stairs and into the building. Dave is in the open doorway to his apartment smiling his huge, pearly white Hollywood grin.

"Good morning, bro," he says. "Where is Crispin?"

"Trying to park."

"Why? He could take my space. I'm ready to go. You saw my Bronco right out front, Scottie Pimpin', didn't you? I'll drive. You know that I always drive."

"Always, D Rock. I told him you always drive."

"Why didn't he listen?"

"He's like that sometimes."

"Sorry about my place. You know I wish you could stay here."

"It's cool. When are they leaving?"

"A few days. I tried to call you back."

"Bad cell service in the mountains."

"Frank come back to the room with you?"

"Yeah. It was a total dive."

"The place I told him to take you is a nice place."

"Frank said they were totally booked."

"I should have gone up there. They usually hold a few rooms back because this is Hollywood, and you never know when someone important will show up and need a room."

"Right. We weren't important enough to buy a room from them."

Dave shrugs. Looking out the window he asks, "That him, dude?"

"Yeah. I'll get him real quick."

"I'm ready to go."

"Dave, he is coming all the way down from Humboldt. Can't we let him inside?"

"Sure."

I notice Dave's American Indian neighbor taking his wolves out for a walk as I let Crispin in. "Those are real wolves," I tell Cris.

"I thought so," Cris says. "That dude an Indian?"

I say, "Full-blooded. He has lived here for at least a few years, I guess. I remember him from last year."

We enter the apartment and Dave and Cris get acquainted. They don't know each other well at all but met once or twice the summer after high school or in Athens. They mainly know of each other through me.

"Dave, I decided to write a book about this trip," I say.

"Did you tell Frank about it?" he asks. "He writes, you know."

We all pile in Dave's black Bronco out front and head. Just the boys taking the Bronco to the beach through thick beats. The Game is playing. Dave loves Game and says, "I can't believe you guys aren't more into him."

The song ends. Dave turns down the stereo.
"Like I told you..." I say from the shotgun seat, "all we listen to is Atlanta rap. There is so much shit coming out from The ATL right now. Just wait, you'll see."

"Like Outkast?" Dave asks.

"Obviously, and like Ludacris. We've been listening to a lot of Young Jeezy, other new stuff. Me and some brothers I was hanging out with at the trap on Peachtree, but I can't hang out like that anymore."

"Most your friends black now?"

"A lot of the dudes I hang with in the city, or was hangin' with."

"I'm real tight with Dallas Austin now."

"Wow."

"He's out here now. Really, really good guy."

"I want to be a mogul someday."

"Right, bro. Am I in your book a lot?"

"I haven't seen you a lot, and the book is what I see, but yeah, of course I'll talk about you some. We came down here to hang with you."

"We're hanging right now."

"True."

"That's the skateshop where I buy all my stuff. Need

anything?"

"I'd love to go. I already went to the skate shops in Santa Cruz, and I bought my son a cool purple Alien Workshop deck; he wants to skate."

"Awesome. I have a white vintage Christian Hosoi Hammerhead."

"No way. He was by far my favorite skater."

"We'll stop in the shop on the way back if we have time. I want to get on down to the beach. There's something I have to do later."

"Okay."

Dave touches the bill of his ballcap and says, "You like my hat, don't you? It's from the set of Dogtown and Z Boys.

"I want to start skating again," I say.

Dave asks, "You good back there, Crispin, with the wind and whatnot?"

"Great, Dave," Cris says.

I tip my head to Dave, and the rap music comes back up as he punches it. Dave breaks out a handmade aluminum foil pipe full of kind bud and says, "I use these because they are disposable. I call it my no contest pipe."

Crispin laughs when the pipe is passed back to him and he sees that it is made of aluminum. They would never use anything except for the finest smoking devices up in Humboldt County.

"You should get a medicinal card, Dave," I say.

We are finished with the weed, so Dave crumples the pipe really fast and shouts, "No contest!"

VENICE WALK:
(-Los Angeles)

On Venice Beach, which generally speaking does not mean the beach, it means the walk, the freaks from the classic Chevy Chase comedy, Fletch. It means those world's most famous outdoor hoops' courts from movies like White Men Can't Jump and American History X. White and Mexican couples and wayward teens and hippies, seemingly every group from or in LA out for a stroll in the sunshine and beach breeze.

And the next paved row over - separated by a small parcel of sand -is for bikes, roller blades, skates and skateboards. Then the sandy beach itself full of people walking and laying out and tossing a ball or frisbee is followed by an ocean full of skimmers, surfers, boogie boarders, body surfers and swimmers. This is the SoCal recreation lifestyle.

Strutting, we do the Venice Walk and see the meatheads getting even huger at the famous weightlifting section known as muscle beach. We smell the salty ocean air and the enticing grease of street food. We appreciate the artistry displayed in some of the commercial booths, while scoffing at the cheesey stuff in others.

A big group is gathering near us in the middle of the wide sidewalk. Dave says, "Let's watch this. All the regulars like this dude."

"Let's do," I say, remembering from my honeymoon. "This is a good show."

The performer does contortion and fire breathing tricks and teases the crowd. He earns his money as his jambox blares that great old "I Love LA" song. Hearing the still familiar refrain: "We Love It," we have to admit that we do. This is LA.

After the show we walk and see bright colors reflecting LA's vibrancy. We see some artists hanging out in an upstairs apartment, above the fray of the street scene.

Multiethnicity is major understatement here at Venice; every shade of person is represented. Nearly everyone here has that LA look: beachy and casual yet somewhat of a stylish fashion victim. There is a certain urban hipness and edginess to the crowd of thousands out today.

"That's really bad guitar," I say about the tone-deaf emanations of one super dark-skinned man in a dress playing electric guitar on skates.

"I'll cut off my ear for a hundred dollars," one drunk shouts out to the crowd.

"Very Van Gogh," I say to Dave. Where is Cris? He must be around.

Just Dave and I alone talking, me explaining my two book concepts to him: "The character based in my novel that takes place in Atlanta, will be loosely based on me several months ago, how I got bad off."

"What's that character's name?"

"He may just go by Van. Why change what works?"

"True enough."

"What I'm researching now is Van's memoir, memories of Cali."

"That the title?"

"I'm trying to decide what to call it. Planning for it to be my second book, so I have time to decide all that."

Emanating from one artist's booth we hear: "Everything is on sale today." Products for sale. Is everything in Los Angeles a product? It's so commercial, superficial, culture of commerce. San Fran is more provocative, more: "Have you ever considered this?"

Bauhaus is being played from an overhead apartment.

"Remember those days, Dave?" I say, nodding upward.

Dave answers: "Dude, I wore makeup...and there were no cameras."

"I miss the Smiths and shoegazer crap like that," I say.

We are walking by a long row of shirt shops, with me thinking: I should have sold shirts to these places. I should still, but with places like these, these tourist shacks, it isn't a business card you want, it's on spot payment for product. And I don't have any product on hand.

"Leisure pursuits are such big business in California," I say to Dave. "I read in the paper that Santa Cruz and Huntington Beach are arguing over which one is the real 'Surf City.'"

"I like to surf right around here," Dave says. "Santa Monica is fun."

I pause then ask, "How far is that again?"

"Come here."

We walk off the shopping strip, through the paved path for cyclists and skaters, out to the sand. The sky over the beach is dark blue with hints of pink and silver. Dave points to a major beach enclave at the horizon of our vision and says, "You see that? That's it."

"I knew it was close to here. It's pretty fun there."

"You wanna find Crispin and walk over to the drum circle?"

"Let's have a beer somewhere."

"Where is your buddy, again? He reminds me of Crispin Glover."

"Right. Who knows. I was trying to keep an eye on him."

Dave sees Crispin in a merchant's booth and says, "There he is. He's looking at belts or something. He needs a tracking device. You can't just walk away from your friends at a place like this and expect them to find you. This isn't a bar."

"Right. He's just...like that. But he usually appears when needed."

"He's cool otherwise and all. Go get him, Van."

I walk near Cris and keep my eye on him. I stop by a booth a few slots down. I decide I need something cool and buy a classic shade of brown leather with white "V" bracelet with two silver "USA" snaps and put it on.

Then I get close enough for Cris to see me, and he nods and we walk over to Dave.

Cris says, "Did you guys see the Sacred Geometry Man paintings?"

"I'm not sure," I say.

He says, "You'd like that stuff, Van."

I say, "You saw us talking to that dude, in the orange shorts. I loved those bright, swirly paintings. Reminded me of Van Gogh's Starry Night. Dave is going to show him at Bicco."

"Good stuff," Cris says. We're all grinning.

Dave says, "Let me buy you guys a slice and a water."

The pizza is good, reminiscent of New York street

126

pizza. Cris takes his space from us again, and Dave says to me, "Are you and your wife getting back together?"

"No, I don't think so," I say.

"Oh," Dave says, looking right through me with intensely caring eyes. I melt. I want to cry.

"How's your pizza?" Dave asks, changing the subject to let me regain composure.

"Great," I say.

"I need to talk to you soon, Van. I want to make sure you're okay."

"I am. I will be. I am."

"I need you to go ahead and get okay right now. Be a man, Van! Stop being 'The VAN' for a second. You can't use blow and be okay right now, understand? You don't want that in your life. You want a life. You had a life, and you have a life. I need you to get it back together. Go ahead and change, grow, recover. Then I need you to blossom."

"...Thank you, Dave."

"Don't thank me. I was there! I was there, Van."

"I know," I say, contemplating that Dave had a major blow problem in LA for a time before he went clean. He's been through it.

He says, "We'll talk about Madeline and you later, when it's more private."

We look up and notice Cris eating by himself on a bench. We walk over to him and then all leave the main walk together for a nearby bar.

Dave has something to do and will be leaving Cris and I to form our own scenes soon. End of this little trip is Dave and Cris and I in a famous bar called Town Hall, they've been open since 1915.

Dave tells us we should get The Thomas Guide to Los Angeles, a compendium of LA maps better than any GPS, and I'm thinking I'd rather hang out with my best friend in person more than see the city.

Cris and I audibly decide we like it at this local bar enough to have a few rounds as Dave finishes his Newcastle with lime and leaves. Cris and I don't need to say much while we drink two beers and a red-headed slut shooter each. Then we let a taxidriver do the driving while Cris gets to see the city differently than he has before, because he isn't behind the wheel for once.

LOW-SLUNG AVENUES:
(-Los Angeles)

I came to a decision in the taxi: Since I've been to LA several times before, I want Crispin to have control over what we do. It should be more about him than me.

So back standing beside the car after a long, decliningly tipsy cab ride to the Wilshire area, I make suggestions. He shoots them down: Santa Monica is over near where we just took a cab from, so he doesn't want to go back that way. He isn't up for heading straight to Hollywood or going to a museum now. And it's too hot for a beach; he doesn't want to be in the sun. He works outside and "...that's hot enough."

"I'm sure," I reply. "But the beach will be breezy."

We enter the vehicle as he says, "That's all we did in Santa Cruz, practically. That's all we have done is hang out at the beach. We just left Venice today."

"But we didn't even go out all the way to the water. I was thinking of maybe body surfing the golden coast of Santa Monica this week."

"I'm not getting way out there in the water. We drove all this way to LA, and now all we have for me to do is drive or sit around a beach. This town is all about driving."

"All about it. That's the drawback to this city. It's like Atlanta: drive, drive and drive. You okay to drive now?"

"I'm fine now, Van."

We drive and drive and drive and see much of the widespread, low-slung mega-city that is Los Angeles. We know at night the famous Strip will be aglow, and the hills will surround us in twinkling lights. By day, the air in Los Angeles has a deserty, beachy, sunny warmth. I'm up for this place.

Southern California's almost tropical touch hits us and we ride it down the crest of hills, around the town. The music is pumping. Plenty of pretty things to see as LA is thronging around us. We sense it, yet we feel confined to our automobile, removed from the action.

Alas, we decide that we will do a lot of driving around today in an effort to take in as much of the city as quickly as possible. After all, driving is at the heart of the

128

entire invention of sprawling modern Southern California itself. SoCal is freeways, fast food and spread suburbs. Car culture comes from and thrives here. We are bumper-to-bumper in Los Angeles or barely flowing or rolling pretty good in the Intrepid, all around this expansive urban ocean. Cris tells me he needs money orders for bills. We somehow can't seem to find anyplace that has any, but we keep looking and driving. Los Angeles is a city of seemingly endless, distinct, yet somewhat similar neighborhoods, representing all world ethnicities, all social strata. A behemoth so grand and disconnected that motorized vehicles are the only viable travel options.

We first drive around the Wilshire area as I get my bearings. Next we drive the golden triangle of glitzy Beverly Hills, then ritzy Bel Air. We reach the collegiate area of Westwood and the UCLA campus.

Passing the front of the school I say, "You see LA today, Crispin, UCLA."

"Funny," he says.

"I think it's funny UCLA is in such a nice area and USC is in the hood, practically. Yet, USC is the expensive private school, the University of Spoiled Children."

"You make that up?"

"Nah. That was in Less Than Zero."

"What could UCLA stand for?" Cris ponders.

I suggest: "University of California, Latinos and Asians."

"Not bad."

"Not very white or black here is it? Not like Atlanta."

"Pretty off white."

"Definitely pretty. You see her?" We are driving past a hottie.

Cris nods and says, "Who could miss her?"

"Me. If she gave me the chance to."

"Westwood is or isn't UCLA?"

"The Wizard of Westwood is what they call the old Coach of UCLA; they won like ten hoops titles in a row, but it's the next area over. Kind of like town and campus in Athens, I guess."

"I love college," Cris says, grinning broadly.

Giggling, I say, "Me too. You see her?"

"Like I said about the last one, 'Who could miss

129

her?'"

"Football out here is USC. Basketball is UCLA and the Lakers."

"I still can't believe they have no NFL team. This town sucks."

"That is ridiculous with like fifteen million people. You want to come to a Georgia game with me this year? We are looking good."

"Yeah. I love college. Greene still quarterbacking?"

"Graduated with the most wins in college football history. D.J. Shockley is taking over."

"Great name."

"Right. Reminds me: my rap name is AOWB: Any Ol' White Boy. I'm going to have my character rap in my Atlanta book. I have one song. It's an anti-racism song; it's anti reverse racism, which is still anti-racism."

Cris smirks then says, "How does it go?"

"The main hook is like this: 'Don't call me WIGGA 'cause I'm Any Ol' White Boy, I'm not your little Ghetto boy, Boy Toy. Don't call me WIGGA, Don't call me WIGGA. You can't say that!' etcetera."

"Wanted to hate it, but that actually sounds like a hit to me," Cris says, grimacing.

We park and get out of the car and walk around Westwood for an hour and it almost feels like college - there's a certain palpable young cool vibe. We pass a few interesting hookah restaurants and stop into a hip clothing boutique where I grab a card. We decide not to walk around campus.

We get back in the car, and I'm contemplating the lay of the land of Los Angeles. The Cali sun is in full blaze as I decide to push again for the new Getty Center, a huge, air conditioned, new museum which I read in my LA travel book is nearby.

Cris declines, saying, "Just not in a museum mood today at all."

"I will be hitting Basquait before I leave LA, but that new museum is supposed to be exceptional. They spent literally in the billions on it, and the same architect that did the High Museum in Atlanta built it, Richard Meier."

"Let's just choose one museum and go before we leave."

130

"Basquiat, then. Done."

So just rolling, which would be okay, except it is summer and the air conditioning does not work, and Cris is suddenly in a mood to complain again. I'd rather be entertained than aggravated.

We stop by Bicco and have a beer and appetizer, just to get out of the car. Dave and Frank are not working now. A girl named Natalie is working the bar, and she has great eyes and a cool look. A bit of a bad skin day today for her, but she seems really fun. She and Cris make eyes, which amuses me. The waitresses seem to be cruising us too.

I have eyes for a brunette voluptuary who looks like an artist, and everyone in the room has eyes for an exotic beauty named Priscilla. When I briefly met her the other night, I told her that "I love the King." She got the Elvis reference, and Dave liked that line. These other girls are new to us, and there's a definite flirty vibe in here.

Warren is working lunch today, too. "I spent the night out in the desert listening to coyotes howl," he says. "What are y'all doing out in LA, besides hanging around with Dave? Just a weekender?"

I tell him - loud enough for the cute waitresses all to hear - that I'm traveling indefinitely and writing a book about this trip.

When he walks off, I say to Cris, "He's very likable. Glad I didn't bang his mom."

"Yet, you mean," he says. "Too late for that?"

"I think she's leaving tomorrow. I called her once and left a very general message. She seemed down for whatever. She said she once hooked up with one of his friends, but she was trying to be ultra-careful not to do anything like that again in front of him, since he got pissed. And she's staying with him."

"Pretty nice-looking broad. Sure you don't want to call her?"

"Pretty sure. She's borrowing his cell - maybe to avoid roaming charges or something - and the number goes to a voice mail they're sharing while she is here. That doesn't work too well in this situation."

"She dug you though."

"A lot of 'girls' her age seem to these days. Getting

131

older."

"MILF hunting now, are we, Van?"

"Not really, Cris. ... But I'm almost thirty-five, so the dating demographics are shifting. I'd take a twenty-four year old if she was sweet and smart and knew culture."

Warren is back asking what I studied at UGA. I have on a Georgia hat now and told him the other night that Dave and I had gone to Georgia together, after knowing each other in high school.

"Communication," I answer. "Speech Communication, then I eventually got licensed to sell space in Atlanta and got into commercial real estate. I was looking at maybe going to grad school to become a city planner, but I very recently decided to start writing instead."

"City planning," he says. "So you get what a joke LA is?"

"It is the joke," I tell him, and he walks off again, nodding.

I say to Cris, "Fun to flirt a little with these girls without the boss around to chaperone his staff."

"I can't believe he isn't cool with that," Cris says. "Well the beers aren't free without him here and these girls are working, so we should head out soon. You want to wait here while I go shop next door?"

While he is gone, the curvy waitress comes by and starts talking to me about the book she heard I was working on. She is an artist. I knew it. She paints and two of her paintings are on display in the restaurant. I ask for her number, and she tells me she is too involved to give it to me. Cris returns and pays the tab to Natalie. She says to him, "I hope to see you again."

I think he's a sissy for not asking for her number, especially considering that he obviously tipped her huge. I almost ask for him, then decide wiser of it, because I don't want to make him look as shy as he actually is.

On the way to the car we overhear a brother in a Bermuda hat: "It's California. You gotta get money."

Back in the car, I ask Cris what he bought at the store.

"A metal weed grinder and some rolling papers," he answers.

I'm bored with his purchases because there is more

to California than suddenly semi-legalized weed, yet I'm excited about LA after talking with hot, interesting people.

"Day two for us today," I say. "By day three, we will be like, 'Maybe I will go out for commercials. Maybe I can act. Or I can write! I'll be huge.' People get starstruck so fast out here. Day two..."

"I ain't playing that fame game shit."

"Just an LA joke."

On freeways and seemingly endless city streets, we drive without much direction as Cris gets more and more frustrated that he can't find money orders to pay his bills. We stop at any gas station we see and ask for money orders, without luck.

LA has beauty but seems now to me too much a variation of the same. Neighborhood after neighborhood, shop after shop, area after area. Daytime LA in the heat of the summer with some cool neighborhoods, but nothing compelling to do. And I see the grime.

Cris isn't up for my new suggestion of a rooftop hotel pool. He doesn't have any ideas but knows what he doesn't want to do. He says he hates LA, like he knew he would.

At least we are both enjoying the street art we are seeing all over town: colors of expression popping in posters, graffiti, murals and fashiony people. Big city art, making sure statements that real artists do live here amongst the obvious commerciality of Hollywood.

Cris notices he's running low on pot so we get stoned with some of mine. I hear the unmistakable whine of Morrissey as I flip around on the satellite radio but don't stop on that for more than a second, because I remember that Cris despises it.

I say, "We should just go to the Santa Monica pier and hang."

Cris says, "I want to hang with someone that wants to see me. I can't believe your boy bailed after a couple hours."

"He's busy, and he just took us to Venice. He's involved in his life and has a hectic schedule. We don't really need him to have a good time."

"I know. I'm just not used to a supposed friend not taking time."

"My fault. I should have gotten him on the phone

133

first before we headed down here. By the way, I was fifty times more bored in Humboldt. It's not like he isn't a friend now. It's a busy pace in this place. It's like me, in Atlanta. Remember how I was, running a major operation at work, wife and kids, always typing on the stupid pager or talking on the phone?"

"You still took the time."

"I did and Dave will when he can. It's just a lot, running a restaurant, going to auditions, staying perfect-looking all the time...imagine."

"I don't want to."

"Don't then. Never mind. Why don't we call your boy Potter?"

"He didn't sound super excited about hanging with us either."

"Probably just busy. I'm sure he wants to hang."

"Everyone thinks they are so fucking busy in this town, so important, it's a fucking joke."

"Cris, I know it's a joke. The Industry. This town. Lighten up."

"I want to light a nudder en up soon, but I'm almost out of weed. Can't believe I have to buy weed in this God forsaken town. I'm from Humboldt."

"You live in Humboldt. You're from The ATL, remember?"

"Fuck that place, too. Fuck Atlanta."

"Okay, Cris. Soon as I get back. This is only Hollyweird day two. Don't worry. These are typical day two anxieties. Tomorrow is the day you start to believe. Day four is the day you become huge."

"I'm not playing that fucking game with you."

"Okay. But you could have been huge."

I know he's pissed off, but I'm so suddenly frustrated with his attitude that I don't care to stop razzing him.

"You keep joking about that," he says. "I don't want to be famous."

"Very un-American. Not even a little?"

"I don't want anyone in this fucking town to know me."

"A talent scout just may see you."

"I don't want to be in love with life like you and Dave."

I pause for a long time relishing that comment before saying, "Wow, okay."

"Roll us another joint, ole boy," Cris says.

"Aye, aye, Cap'n," I say, resigned and annoyed.

He grabs his weed out of the console asking, "How much is left? Fucking shit!"

"I can find more," I say calmly.

We start to listen to the White Stripes' new record again, switching from the satellite radio. We've so far been unsuccessful in our efforts to overplay this record. It's that good.

"I have to be like that you know?" Cris says, after about five minutes of us saying nothing while I rolled a joint. It is lit.

"I know you are like that," I say.

"I have to be intensely not into shit, so I can also be so into shit."

"You hate it when you find out that it isn't always a party, not always your party."

"Shay...dats right," he says in Jimmy Stewart's voice.

I actually don't feel like being super-stoned today, but this beats the tenor of the previous conversation. His mood has changed.

"Smoke the rest of that alone," I say. "I'm done; I think you need it more than me."

"You all good?" he asks, sounding genuinely concerned.

"Not really. I'm still having trouble breathing."

"That may be from trimming, breathing particle matter."

"Great. I just thought it was from smoking."

"Occupational hazard," he says faultlessly.

"Another thing I didn't bargain for when I came to work on a quote unquote ranch. You should maybe smoke a little less in the near future, buddy. You get wound up if you happen to be not stoned for an hour."

"Shay, whas da big idea getting in my brain like dat?"

"My bad, Cris. I'm a little manic today."

"You? Manic? Never!"

"Hey. You're in my brain, too."

135

We both laugh.

"Let's have a good day," Cris says.

"Fuck you," I say, and we laugh again.

LA is fun to see, fun to look at. Mile after mile after mile of cute businesses, many of them independently owned and I like the endless housing. Avenues carry us past all these businesses and apartments and houses, with alleys in back of every row of development. And every mile is developed. Flying into LA in the past, I saw the city of lights that I feel now. The sprawling mass of humanity.

So many pretty young women are out bopping around town today, in their perfect little outfits, trying to look casual in $400 worth of casual wear, carrying a $1,000 handbag.

It's a funny joke, a big sprawling laugh. But the traffic is nothing to laugh about; it's horrible and not reserved to the highways; side streets are packed with cars. Where are these people going? Nowhere fast.

We stop in the middle of the city for coffee and to walk around a few shops. Good shopping in LA, expensive, but you can find anything and everything. Lots of affected LA pretty people working the boutiques, sipping skinny capuccinos in the café.

Back in the car I say, "I need a new image for fly-wear. My image...fly-wear is a bit late 1990s, early 2000s. It was ahead of its time. I did that type of shirts before everybody did them. As you may recall, fly-wear was 'surf-skate-dance-urban'. Now I'm more into just urban-urban or strictly art. I want to really make it art, yet keep the old focus on intense color. I may even change fly-wear's name."

Cris says. "Remember when you and Alex and Rooster had that other label before in Athens, DIGGS? That was a good name. Why don't you just go back to the old name?"

"Because I'm not focusing on the past right now."

DIGGS is so last millenium. I need to think of something more modern, slip into something. Slip into something more comfortable. How about Slip-Rite? Slip Right into Slip-Rite Threads, trademark. I like that. I decide not tell Cris the name yet.

"We should call Dave, again," I say instead.

"Go ahead," Cris says, handing me the phone.

I dial, and he actually answers for once. There are girls getting naked in Hollywood at the Deleanor Hotel pool; Dave says we should go. He has a friend working there that can get us in and the place dies down when the sun sets, before it cranks up again.

"Naked ladies and cocktails. Sounds good," I say after I hang up.

"Definitely." Cris chimes. "How far is Hollywood?"

"Everything in this town takes thirty to forty-five minutes."

"Let's go."

We head back over to the Strip. I find it easily and am self-impressed with my navigational skills.

I babble: "I'm actually starting to know a little of LA. This main part of town anyway. I was around this area last year. Here and Dave's neighborhood, of course. Everything we saw today so far I'd already seen. Good to get some things off the list for you. Too much car time, but you at least saw a few different areas. Maybe we can do some things that are new for us both. Hollywood's next. Off your list."

Cris says, "You've already seen everything in LA, I think."

"Most of it finally, I think. This is my third trip here. When I travel, I try to be somewhat educated on where I'm going and see as much of it as possible. I read entire guidebooks before I travel."

"You could probably write them, Van."

"Probably. I never made it out to Malibu yet. I haven't been to Silver Lake – that's where Beck is from, or at least lives. I can't wait to hear his next album."

"Is anyone really from here?"

"Right. It's like Atlanta. People move here."

"I got sick of that in Atlanta, carpetbaggers." He sounds disgusted.

"Me too, although on the other hand, I'm a bit of a scalawag."

"What does that mean again?"

"A Northern sympathizer. It's a derogatory term they used in Civil War days originally, I believe. Likes the urbanization and some of the forward thinking and progress of the North but lives in the South."

"Yeah. Me too then, I guess. I love New York because

137

it's so huge and small at the same time.

"It's kind of a long roll down the Strip to Hollywood from here. We could stop at Bicco along the way for a quick free pizza to go. Dave's working now, and I could call it in. I'm really hungry all the sudden."

"Let's just get there, Van, okay?"

"But that place right there has dollar beers, cheap hot dogs. Travis and I ate there last year, the night we all eventually ended up at this late night commercial party house in the hood...bars close early here."

THE REAL AND THE SHOW:
(-Los Angeles)

We have hot dogs and brews in an old train car that has been converted into a restaurant and plopped down right in the middle of the chic boutiques, hotels and bars of the Strip. Customers in the place consist of a few business people in blue oxfords, two Asian Flyboys decked out in yellow and orange Gucci shirts and dark shades, a chubby Mexican B-Boy wearing a slightly cocked LA Dodgers cap and huge plain white T-shirt and us in our ATL-meets-Cal finest casual wear. Nothing like a cheap hot dog, in overpriced urban clothes, on prime real estate, to make me feel like home.

"Not so hidden, hidden gem of the city," I say.

"A dog is always good," Cris says, through the relish of his second.

"A hot dog isn't a real solution to anything, but I love this place."

We get in the car and leave for Hollywood. I switch the music to local radio and suddenly start to crave the cocaine that Cris has with him. I remember how bad it feels to be strung out, then I feel a strong twinge of addiction. This is nothing compared to what I've already been through. When you tell yourself take a left, and the cocaine takes a right for you, it has taken away your rights. It takes away your freedom.

Relapse is generally part of recovery. That's usually what happens, and the key is to make it back out before it gets me again. Even though I know the damage that drugs can do and have done to my life, I want a key bump. That's addiction.

I say, "You remember the most likely to die from drugs list we were talking about the other day?"

"Yeah," Crispin says quietly. "We were next up, ole boy, in line."

"I think we both have finally taken our names off the list. I know you have." Have I? Yes. Please help me to overcome my addiction, Lord.

"You know what," Cris says after a pause for reflection. "That feels good. That's one list I don't want to be on."

"Me neither. You're much better…off the hard stuff, out of ATL."

"Thanks, I guess."

"You had a different personality I hated at one stretch in Athens, and I saw the city and hard drugs start to do it to you again in Atlanta."

"I was a junkie in Athens on that stuff. That was all I could do."

"Speaking of junk, you don't use heroin anymore at all, do you?"

"I have a small…taste every now and again."

"That's the kind of thing that keeps people on lists…permanently."

"I know."

"It took Wes, one of my Weses."

"I know. That and blow."

"Anyway, I'm coming off the list."

"You still use, Van."

"I will use tonight…if you break some out. I haven't been able to stop entirely, yet. That's true. I'm embarrassed about that actually, but I'm managing my addiction now, at least."

"That's what they all say. All addicts think that."

"I know. I hope I'm better. I'm better. I know I'm better."

"You are…but you aren't out of the woods yet."

"I can see the edge of the forest at least."

"You want a bump?"

"Yeah."

"Just testing you. Let's wait for tonight. We may meet some hotties that wanna party. Recognize us as two loked up Gs"

The sun is threatening to set as we enter Hollywood, so we skip the pool at the Deleanor Hotel completely, thinking it already too late. Just driving and admiring the young Hollywood freaks out in their outfits.

"You are so tough," I say about a particularly obnoxious Goth guy.

"Total punk bad boy, dressed in that shit," Cris jeers. "I'm scared."

"We should still go to the Deleanor maybe."

"You had enough car time for a lifetime? I have. Wanna head back the other direction?"

"I guess."

We see the famous Chinese Theater and the Walk of Fame stars. We see Hollywood High School. We are just zooming aimlessly, still.

We pass the Hollywood Bowl as the Red Hot Chili Peppers are on the radio singing about California. They always sing about Cali. Then Beck comes on, and I wonder if he's in town. This is similar to the Atlanta stations that play only ATL rap. All Cali, all the time.

Thinking of home has me feeling depressed about my impending divorce and low, after being so high recently. It's coming in waves. And it's unfortunate that we can't just stay at Dave's place; that would have given us a home base and I'm feeling so far from grounded.

I tell Cris, "I'm super-depressed about the impending divorce."

He makes me feel worse by trying to cheer me up, telling me I'm in the perfect situation. He says, "You have the dream already. You have two kids, two sons, and you don't have to be married anymore." He somehow fails to get it.

Cris tries to make a call then rants, "I'm sick of leaving messages for people and sick of you leaving messages for people."

"I know. People are busy," I explain, mainly explaining for Dave.

"At least when I go to New York, I get people on the phone to..."

"New York is actually a busier place than LA," I interrupt.

"New York is the real."

"The real. Good nickname, Cris. NYC should be known as the real."

"Right. LA is...a joke." He sounds truly disgusted.

"To me it's not so much NYC versus LA, as it's NYC and LA, The Real and The Show. Big, beautiful America. ... We showed up in LA practically unannounced, and this is just what happened."

"That was your idea, Van."

141

"I was trying to be spontaneous in my life again."

"Don't worry about it then."

We are quiet for a long time, rolling along and looking while we think. It's interesting that the big memories, the important stuff that you should remember about people is often not what first comes to mind. Obscure minutiae may overshadow big events when I recall friends. Earlier Cris mentioned an old friend, Shawn Nutt, and the first thing to pop in my brain was Nutt's smirking face when he was picking on me while he drove me to Jersey City Heights from Brooklyn. He wanted to get a bagel before he dropped me off to family-it-up with my wife's family, and I was way too hungover to eat, and that so doesn't matter in the history of me and my good friend Nutt, but that's what I remembered first. Then I remembered how fun it was in Brooklyn with Nutt, what a good friend at heart he really is.

I remember living with Nutt my next-to-last summer in Athens, and when our crew first met Nutt and ScottMo years earlier. I remember when Nutt and I got jumped in Atlanta after the first Cypress Hill show. And I have feelings of friendship that are emotions, not words. I have to remember to think of the big stuff about people.

We see a sign for Century City and I ask Cris if he knows that Tom Petty is a distant cousin of mine, because Petty has a song by that title. He tells me I have told him that around a thousand times.

There are many of these fringe cities built around movie studios in greater LA. We stop at a pub in Century City, and we have beers and fish and chips. The bartender is obviously a rocker.

A nice guy writer is here who seems to be some sort of hetero groupie of the bartender. The writer is obviously a regular at this pub, as the staff all seem to know him. Hearing we are from out of town he says, "The thing about LA is finding your niche. I write. It's good for that, and I live near here. I hang here."

The rocker bartender turns out to be from England - I generally love the Brits because of their off the wall attitudes - living in LA to do his music. He loves LA, "...but, you know, I have to work."

The writer seems to be the type of slightly socially awkward guy that goes to a bar and talks to the staff instead of having true friends. I understand that. He needs connections, like the rest of us, and it's easier to just talk to the bar staff. You know where to find them; they're interesting. So what if you in essence have to tip them to hang? That's how it works.

The writer suddenly opens up and it's too all about his work. I'm not that interested in how someone writes treatments for scripts.

LA may talk about itself more than any city ever has, even New York or Paris. Los Angelenos always tell the story as if they are on film, because to them the cameras are rolling. They see their lives as movies. They tell the story in flashes, because to them the camera bulbs are flashing. Many in this town have such overblown egos about their professional identities. There are always blowhards around, bragging about their mostly boring careers. Tinseltown. The show is always on in dreamland, Hollywood USA. I want to figure LA out, and I think I'm beginning to. I'm cracking the nut.

BEDBUMPS:
(-Los Angeles)

Cris breaks out a little more of the blow after dinner. He passes it to me under the bar counter. I surge adrenaline when I have it in my suddenly sweaty palm. I go to the bathroom and do a bump. Then I fixate on the few girls in the pub, stripper types. I don't feel great, just good.

We have a bourbon drink, Maker's and soda. I enjoy the strong oak flavor, and the food was pretty good, but I mainly just want more blow.

I try again and do not get Dave on the phone. We leave and go find a quite-a-bit-nicer-than-the-last-one motel. We are tired from all the car time and the heat. We have freaked out, driven, hung at Bicco and seen the city, mainly from the car. I feel guilty that it hasn't been more fun, but I'm somewhat at the whims of Crispin since he's driving and has most of the money.

We've been friends for so long that minor adversity should be no more than a joke between us, and then it is. We are friends, friends that missed each other and are reunited and in a not bad place to be, California, with money. Things could be way worse. We laugh it off.

I call Judi but get her sultry stripper-sounding voice mail. I call my friend from last year, Dave's ex's roomie, Sasha and get her corporate-sounding voice mail. She's a top pharmauetical makeup sales exec.

The phone rings. It is Judi. She's working tonight, but if we are up for a very, very late night we should call her back. I tell her we may not be up that late tonight. Hopefully, we'll see her. I would love to see her again. She says Dave mentioned something about us all meeting up tomorrow night. That'd be good. I haven't heard that yet, but I'm down for anything fun that Dave suggests since he knows LA best.

Judi knows the place we are staying, right by CBS, and she will call back if she is coming by after work. I tell her she's welcome. We are partying a little, but we are basically relaxing more than anything; just catching up. She asks if we have been friends a long time. I tell her we have. She loves friendship, loves her friends. She probably won't come by, but she will def hook up with us again. She called back at least.

"I like that," I say.

"What?" Crispin asks, raising an eyebrow. He is chopping lines.

"The fact that she called back. Sasha is supposed to be my friend, all anxious to see me again, but she hasn't called me back. My interest is currently shifting to Judi."

"She coming over to blow us...or to blow you?"

"Highly unlikely, something about her I like though."

"It could be that she is super hot and totally down."

"That could be it."

We do a line, then I say, "Being across from CBS is appropriate. Television rules America. Everyone thinks of movies when they think of LA because we all love a good movie. But when you think about it, TV is what really shaped America. And TV is as straight up LA as Coke is Atlanta."

"Dave on TV all the time?"

"A different campaign once or twice a year, which is all the time for an actor doing television commercials. He's done Nike and Coors Light and Chevy, Red Lobster and stupid Zima. He was in a Vegas commercial with Dennis Hopper. My friend is the man, but it'd be nice if my friend would take my call more often," I say as I snort a line. "That'd be a bonus. He's LA-ing me. He's fuckin' LA-ing me."

We feel like having another beer. I would love to go out if anything cool is nearby. We do another line of blow and I'm amped. Now Crispin really wants a beer, but he doesn't want to drive anywhere. I suggest we walk. He's tired and needs to make a few phone calls, preferably private calls, but he will pay for the beer. So I walk to get the beer alone. Walking to a convenience store and feeling edgy and slinky. Then I see a - looks pretty cool from afar - local bar. On the way back from the store, I remind myself of the old me, those months of walking around Atlanta under the premise that I was in the city only to work, often high on cocaine and paranoid. Hating my life. The energy in LA is different, but the drug is the equalizer.

The first few lines are still fun and I feel high and sexy now. It is the addiction that is terrible, the desire to abuse and the mood swings that follow. And I do have a bit of the paranoia. I look high.

I wish I'd never tried the stuff. I'm still addicted. I want to get back to the room, do more blow, not too much, just more, which may be too much, and then wait a few minutes, then go to the bar, but not be carrying any when we get there. I already look high. I didn't feel so high in the room, and now I look and feel high.

"God, help me to overcome this addiction," I say as I race up the motel stairs to do another line. The irony of the moment is not lost on me. I have to shake this grip.

Cris doesn't want to go to the bar; he is tired. We do blow until it is gone. I'm glad to see it go. Coke is just too much for me anymore, and I'm in a deep sweat and relieved to not be in public.

We hear a woman, perhaps a prostitute, getting screwed through the wall. I don't even know if it is real until I ask Crispin because I sometimes hear things and see things when I am this wired. I'm sweating bullets and fixating on the sex sounds.

Remembering now how I started hallucinating in the shadows. I was actually seeing shapes having sex in the shadows back home, trying to fixate on sex so I wouldn't fixate on getting busted. I was losing my mind. But I have slowed down. That is good. Now I just have to stop.

She is still getting fucked next door, and I want to fuck her. How can you want to fuck sounds? Not sure, but I definitely do right now.

Cris is right about my sexual fixations. In the past, I always fixated on sex when I was high. That was bad enough. Then I started always fixating on the police. They were after me in my mind when I was high, because I was an obvious cocaine user with a twitchy mouth.

Plus, I hung out with a black guy that was ten years younger than I am, and we stood out. We both dressed flashy, and we dressed so differently from each other. Classic dealer and his customer look. He sold me drugs almost daily for some months, and it was oh so obvious.

Things that seemed fun and experimental when you were young could quickly turn dark when you were not in control. It stopped being a decision. The drugs did the deciding.

"Not so cute anymore," was how my mom described

it, with masterful understatement. I...and not just me, some of my party-boy friends too, we were fucked. Some of them were dead, some had addictions that required self-medication; addicts require medicine.

You had yours, now stop. Live. Go into the light, from tomorrow morning on.

The woman next door is leaving now or maybe he is. He's finished with her and someone is leaving. I wonder if she's staying behind. I stand up and listen closer and think about going outside to see if I can get a glimpse of her.

"Stay in the room, Van!" Cris says. It's an order.

I listen to him this time, thinking that it may actually not be too wise to leave the room this late. I'm in a crime-filled city and visibly high on drugs, sweating and twitching.

I lay back down and fall asleep thinking two thoughts: 1. We need to have some fun and 2. I need to stop using. I am praying for help overcoming the addiction as I drift off deep.

Then the phone rings. It's Judi, getting off work, and I'm still up.

SHINE ON, YOU STAR:
(-Los Angeles)

By the time I'm alone again the next morning, I'm glad we came to Los Angeles. Outside, I stand on the cool tile and glance at the figure eight-shaped Hollywood pool and feel the energy of the scene. The vegetation is tropical and the desert chill is lifting to another warm, bright Cali day.

"Let's get something great to eat, ole boy," Crispin says as I re-enter the room and plop down on my bed.

"Sounds...great...bro, " I say, fading all Cali. I am immersed.

We gather our stuff quickly, drop the key and enter the vehicle.

"What you want ta eat?" Cris asks. "You must have an appetite."

"Bicco."

"Again? We were there last night. Well, not last night but the night before last and yesterday."

"I know, but they have such a great breakfast, return to the scene and see the staff."

"Dave working?"

"I'm sure, and if not, even better. We can talk with his staff unencumbered again."

"Thought you were kidding about that before. He's really not cool with that?" Cris is incredulous.

"Not really," I answer matter of factly. "He has to control everything. It's funny. He's always right, usually, but I wouldn't mind some more waitress time without the boss around. I like that curvy one and who wouldn't love Priscilla. And that Nat likes you."

"I thought she was checking."

"She was. She was on you, money."

We are heading to Bicco, but first, the all-important money orders. Thankfully, the gas station where I bought beer sells them.

Exiting the motel parking lot Cris is saying to me, "It's hot as fuck during the daytime in LA."

"It's hot as fuck, Cris," I say, after a pause. "It's hotter 'n fuck in Humboldt during the day, too, but it ain't as hot as this."

"Not even close. It's hotter 'n fuck today."

"Yeah it is." I want to agree with Crispin, even by repeating the stating of the obvious, which is a very old routine of ours.

As we pull up at the gas station Cris says, "I have to go in here and get these money orders to pay some bills. I need you to go in, maybe, and buy some of them."

I'm trepidatious but feel obliged and say, "Okay, I guess. Why?"

"I just have a whole lot of different bills that I have to pay, and it ain't that cool to be walking into a convenience store with a big ass wad of cash and starting to roll off a long list of money orders you need."

"Because it makes you look like a drug dealer? Imagine that."

"Right. No need to be obvious."

"All right, I'll buy a money order in my name and you pay bills with it. Is that how you want it to work?"

"Forget it. Forget I asked. You're gonna blow it anyway."

"Okay. I'd rather not if I don't have to, I guess."

"I'll take care of it. You break up our weed. Use my grinder and grind some shit up for a joint but don't roll it. I will roll it when I get back. There's the gas station, on the other side of the street, the wrong side, of course," Cris moans.

"Of course," I say in a consolatory tone.

"Let's see, my list...you want anything?"

"I'll get out in a minute and buy a drink. I'll get you one."

I enter after diligently grinding weed and buy two Crunk Juice energy drinks and a Fifth Avenue candy bar. "I need one of those," the African cashier says to me. "Those drink."

"Get you a Crunk Juice and Five Ave.," I reply.

Back in the car Cris says, "Nice job not talking to me in there."

"Are you serious?" I ask.

"Yeah," he answers, sounding sincere.

We drive to Bicco and have egg white omelettes under the patio's yolk of a sun. Dave seated us outside where the male Mexican waiter was serving, and I think it was by design to keep us from his female staff.

It is a typically nice day, and we are off the hard stuff and in good moods, so we drink two mimosas each. There are crayons and the tablecloths are made of paper, so we color on them, me doing the cover art I designed for pOp 101: Prince of Peachtree for Cris to see. He likes it.

Our old friend Ramon calls Cris. He is heading to Las Vegas in a few weeks and says we should meet him there if we can. We can stay at his suite if we want; it will be huge.

The lady at the table next to us is a promoter of some kind, apparent from the conversation she is having with a male companion. Two of her work cohorts show up randomly as we are just finishing our food, so we give them our table and go inside.

Dave is standing at the end of the bar talking to the health inspector, schmoozing her a little while she finishes an inspection. She is sternly holding a clipboard but looks to be softening under his charms.

I go to the bathroom, and when I come out Dave says, "Crispin just stormed out!"

The health inspector is gone and so is Crispin. I'm confused.

"I asked him not to sit at the bar," Dave says.

"Fuck, Dave" I say. "He is sensitive."

"It was the health inspector, dude. Do you know what a big deal that is to a restaurant?"

"Of course I do. I better go get him."

I pay the nice waiter a big tip on my way out. Dave buys the meal.

I walk outside where Cris is parked on a side street in front of a parking meter. He is in his car, fuming. I get in. He says, "I'm not mad at Dave anymore, now I got a fucking ticket to be mad about."

"That sucks," I say.

"I hate this fucking place!" Cris yells.

"Wow...you all right?" I ask, genuinely concerned.

"Yeah. This place just sucks."

"I like it here; it's great!" I say in my Andy Warhol impersonation voice that is an attempt to amuse him. He doesn't get it.

"I know, Van. It wouldn't be that bad, if it wasn't so fucking hot, and if I hadn't gotten that ticket. Let's go."

"Okay. What is the ticket for?"

"Expired meter."

"No big deal."

"It's a big deal to me."

"I'm sorry."

"And if we weren't...I'm about to run out of weed... Fuck!"

"I'll find you some if that's what you want, homey."

"Yeah...fuck. I can't believe I'm paying for weed. I grew a whole mountain of herb."

"Some of the best herb," I interject.

"And then I get nothing, none, and Swiftboy bails, and I pay a hundred fucking dollars for some pot I don't want. It's insane."

"That is insane. I can't believe you didn't take more of your bud."

This is a typical theme of our friendship. I have always tried to get Crispin to see his part of responsibility for his own happiness. He always blames outside factors outwardly, while quietly he is frustrated at himself. I wish he would grab life by the reins and let nothing get him down, but these days it seems everything gets him down.

"UGGH! I hate this place. A hundred and something... that's how much it is, too. How much is that bud you are talking about?"

"I don't know. I just meant I would try to find you some, if you want. Dave or Frank or somebody knows somebody with weed. I'm sure."

"You sure?"

"Nothing is 100%, but yeah, I'm pretty damn sure we can find weed. We found a lot more than weed already did we not? This is Hollywood, California. The sign was changed once to 'Hollyweed.'"

"Sometimes blow is actually easier to find than good weed."

"I know...all too well. I'll find you some good smoke."

"Okay."

"I was just thinking, when you said you hated this place, about an 'I H8' shirt concept. Like 'IH8 ATL,' I-H-number eight, A-T-L, or NY or in this case LA." I'm trying to change the subject. "Think of another shirt concept if you can, at any point, ole boy Cris."

"I didn't think of that one."

"It was inspired by you then, I H8 LA is dedicated to you, sir...I hate Los Angeles. ... I don't of course; I fuckin' love it. I need to jot that."

"You should."

"Do you have any paper?"

"No. Yeah, somewhere, maybe in here."

I first grab his medicinal marijuana card then put it back and use the back of the envelope for the ticket to write "I H 8 ATL," in pencil. Once I have written something down, I remember it, so I wanted to write that down to remember the concept. That would be a funny shirt. I H8 NY shirts would be good for fans of opposing teams playing the Yankees. I'd wear one if the Cowboys were playing the Giants...or if they were smart enough to actually have real college football up North. I aim to pontificate on sport further, but he notices what I have done and freaks about the envelope.

I calmly and confidently say, "I'm pretty sure it will still get to The City of Los Angeles, as it is pre-addressed and will contain payment."

"But you knew that was mine," he says, tense and annoyed.

"Keep it," I say, departing the vehicle.

I'm not feeling this again, and I've decided that for the rest of this trip I have to feel it, or I simply will not do it, will disengage. I have put myself through too much the past few months, and I'm not going to subject myself to Crispin's negativity. I may have had more fun alone.

"Shine on, you star!" I faintly hear Cris yell to me as I venture on my own for the first time. Go Van. LA, walking, and I'm in a cool area for doing so.

I'm not upset, just working on my Bible of Truthiness, more galvanized by being called a star by Crispin. He meant that. He wanted it initially to be derogatory, when he first thought of it and started to say it, but when it came out, he believed it. He knows a star when he sees one and is a starfucker, so I really believe that I may be on to something if he called me a star, a shining star, like that. He knows that shit, and I could hear the change in his voice.

So, walking, so, looking. Nice day again today. I left

my UGA hat and my bags, but I had to break away. I see myself in a store window reflection. I look so The VAN in this black shirt that says ®andom, my stud glasses, good jeans, messy product hair and this cool bracelet. My life as a poser, I think. That's a good one. I need a new pad and pen. I need to write.

And I should get business cards from more shops for my fashion, so I can send them brochures when I get that together. Or my new fashion label. ... Get busy! I've seen hundreds of stores that I should have grabbed cards from, but I haven't wanted to inconvenience my sensitive buddy. I wanted him to have fun. I figured me having fun with him, near him, would help him have fun. Guess not. I'll just do me.

He has too many preconceived negative ideas to have fun anymore, I guess. Things have gone less than stellar. I feel that too, but maybe he just doesn't like me so much anymore, which is fine. I can live with that.

Differentiate yourself from friends that you don't want to be like, Van. Stop worrying about every stupid friend you ever had and work on yourself. I can do this. If I write and sell fashion and maybe even manage a great band or just promote art of some kind, I can become a mogul, sort of a mini-mogul first. That's very striving ATL to want to do that.

I was an all-American golden boy when I grew up and want to be my own hero again, not some anti-hero. I have so much to offer when at my best. Eventually, I will be a mogul and mogul maker. I could help people and give back and be a valued member of society. That would be much more...huge than just growing weed or acting in TV commercials.

Cris is jaded from that mountain - glad to be away, yet already misses his mountain, his fresh air, his weed, his dog, his mommy, getting laid.

His mom will be here soon, in California, and he will get laid as soon as he gets back to Atlanta. Can't he just relax until then? Fuck him if he can't have a good time. Maybe he just misses the comfort of a woman, and this town reminds him of that a little too much. Or maybe LA is too like Atlanta, hot, sprawling and materialistic. Especially LA with me, because I symbolize ATL to him. He left Atlanta for a reason. It was too much for him. This is too much for him, too. That's his deal.

I need a male friend I can relate to. I need...Dave, really. I need him to try to talk me through this. We have hardly talked, and I could use a long chat.

Half-baked plans don't always come to fruition. Everyone knows that. It would have been different if we had stayed at Dave's place, if we had not spent the first night geeking on blow, if we had spent our days at the beach, hitting the bars at night after eating some nice dinners. That was what I envisioned. That and seeing the sights and good friend talk.

I say aloud to myself: "I don't want to be in love with life, like you and Dave." That is one of his greatest lines of all time. If Crispin had just given me that and nothing else, we would still be cool. He's done enough for me at this point in our lives for me to love him for the rest of my days. I just don't want to be around him anymore. That jerk really needs to get laid and everything will be fine.

I just need to live. I need to think. I need to feel. I need to heal.

I'm not Cris. I'm not my sometimes misogynist father. I'm not the greedy people I've worked with in the past. I'm not Dave. I'm myself.

And I've been through enough. Stop thinking about other people and think about me. Stop using blow all together. Find more constructive things to do.

Cris will just leave my bags and go on his merry way, I hope. All I need is my bags...and my new blankie. He did not help me through this, but maybe Dave will. Being around Dave makes me feel better. I should call Dave.

I see an ad for Basquiat and then ask a car salesman how to get to MOCA by transit, which is a joke on LA. Then I stop at a pay phone at a Burger King and call Dave.

"Hey, D."

"Hey. What's going on?"

"Not much. Just going to the museum, I guess."

"Which one?"

"The one with Basquait."

'That's downtown."

"That's what I hear from the car salesman I just asked. I'll take the bus. I've been to that museum before. I can take care of myself."

"Yeah?"

"Yeah."

"Fuck that. Crispin wants to take you."

"Oh yeah?"

"Yeah. What happened?"

"We just aren't getting along. I'm fine. It's all good. Did he call you already?"

"Yeah, and he is fucking coming to get you, Van. What the fuck?"

"I don't know, whatever."

"Where are you?"

"At the Burger King, the one near your place actually."

"Stay there."

"Tell him to meet me at Luna Park, or in front of Luna Park. I need a drink."

"Hold on...that's him on the other line."

"Okay."

Twenty seconds later Dave is back on the phone, "Luna Park. You guys, stop! I stopped that shit. Van, just stop it."

"No problem...I..."

"Shut up. It's done."

"Okay, D, whatever you say."

"He called wanting to drop your shit off; that shit is done, got it?"

"Got it."

"You are supposed to be boys."

"We are boys."

"Then drop it."

"I already did, before I called you."

"Good. ... We are going out tonight, too."

"Great! Finally. Where?"

"Hotel Deleanor. Be out in front of Luna Park."

Luna Park is closed between lunch and dinner, so no drink, but the host tells me that I should come in tonight, "It is inner child night."

"That sounds great. I will be back."

So, out front waiting. Here comes the Intrepid, and I'm so relieved.

"I'll be your best friend if you talk to me again," Cris

says.

"You already are," I say.

"Drink, then?"

"Closed. Inner Child Night tonight though; we should return."

"We should."

"Basquiat. Let's do Basquiat. It's on me."

I want to buy the new Crispin something; I always used to pay.

"CLITORIS ©"
(-Los Angeles)

Back in LA from Acapulco during our honeymoon, my new wife and I took a then brand new subway train of the METRO system from Hollywood to the downtown area of Los Angeles. We had expected so much more activity in the Central Business District of the largest city on the West Coast. Los Angeles is sprawl and low urban density, even at its core. And though an effort to revitalize Downtown as a standalone attraction was evident, an overall level of any real excitement lacking.

Crispin and I head toward those towers now. Contrasting with the huge population of Los Angeles, the skyline itself consists of relatively few tall buildings. None of them seem to be of much design consequence to us, with a strong exception being the glowing, crown-topped tallest building in town. The impact of the overall cluster of tall buildings is not there for me, the structures unimpressive in number and dimension.

I say: "Atlanta's skyline just puts it to shame."

"It really does," Cris says. "I'm surprised."

"I think you'll like Basquiat's stuff," I say. "You see the movie?"

"Part of it, I think," Cris says. "It was on somewhere I was. Is it a little slow?"

"It is. Pretty good film. Anyway, I'm glad you haven't seen it, or all of it, because it's very watered down. His life and perspective was more than is represented in the film."

"That's standard in movies about people; I hate that."

"Art should be real or more real than it usually is anyway."

"I like real shit."

"I know you do. That's what I'm trying to do is be real with this, but today is not about the book. It is about one Jean-Michel Basquiat, in many ways my favorite. He isn't the greatest painter, per se, far from it, but his themes are really interesting, and his use of color and imagery, iconography is really amazing. Especially color, he uses great colors."

"Yeah I like 'coloreds' too," he jokes. "He was a black guy, right?"

"Yeah. The most-famous black American painter, and he really isn't...he wasn't all that famous. He was a famous modern painter."

"But not compared to Whitey?" he cracks.

"Not compared to some of his historic white counterparts, but at one point he sold for the single most. ... We should smoke, if we can, because his stuff is especially drugged out. He makes you feel like you are on drugs even when you're not. He uses a lot of words in his paintings. You'll see."

"I'll see."

"Julian Schnabel directed the movie, and I admire his paintings too, same basic modern art movement, Julian and Jean. And I thought it was cool that he'd been chosen to direct. But painting is not directing movies, and it was his first film. I liked it okay, I guess. I like most movies about the lives of artists, almost always like those."

"Maybe there will be a movie about you someday, Van."

"That'd be neat. Tell you what, dude, I'm gonna pay for the admission to the museum and buy you some snacks at the snack bar for saying that."

"You don't have to do all that, ole boy."

"I want to. Did you know that Cali was named after a fictitious land in one of the Spanish Novels of Chivalry?"

"Sounds about right. You learn that in school or a travel book?"

"Internet."

A total dude pulls up next to us in an electric car bumping 311. I'd drive one of those or a scooter and be just as happy. Actually, riding a bike everywhere was when I was happiest, as far as commuting goes.

We make it to the spread of Downtown buildings, and then we smoke while we drive around them. We see Union Station. We see a sign that says "museum parking" and park and get out.

"This isn't MOCA," I say to Crispin, as we enter a huge commercial artist work space.

"I figured that out, too," Cris says, grinning and looking at the glass sculptures around us.

A bunch of scruffy artists are standing around, so Cris asks one where MOCA is. He seems to have no idea what Cris is talking about, so we both just shrug and leave. We get back in the car to drive around the block again. So many artists, designers, production people live off the resources and opportunities that The Industry creates. That's wonderful, but how could you be an artist or art student and not know where the museum is? Maybe he was just too busy being the dilligent and difficult artist to help, or maybe he thought Cris was asking about coffee.

Circling around Downtown, we see a sign for MOCA this time, so we park. As we walk up a hill past a long row of parked buses, I'm thinking about scene setting, about painting a picture with words. Jean used words in his work as scene setting.

Downtown is full of commercial activity today. Walking, we get in a little of that familiar big city, Downtown, weekday hustle-and-bustle. We surge up the hill in response to our great endorphinic moods. I love cities and transportation and developments, city planning and architecture.

I ask, "Why does LA not have a great Central Business District for architecture? They invent everything else out here. Though a few have nice Art Deco touches, why not more great buildings?"

I think of home again, the Atlanta skyline's great rocket ships for buildings, sprawled for miles up Peachtree through an urban forest.

Then I see the shiny new twisted metal Frank Gehry building across the street from the museum and take it all back: "I guess LA does have a great new building after all."

"By whom?" Cris asks, knowing I know the answer.

"Frank Gehry. He did the Bilbao. Madeline and I saw this place as just a shell under development on our honeymoon, and now look at it. How gorgeous. I haven't been Downtown since then I guess."

Just a shell, like a divorce, just a shell of what it was then. Our love was not perfect but it was gorgeous, I loved her so much then. She loved me too, and it was nice to finally be married after dating and being engaged for so long. When our marriage finally started it was just nice.

We cross the street, as I sift through memories of

159

us together. Then my thoughts shift to the madman that is Basquiat. I'm present in Los Angeles for a big city cultural experience. Here comes The VAN, Jean.

There is a Basquiat merchandise stand upstairs out front. I love the merchandise but do not buy anything because my money is running out, so I just pay for our admission, and we enter the museum.

We walk around mostly separately, which seems the norm for us when we are together. We don't stand in each other's shadows, like I have done with other good friends. It sort of refreshes our friendship.

I'm energized, in a dream world, reading every word that Jean wrote on his paintings. Tripping, as I expected, on his use of color, the powerful imagery of racist America, of fame, of being black and famous.

This one is about LA. He must have spent more time here than I realize. Sexuality, repression, colors. That one explodes. Those strokes are very deliberate, a puppet master toying with his audience.

Is his work lacking? On a Master level is something missing? Yes. Many things are left out, erased, partial and repetitive. It is much more rock band than average art show. It has an edge, a tangible intensity.

Pink. Blue. Basquait's beautiful shades of pink and blue exist in a world that also has a darker side for him. A confusing world is what Jean showed us, is showing us here. He is an observer and reporter, and he is a star, an art star. This show feels a bit like a rock concert.

He was drugged and confused and amazed and half-interested or too interested. A mascot, too, he thought of himself as an art world mascot, a token blackey in a high money white world. It is an interesting perspective.

You can see the drugs taking over his brain in the process, in the later works especially. Perfect show to bring Crispin to. I hope he is enjoying this, at least somewhat. Jean was angry, confused, drugged and unsure, like Cris. There are many things that Cris doesn't like about America, and Jean noticed some of those things too, through his haze-filled painter eyes.

I notice too. I notice commerciality and selfishness as sad cornerstones of American society today, and I don't like that one bit.

160

Race has intrigued me for quite some time as a concept.

Fame, as a concept, is a newer fascination for me. I never really wanted to be famous before for anything besides catching touchdowns. Fame fucked Jean up, obviously. I don't need to be anymore fucked up than I already am.

"Heal me, Lord," I whisper under my breath. I want to show the world something. Jean showed the world something, and that is why he matters to me. That and his proper use of bold color.

Word use in his paintings: "bang: to inject" and "bale of straw: thin blonde girl" are defined. Some are not. "Corpus." My nanny was from Corpus, and the word itself has profound meaning. "Clitoris ©." He copyrighted, in his mind, the word, clitoris. That rules.

"Money Orders" - This one is about his friend. "Ha, Ha. Cris needs to see this." He's been freaking about money orders the whole trip.

Imagery, iconography, crowns. I like crowns drawn over things. I want to do a book that is like a Basquiat painting and a Beck album.

Remember to draw a crown over my own head, the head of the narrator. Just did it in my mind. Cool. I'm so stoned and manic and thirsty. They keep it cool in here, but I'm just so thirsty. Where is Crispin? There he is by the snack bar.

Cris doesn't want anything besides a smoothie, so I have two bottled waters and a macchiato, and they make him a strawberry and banana smoothie. We chat at a café table, and our fight is over.

"His art was an effort to drown out problems in many ways," I say.

"So were the drugs, I guess," Cris says.

"This project is an effort to drown out the sorrow, maybe?"

"Maybe so. Look. I know you are hurting...and I am really sorry. I think that may be what you need to hear right now from somebody."

"That just means so much more to me right now than you even know. I can't even express it fully in words. I'm real sorry, too."

"I know you are. You're going to pull through this

161

rough stretch. You are loved and you're a good dad and good person that just...got off track. Way the fuck off track with the drugs and the affair and a couple of your buds died and you woke the fuck up or tried to, and now you're going to be okay. I just had to make sure you was gonna be good. Lord knows, I've...'What track?' had been more like the question for me before. I was so far from on track."

"You're on it now, Cris. We'll both be fine. I just really miss my kids and want to head for home soon. You think we'll make good time on the way back East?"

"Direct. We will get there as directly as possible, once we head."

"I was thinking of leaving from here for some reason, Cris. I just keep thinking that would be the thing to do. We are south and I live in the South. We could head through Texas and New Orleans and stop."

"We have to get my dog. And we are going to The City and Napa."

"I know. I was just thinking...geographically it makes sense."

The sun is setting behind the tall buildings already, and I have a sense of cooling calm I haven't felt in days. I love to travel and have nice experiences, and good art and friendship can be so therapuetic to me. Glorious America is such a nice place to be.

Cris says, "You must be low on money by now."

"Yeah, starting to run low."

"Maybe you can get some good trim jobs still, up north."

"Maybe. I wouldn't mind working. You still going to be able to help me out with some money to send to the Mrs.?"

"Yeah. I'll give you a grand to send her for bills and whatnot...and you can get me when you're back on your feet. I may end up charging you a very small interest amount just to make it worth my while, but I wanted you to come on out here to California and check it out...and I know you've spent most of the money you have with you."

"Thanks a million, dude."

"What are friends for?"

"I was just asking myself that earlier today. I remembered."

162

INNER CHILD NIGHT:
(-Los Angeles)

We leave and are back down the hill quickly. Instead of getting right in the car, we decide to walk to a groovy little Cali-Mex taco joint right near the pay lot where we parked. We wisely opted for close and quick fish tacos over LA Friday traffic.

"How did you like Basquiat?" I ask Cris in the restaurant.

"Are you kidding me," Cris responds. "I loved it. Was he on smack, or what?"

"He died of that shit, and blow, eventually, in his twenties."

"Fuck that."

"Cris, tonight is the night. The night. We are going to have Sasha and Valentina and whoever else hang at Dave's. Some corporate power girls and models, you know? Smart, sophisticated pretty ladies. His family has vacated the premises. Then we are maybe going to dinner at Luna Park or somewhere else good. Then we finally get the old King to go out with us at nighttime. It's always good to have Dave around, and we are fuckin' goin' out tonight...all night, if necessary."

"Shay, dat shounds...like a good idea, ole boy."

"This is some neat local art for a taco joint. LA has a vibrant art scene. This one of the skyline that's disintegrating is interesting."

"Basquiat live here, Van?"

"He spent time here, but he's NYC."

"They have an art scene there too I've heard."

"You think?"

While his phone rings: "You're sitting on my phone. Pass me that."

"Who is it?" I say, as he checks the caller id.

"Potter."

"Good."

"He finally called when we have plans," Cris says, discouraged.

"Fuck that; it's cool. Bring him. We bring him. Bring it on. We party like huge stars tonight."

"I may play that game with you after all, just once," Cris says before answering. "Potter, what up my homie? Yeah...yeah...fuckin' me and Van and Van's boy, our boy, Dave. Definitely going out."

"Tell him to meet us at Dave's on Cockring," I say to Cris. Then to myself I say, "Yeah, boyeee. Oh, it's fuckin' on tonight, like Jean."

Cris says: "See ya!," in the phone. Then to me: "He's gonna meet us for dinner. He has to shower up first and whatnot."

I sing: "Tonight, tonight. Tonight's the fuckin' night. Everything that we've waited for on this trip happens tonight, in la-la-land."

"I loved that art show, Van."

"I'm so glad, Crispin. I knew you would. I knew he'd reach you."

"Let's have a great night tonight, homeboy...like old times. You want to stop for a Thai Tea too in Tokyotown, or are you through?"

"I'm set," I say, hoisting my delicious lime-aid: "To old times...bro, we need a real drink before we cheers...so, let's pick up some booze, cheers it up to old times and..."

"Ya know, Van, old times were great, but this is post come up. These are the new good times. This will be my now time. This is my time."

"I like that, Cris."

Wow, I think, redemption. Our friendship is bigger than that lame drama.

"How's your tacos?" Cris asks, clearly enjoying his food and the change of mood.

"Incredible," I answer. "I'm almost finished with mine".

"Mine too. I'd love to hit Mexico."

"Gordon and I used to drive to the border then walk across."

"Exactly how far down is Diego?"

"Like two plus hours or more depending on traffic, but it's totally worth it."

"Just not up for driving."

Back in the car, I'm thinking of the less fortunate in the City of Los Angeles, the impoverished in the hoods, those immersed in gang activity. I've read of life under these bridges, where the crack smoke flows but there is no flowing water. LA is a bit like a whore in that it always seems to look better from three blocks away. Glitzy exterior; grimy interior.

Sitting in traffic, thinking of all the people that comprise Los Angeles. The Mexican families, the struggling actors, the surfers, Hollywood movers-and-shakers, the rich families, the business people, the UCLA and USC kids, the hangers on that ride coattails.

God's sun was shining so strongly in the summer in Southern California today that I'm thankful for it to fully set. Bring on the night.

"I'm ready for that desert breeze to start blowing," I say. "This wouldn't have come close to working, Cris, this trip to LA without Johnny letting us leave the dog at his house."

"I know," Cris says. "Barely worked without her."

"Can you imagine? Having a dog with us in this heat."

"That would have sucked."

"You know what doesn't suck? Hanging out with Dave. Go ahead and expect a lot from tonight."

As we roll near to Dave's place, we see the diner from Pulp Fiction again. I say, "I had a 'Bad Mother Fucker' wallet."

We reach Dave's, and it feels relaxing to be inside the apartment. I missed this place, this neighborhood. Same as many cities, a street's name in LA may equal an area's name; this is Mid-Wilshire.

"You getting some good material for your book, Van?" Dave asks.

I say, "Yeah, I would have to say that I am. It hasn't exactly been what was expected, but some interesting enough stuff has happened."

"I really think you need to talk to Frank about how this project is coming along. See if he can help you with this."

"Okay, I will. Should I get his number?"

"You'll see him at the restaurant."

"He and Jo coming?"

"No, they can't. My restaurant. ... Thoughts on eating tonight?"

"Luna Park, right here in the neighborhood."

"I thought you had a liquid lunch there today."

"They were closed, but tonight they are having Inner Child Night, with like baby-style drinks and comfort food. I am being new in this creation process, so I thought it would be appropriate."

"Oh, it is appropriate," Dave says. He walks down the hall to touch his hair in the bathroom.

Cris is finished rolling a joint and says, "When Dave comes back in here, let's get small." He and I love old Steve Martin standup. "Does anyone even listen to music in LA?" he asks.

"Of course they do," I say. "Jane's Addiction is from here. The Doors are from here. Chili Peppers. Beck. The Eagles. The Beach Boys. All the bad metal too. Guns n Roses. Punk Rock: X. The fuckin' Go-Gos."

"I know, I know. I just mean there is always a movie on everywhere you go," he says, gesturing to Dave's TV. It is starting to upset me that he and I are on opposite sides of every conversation.

I say, "This is a cool movie: Collateral."

"I haven't seen this, but Tom Cruise is always the same."

"Tom Cruise is actually a pretty good bad guy in this."

"Who'd a thunk it...Mr. Top Risky Gun Business."

"Right. This is right here. This takes place right here."

Dave has re-entered the room and the conversation saying excitedly, "All of it takes place in this neighborhood and Downtown."

After we smoke and talk about Humboldt a little, Cris asks to use Dave's bathroom to clean up. As he does, Dave talks to me about the nuts-and-bolts of my writing for about five minutes then departs.

I'm all alone in the living room and check out the new additions to the artifacts on Dave's coffee table. A hand, the five fingers of the hand, a glass statue of an angel, a huge laughing Buddha I love. I laugh to myself remembering Nutt commenting that Dave's rooms in Athens always looked like museums.

I walk into the small adjacent office, after grabbing

a fresh beer out of the refrigerator. There wasn't much to see in his kitchen except a card from his financier brother showing off the kids, a bunch of gourmet chocolate, a half-eaten leftover Bicco pizza and the beer and champagne Cris bought. I bet that chocolate is for the ladies. It's probably a prop for ladies. Dave doesn't eat it himself much.

On the desk, I see Dave's new promotional sheets, his shots. He is shirtless and shaved all over. Jewish but he could be Italian or Latin. He is buff but not too buff. He is actually bigger now than when these were shot. He may be getting too big. I should tell him he looks better lean. His eyes are searching, yearning. Pretty good.

LA flesh, this town shows flesh. You see a lot of skin, and it's good-looking skin usually. If it's real LA flesh, it should look good. Dave shows a lot of flesh in his sheets or whatever you call these. I wonder if just a head shot would be a better promo for him. Maybe you need both.

"Come back here, Van," I hear Dave call from the bedroom.

"This is my new demo," he says, as I enter the room.

He cues it and it starts and Patrick Dempsey is in it, and another recognizable actor dude is in it. Dave is the star, almost getting hit by a Ferrari in the back alley behind the restaurant he used to manage. It's driven by the other actor dude. They have a verbal conflict. Then it switches to Dave on the Sci-Fi Channel singing as camp counselor, telling a scary story. Then it's back to Dave and Dempsey – they've pulled an identity switch trick to fool the other actor dude for being an ass. Dave is in the valet outfit now instead of Dempsey. They look enough alike. Dave drives off, stealing the Ferrari. I laugh and say I like it as it ends then starts back up. "Bonus:" flashes across the screen.

Music plays. It's Dave as front man with a band. He's covered in tattoos, playing frontman with guitar. The song is good.

Cris comes in saying, "I thought no one listened to good music in LA, what is that?"

"It's Dave," I say. "Dave's demo."

"I really like that, Dave," Cris says. "I thought that voice sounded familiar to me."

"How many songs?" I ask Dave.

"Just this one. It is thrown in at the end. It's a scene

from an indie film I was in. Most of these guys worked in my last restaurant. That's how we get to practice. If we aren't getting any big roles, just make an indie film."

"That is cool," Cris says.

On the screen, Dave is shirtless in a shower wearing boxing gloves, looking forlorn as the music repeats a catchy refrain. It's interesting cinema, with Dave as a boxer after a fight.

Dave leaves the room as I re-start the demo for Cris saying, "Out here, everyone you work with at your McJob are actors, screenwriters, musicians, something."

"Right," he says.

"Kinda like how everyone we knew was in a band in Athens."

I walk out of the bedroom and Dave is in front of the bathroom mirror making final touches.

"Do you ever miss going out?" I ask him.

"No," He says. "I just miss getting ready."

I raid Dave's closet at his urging and try on a few things and find a shirt I like for tonight. We are all in our own worlds yet together. This is much closer to what I had in mind for the trip. I have a sense of relief.

A few minutes later, Sasha and Valentina show up. Valentina is Dave's ex-girlfriend, a German model. She looks at least a year older. I can see that she is aging some, but she's still a gorgeous woman. She was once on the cover of Elle Magazine and more recently she has been in videos with Mark McGrath and Bob Dylan's son, Jakob.

Sasha looks at least as good as I remembered, which is not all that attractive when you take in the radiance of a Valentina in the same room. But she is a very nice-looking woman. She is very top-shelf, upper crust Los Angeles. Her stance, attitude and voice, and her style of dress all show her power as a corporate girl, an independent woman.

Their friend Ryan shows up ten minutes later. He has white, cropped hair and a gregarious, inclusive grin. His T-shirt says "QUESTION." I immediately like him.

And we pop the champagne. The girls stick to bottled water, which is so "image is everything" LA lame. A few calories can be a good idea. We have a toast anyway, to the night.

Dave says, "We could go to El Carmen first for a few

shots, if we all feel like getting in our cars and driving."

"That's the Mexican Wrestler tequila bar," I remember aloud. "I like that, but I'm sure the ladies need real food soon, Dave."

"We could go eat Indian and watch Bollywood videos on the big screen at Electric Karma before hitting the hotel."

I say, "Let's just do that Inner Child Night at Luna Park right up the street." And we are off.

Later, I'm in the restaurant talking intensely with Sasha. She and I have an immediate need to disclose to one another. It is nice. Valentina and Dave are immersed in "we used to date and now don't" banter. Their eyes are hungry. They always want to fuck each other when they are near. I remember that being funny for Sasha and I before. We were in a group of four and she and I were just being friends. I was safe to her, since I was Dave's friend. I was leaving. I was married. By the end of the trip, we had developed some feelings for one another, a small affinity. Nothing happened romantically. I think we were both relieved I behaved.

Potter shows up and is added to our table. Good, I think, a verbal "date" for Cris. He is from back home but rugged LA cool now, a reality show carpenter and building and furniture designer by occupation.

Ryan has the air of being a date to us all. He makes us all laugh and smile. I like the fact that his flamboyant yet still manly personality is outshining Dave. Everyone is chatty, and the girls are playing with their food, the boys are noshing hard, some of us are quickly getting drunk, buzzing. The whole room is buzzing and hiving more loudly now suddenly, and we are the stars of the show. Customers at other tables watch us party and want a piece of our group's energy tonight.

And the DJ plays sweet, sweeping music that moves and enchants us, almost as if we were children. The waitresses occasional thoughtful interludes and our own pleasant conversations guide us through the tasty meal of comfort food, as cocktails flow and our buzzes hive louder.

The waitress is a fun, funny girl. Her heart just melted when she saw all of us; she needed a good-tipping table that badly, I guess.

Everyone is attractive and dressed so well that this

169

must be Hollywood. We all seem so happy to be here that it reminds me of a hipster magazine advertisement. Ryan starts beat-boxing to the music over yet another baby drink. We are getting small, the mashed potatoes and fresh juice cocktails are helping. He is phenomenal, more playing a vocal instrument than just plain beat-boxing. I look at the new, fun art, these faces and the paintings on the wall. I start rapping about good food, art, people...how some evenings are unequaled.

The waitress stops by saying, "The rice pudding is out-a sight."

Potter and Cris leave to go get high off the Humboldt weed and catch up. The rest of us stop by Dave's and have a chat and smoke up. Ryan makes some more alien mouth music, and I tell him he should be signed. He says he will be within the year. Ryan and I have beer together and a toast to the good cheer of the evening, and then it's time for the club. The night is in full swing.

The ride with Sasha feels like togetherness. I really do connect with her, and this Mercedes is awesome. She is a city girl, a corporate city saleswoman. Could I be with her? She does look pretty with the colors of city light glinting off her perfectly made up face, as its image is reflected in the glossy new dashboard of this power vehicle that she earned.

"Beautiful night," I say. I'm charged from the energy of the millions around me and think of the book. LA has her lights on tonight, but she always feels so much more Less Than Zero than she does Bright Lights, Big City. Everyone in Los Angeles seems self-interested, and this isn't big building urbane. This is so not New York. This is a different hustle, this somewhat laid back land of self.

While I do love it here for recreation, Los Angeles is ultimately not for me. I'm too urban East Coast, too glorious green South for LA.

"You want some star power?" I ask Sasha.

"What? Sure," she answers.

"East West Fusion Like Poetry-Song Nights, Pardon My Intrusion City of Angels, city of lights," starts my rap into her hand-held recorder that I picked up from her dash.

She smiles at me and nods then says: "It's recording."

I can see from her eyes that she is eating this up, so I continue:

Inner child insight
Life's rice pudding is out-a sight
Bring my desert dessert tonight
I'm from Tex-Lanta and you a fan-a
My dirty South vibe and grammar
I don't stammer or stare or fake-care
About air kisses, snitches or your airs
I'm the heir apparent kissed
Go ask your therapist this
You call me daddy, playin' wife
This Cedes is so Caddy-lac Lincoln
This sporting life...ringin'
Like Jordan's strife
I'm two-sport swingin'
Two states of mind
You're Too Short
I'm Outkast and don't mind, see
So get behind me
My reeling real ride
Get inside...The VAN!
Say it two-times
Fast in hush-rhyme
The VAN is the man.
The VAN is the man

I can see from her captivated gaze that, at least for now, she agrees.

STARGAZED:
(-Los Angeles)

This is a town of stars. They may be business executives that really know how to sell, or household namebrand actors on the red carpet, or a blonde with the perfect boobjob stuck in the valley of porn. They may be a locally famous WeHo gay or the straight stud of the Strip. But they all want to be a somebody out in Hollywood, these stars.

LA's glamorous nightlife has always revolved aound swanky hotel bars. New boutique hotels for the fashiony trendist, old classic hotels for the romantic classicist, home to the best bars and clubs in the city. Famous spots like Chateau Marmont on the Strip, where John Belushi died. Or perhaps the Deleanor in Hollywood tonight, where we arrive in flashy style. Tinseltown is a dream.

In my line of vision as Sasha and I approach the hotel club, the palm trees part for a velvet rope, guarded by the hip-looking. I suddenly notice Dave walking up quickly behind us.

"Is my name on that list?" Dave says to the male model/actor door guy as we glide up to the Deleanor's entrance. "It better be."

"Dave!" shouts out Door Guy.

"Good to see you," Dave says warmly.

"Dude, I need to call you and talk about a few things."

"Give me a ring."

"I'll call you this week, or next week at the latest. I have to go out of town. Thanks, man."

As the velvet rope drops, I wonder how many people Dave helps? We enter through a side entrance and then the kitchen, just like that scene in Swingers, because we're so money.

I'm thinking that a son of the South in Southern California works because we are gregarious and gracious. Southerners are far and away the most charming people in America, because it's expected of us. Manners matter out here some, too - they probably help.

And we enter the club. Potter and Crispin soon

joining the original contingent, which was just Sasha, Dave and myself.

Judi is out on the town tonight too. She looks stunning as she joins us, replacing Valentina in the "one to watch" category.

Too bad Ryan had to be at the studio so early in the morning and left with Valentina. I wonder if they hook up ever or are just friends.

I've just met Dave's Cali best friend, Cyril, a pro soccer player for the LA Galaxy second team and an actor. He is a beautiful man, in look, dress and action. We are tight before even the formal introduction.

"Heard about you," he says. "How's your book coming?"

"Great," I say. "Were you in an independent film with Dave a few years ago? I think I saw some raw footage of you and Dave where you guys had skateboards and tattoos and were arguing."

"Yeah. Holy shit, you saw that? You know soccer is my main thing right now."

"Dave told me."

Dave says, "We weren't fighting in that scene, Van. I was giving him advice."

"That sounds more like you, KD," I say.

"What does that stand for?" Dave asks.

"King Dave."

"It was my film...and this, this is my town. You feel me now?"

You never know when struggling actors speak of their careers, but Dave has a track record of notable commercial work and overall success, so I don't doubt him. Dave never knew when he was going to get a big break, but in the meantime he stayed pumped on himself all the time, and he worked at it. He worked his day job too, but the acting was where his real personal focus went.

Dave's close enough to a star to me just for being in so many national commercials and for working hard and being charismatic. The real essence of stardom is charisma, and that oozes out of Dave's pores. Plus, he's a positive life force and good influence on his friends. You can actually feel his energy when he's in the room whenever he's talking, which is often, or even if he's just quietly being present.

When Potter and Crispin showed up earlier, Dave got them in too. I bet that impressed them some; they look stoked to be here. Glad Dave could get us all in, because it is a packed night at the Deleanor.

Pretty LA hotel pool bar scene: shiny, gorgeous, on. Tonight it is all friends and tingly night air. The lights, the pool, the glimmer of light off the pool, lots of beauties, everyone is being beautiful.

Glitzy glimpses all around me: Fancy sunshine clothes, sunglasses inside even for some, slick and expensive jeans and shirts on the men, skimpy dresses on pretty women. And this is one of those lovely nights where things start to go well, where the booze washes away everyone's worries and the night itself is intoxicating, so is the air on my skin, the moon. It is a gleam beam dream, know what I mean.

I love how girls tend to feel it before the guys. They help the guys around them to realize that this is one of those memorable nights, a seemingly enchanted night full of energy and vibe.

When the booze and/or illicit drugs hits a lot of these young adults here tonight, it will only intensify what is already here, an exuberant sexuality, an energy and collectivity of thought and emotion, a cry for decadence.

Conversely, my friend Sasha does not seem comfortable in this world anymore. You can tell that she has known it in the past, but it is just not her anymore. A fine restaurant is much more her scene now. She has refined out and settled down. A corporate girl.

Judi is not uncomfortable at all here, in her tiny dress with her ass hanging out. She fits in nicely with these girls, the LA Persian Princess crowd. I should thank her for wearing that tonight, and I love the hot hostesses in tight white tennis outfits and Vans. Very nice look.

Dave is buying drinks, of course, because that is what he does, and we are having as many rounds as they will serve us as fast as they can get to us, and it doesn't seem to be fast enough, so I go to the bar.

I grab Judi's ass before I leave the group. She seems to suddenly be way more into Cyril than me now. He does have on a great plaid hat.

Walking away alone I think, she actually scolded

me. That is very unlike how she has acted toward me before. Earlier she was threatening to jump in the pool naked she was so revved up. We all encouraged her.

I have a feeling she and Cyril may be screwing soon, the way they were making eyes. Maybe she and I are just friends now.

I go buy another round of drinks on Dave's tab at the bar. The covered, tiki-like bar area is in a crush of thirstily imbibing clubgoers. We are all waiting for cocktails and beers together.

"What up, dude?" I say to a bar patron that walks up smiling broadly at me.

"Hey man. How's it going?" he says.

"Good."

"That's great. You been waiting long?"

"Nah, couple minutes. I'm supposed to be bringing drinks back to friends."

"Me too. It's busy tonight. I love this place, come here all the time."

"I don't blame you."

"You live in LA?"

"Atlanta."

"ATL, cool."

I think to myself that the contrasts and similarities are profound between Atlanta and Los Angeles: the southern capitals of East and West Coast America. Both are sprawling inventions, sunshine car towns, but nothing in the world invention-wise compares to Hollywood.

"Yeah...this is fun," I say as a gorgeous blonde passes and turns both of our heads.

"Couple of nude girls in the pool so far."

"The girl we were with was threatening to jump in nude."

"Was she?"

"Yeah. She's hot. I think she's going to be hooking up with my friend's buddy this time though."

"I'm hanging with some really cool people over there, some real pretty girls. Maybe you should come over and talk to us."

"I might after I drop these drinks off. That sounds cool."

"What kind of shirt is that?"

175

"Corpus. It's local, I think."

"Local LA or ATL?"

"Oh, LA. I do some lowbrow fashion kinda like this back home though."

"Oh yeah? You do fashion?"

"Not real high fashiony fashion, T-shirts and stickers and stuff."

"Cool, with original art?"

"Exactly, I don't use my own art much. I find artists with cool paintings and make deals with them to make shirts of their stuff and outsource the production. It's pretty simple. I keep it pure and positive and simple, so it is called fly-wear."

"That's perfect," he says.

It's time for me to order drinks: "I need two Maker's and sodas and two Belvedere sodas and one bottled water"

"On Dave's tab again?" says the beautiful waif of a bartendress.

"Yeah. Thanks." She remembered. She remembered Dave anyway.

"She is getting you next," I say to the guy. Then referring to an act of acknowledgement the bartendress gave him before she took my order, I say, "I saw that little hand gesture."

"I know her. Hey, you should meet this girl that I'm hanging with that does fashion."

"Okay!"

"Is she your girl?" I ask out of general curiosity.

"No, a friend. She is recently single."

"Okay." My drinks arrive.

"I just need two more," he says to the bartender.

"Comin' up," she says, smiling like the professional flirt that she is.

"You wanna go over there now?" he asks me.

I like his energy, so I say, "Yes. I have to drop these drinks off first, and I'll come find you."

"Do that."

"Which way will you be?"

"Right over there. Do that! I'll be with this brunette with long hair."

The fact that Sasha is here to see me makes me feel a little torn about going over, but she already said she was leaving early, before we even arrived, so she'll be out of here soon.

I'm carrying five drinks like a server or barman might, thinking Sasha and I really talked, and it was nice to have her around. I want to be her friend, definitely and maybe we could hook up...maybe not. I just want to be friends with her right now.

As I walk up, Potter is getting to know Dave and Cyril better verbally, while Judi is sprawled across Cyril on the chaise lounge.

"He was on House Sweep," Cyril says to Dave.

"Were you on there with Franklin?" Dave asks Potter.

"No, I replaced him actually."

"That's cool. He's our good friend."

I go to find my new friend, and he is with this truly gorgeous brunette that does fashion, as advertised. She and I talk that industry briefly while my new friend smilingly listens in.

She's exactly what he said she was, and I do like these people, but I'm sort of wondering what to do and say next. What he didn't tell me at the bar was that she has a big bag of ecstacy in her purse.

She breaks it out, and I buy five rolls with my last $100 and eat two of them before thinking much about it. I still have such strong urges to use drugs.

"He is like Stevie," the brunette says to my new friend.

"They are both wow," he says, as I clearly notice his huge dilated pupils. "Being like Stevie is a total compliment. I think she likes you."

"They are really strong," she says to me.

"I'll be okay, right?" I ask.

"You'll be on fire, sweetheart," she says.

"Two of these ones. You'll love it," he says.

I soon decide to leave the scene of illicit purchase and bid them a nice night and walk back to my crowd. These kids I'm with tonight are a bunch of stars, and I should spend most of my time with them.

"Let's party like stars," I say to the crew, especially Crispin, as I hand him a roll. I hand Judi a roll, too.

"Let's do," she says.

Then I ask who wants the last one, and Cyril takes it.

Look at all these pretty Hollywood hustlers, dreamers. I want to dance. My eyes are shining from the lights around the pool. Light is bouncing off the pool, bouncing off my eyes, and I'm bouncing to the beat on those great loudspeakers.

"Follow the bouncing breasts," I mumble to myself as a huge pair of perfect silicone dribbles by me as gracefully as Kobe Bryant.

Sasha leaves for tomorrow's workday. I'm totally gone, too, almost immediately gone and regretting I took so much. Glad I'm not on blow.

I migrate to the bathroom to urinate, and it looks so fucking cool. It looked cool before, but not like this. This shit looks cool. This is what a star bathroom should look like, in a star place, in a star town. This bathroom is so LA. I'm starstruck.

In the bathroom still, looking in the mirror, I think, I could be a star like this group. I'm suddenly a star like them almost. I'll start out a small star like Dave with his commercials or Potter with his reality TV stuff. Then I'll become a real star. The key may just be to become a star in my mind first. So I'm a star, but I'm new at this.

I walk back toward my California star friends. Dave looks every bit a star. Cyril looks like a star. And in the mirror in that glamorous Hollywood bathroom, I looked like a star. We all look like stars tonight, with these lights shimmering off of the pool on our faces. Even Crispin looks like a star, in his way, like a blue collar star. Potter? Potter definitely has a rugged LA style. Judi is like a female sexuality star. We are all stars tonight in LA. Hooray for Hollywood.

Judi is getting voraciously randy and telling us all she can squirt sometimes. That gets my attention. I was half-ignoring her and she noticed and made sure I heard that.

"We'd like to see that," I say.

Judi's friends from the other night show up. Dave has been having sex with one of them, he tells me in my ear. I think she's the second or third cutest. Judi is by far the cutest. They all play pool near us or hover and drink sugar free Cosmos, while Judi bounces between them and us.

178

Soon Potter leaves, saying he has to be on point in the morning. Cris walks him out. I'm glad someone from Athens paid attention to Cris and made him feel loved.

The lights are dancing higher and faster off the pool, and I'm starting to roll harder. My skin tingles in the desert air as another strong wave of drug washes over my body. I feel good but so overwhelmed.

Not sure how much time just passed. It didn't seem like much at all. But they are closing soon, and we are leaving. Dave is driving Crispin and I. Cyril and Judi are each in their cars. They may have exchanged numbers, but Judi is coming over, and Cyril has to work in the morning. I like him but it's good he won't be coming, because I want to party with Judi tonight.

He has to work and is rolling? Whatever, I feel great. He'll be fine.

"How do you like LA now, Cris?" I ask.

"We love it!" he answers.

"Dave's got girls on the phone. It's Judi and her friends. I heard him say 'your friends' and I'm gonna lick her all over. I'm so fucked up. Let me talk to her, Dave. Dave's the King."

"I know," Cris says, nodding through a foolish grin.

"Let me talk to her, please," I say to Dave.

"Here," Dave says, handing me the phone.

"Hey Judi," I say. "Who made you feel like this?"

"What?" she says.

"How do you feel?" I ask.

"Good."

"Really good or just good."

"Really good."

"I'm glad you feel really good. Who made you feel like this?"

"You did."

"Can't wait to see you back at Dave's."

"Me neither."

"Here's Dave again."

I hand the phone back to Dave. I am aroused in full, and my arm is so tingly that my hairs are standing up on end. Can't wait to see Judi.

Then we are zooming at what seems to be the speed

of light. Palm trees and lights and night excitement. I'm glad Dave's in control because I'm not. I like it best when someone sober and on is in control of the car.

This is fast. This is fast. We are going so fast.

"Cris?" I ask him, his name seeming to linger in the air. The air feels so good.

"Totally," he answers, raising his eyebrows. "Can't believe you are on two of this. You okay?"

"Totally fast, but I feel great."

"Me too."

Next we are in the parking deck.

"Come on Van, come on, keep moving your feet," Dave says.

I'm chasing Dave down the ramps of the deck while he skates. His board is a Christian Hosoi Hammerhead, white, smooth retro deck.

This is fun. I'm running down a loop, and when I get to the bottom, I know nothing will be real, except Dave. He's not even on anything, except some vodka.

"Wow," I say to myself. Everything is cubing. I'm running into Cube Land. Now, there are two Daves. "Which one? Cool...there are two of you now Dave! Holy shit."

"You okay?" asks Dave.

"Yeah."

At the bottom of the deck, I see Cris coming out of the stairwell.

Cris is right beside me talking in my ear as we walk up the sidewalk. "Can't believe you are on two," he says. "Having fun?"

"Yeah. Just glad to be with friends. Dave's my best friend."

"He's the coolest."

"And how cool are we?"

"We are best-best friends."

"I love you, man."

Then, he is singing about thirty yards behind me. Then, I hear a crashing sound, and it's Cris rolling off the hood of a car right next to me.

Dave looks at me, disturbed about the disturbance, and rolls his eyes. Then the other Dave rolls his eyes.

"There are two Daves," I tell Cris.

"Two Daves!" he shouts. "That's awesome. Dave is

the King. One can work and go to auditions and the other one can go out with us all the time, like tonight."

"Right. Which one of you is real?"

"I am," says the one Dave, smiling.

"I am," says the other Dave, with a serious face.

"They are both real," I announce.

"Judi isn't coming," Dave says. "She can't drive."

"I can walk though," I say.

"What?" Dave asks.

"I thought she was. She was when I talked to her."

"She wants to but she's too fucked up to drive. Her girls are coming to get her, and one of them is going to drive her car home."

"Oh...okay. I hope she's okay."

"She'll be fine. I'm going to bed. I have shit to do in the morning, so be quiet."

"I'm going out for a walk. You coming, Crispin?"

"Where?" Cris asks.

"A walk."

"Nah. Be careful."

And then I'm out walking the relatively safe streets of Dave's neighborhood and beyond, strutting alone through a warm Los Angeles night that seems to be only getting hotter.

ECSTASY TV:
(-L-A)

This is wild; this feels so cool; holy shit everything looks so cool; the palm trees; the cars; that engine sounds really cool; buzzz; yeah; car racing engine.

"Yes...Holy shit, holy shit, holy shit."

The air, my skin-tingly with my hairs standing up, sensual, I am almost too alive now. Rubbing my arm is better than sex.

My bracelet is the coolest thing I have ever seen, except childbirth. This is like being born in a way, this trip. They look cool; those guys are banditos; everyone is sooooo coooooool; especially me; strutting; walking smooth and feeling like a panther only a shockwave is pulsing through my super-charged body, electricity.

"Whoooooo am I?"

I can't believe I am really going to be a star. And it IS true.

"A fucking star!"

A star, the stars, the sky, hardly any stars visible, but the night, oh my God the night.

This is, fuck...wow.

Basquiat, you're here?

"You're here, Jean!"

I am hallucinating...at will, and the sky is wide open and I can see the wind. I can see what the breeze feels like, and it feels so good and looks so free. I feel good. It feels good.

"Everything feels so good...L-A."

Try to control your hallucinations, like you could on mushrooms in the tent that time in high school, take that Basquiat painting and put it on those palm trees and buildings. ... I did it. More, faster, more pink, lots of pretty passionate pink. The sky is...a pussy, a warm breezy pussy that is fucking me. I feel like a...oh fuck, yes. I've gone crazy. This is crazy. This is a little crazy.

I am still; walk while you hallucinate. Moving me while I move thee and move with thee. That Basquiat over here to my left with buildings and palm trees on it, inside it, with lights trailing on top of it. Jean, you never painted anything this beautiful, but I take what I made with you, together, me, you, LA and God. I take what I see on my left, what I just saw in front of me but now it's on my left, and I will blend it with what I am seeing now in front of me. Sideways, I did it.

Blue. I love blue. Lights, the lights are melting...put them in the picture too, not just on it.

Those memory mixtures are the best. Never before like this where I could take a memory of a hallucination layered with reality, fuck reality, and blend it with reality, fuck reality. I want to fuck someone. Pretty sure I am fucking now, right now.

Judi, do you, are you? If you are feeling anything close to this, you are probably just rubbing your pussy somewhere. Home in your bed...I'm rubbing your pussy from here. Does that feel good? Telekinetic mutual masturbation is cool. The night air is getting so cool, and I am so hot, sweating bullets. Bullets should have never been invented. Love only. Motion like the ocean's pure devotion. I can rap. Move again. Keep moving.

"Light show tonight. Yo, Bro. Daddy, mommy, I'm a star now, and I don't know if I can take it."

Am I okay?

Is this too much?

This is too much and I'm okay.

Not moving. Move, safely.

Moving now. Stay away from cars and cops because I'm not thinking too clearly.

"Hahahahahhahahahahahahahahahhaahahha"...that was an understatement of a lifetime novel boy.

Novel, how novel is this? How novel is that?

Expert..."I'm a fucking expert in this town!"

We made it all up. This place. Hollywood.

This vision, now make it upside down. YES.

My show; and my movie; my television station:

TV Ecstasy; Ecstasy Television; Ecstasy TV.

"TV Ecstasy."

By me, you see.

I am on television, what a drug.

My movie, my show...

My book...this is my book. Good book.

Note to self:

Write this and let Hollywood try to make a movie about it.

Now, now, now.

Be here now because walking feels so good. I love these palm trees and lights and buildings, pastel buildings and light beams and lights and lights and melting lights and palm trees.

More Basquiat, if you please.

That is? The lights are...

I'm enchanted. It's so beautiful...

So, so intoxicating and just, I'm crying.

Lovely

Lovely

Lovely

Scared for a second, but it's so beautiful. That's too beautiful; I am not scared of this. It is pure beauty with golden trumpets angels with wings.

I can't believe it is getting prettier.

"Wah, woooo...wow. I have rarely seen anything that beautiful."

"Ha, ha, ha...he's as fucked up as you are, Lucy," says a voice.

My hallucinated visions stop. Who said that? Is that real?

"Come over here, bro, and talk to this girl; she's just as fucked up as you."

Now I see security guards, laughing, and a beautiful girl.

Two of each security guard, and two of her, and am I in trouble?

"I want to be with him," she says. She swims or floats to me.

Those beautiful eyes of hers are enchanting. I'm spinning her in circles in my arms and she loves me and the way we look at each other is almost like real love. Those piercing, ice blue eyes, four of them, two of her, more when I spin her faster.

"I love you," she says.

"I know from your eyes. Those four ice blue eyes."

We embrace. "Is this real?" I ask.

"Holy shit, bro," the big security guard says, and I notice that he is a young Mexican, maybe twenty-one.

He continues: "He is more fucked up than you even Lucy. Yeah, bro. It's real, but that is only one girl."

"Okay. I mean thank you, I see two."

"I can tell, bro. What are you on?"

"Am I in trouble?"

"Ha. You mean our clothes. He thinks we're cops, you're cool, you funny as shit bro, but you're totally cool with us."

"I love him," Lucy says. "I need to be around him."

"Are you? You are on it too?"

"What, baby?"

"X, you're not?"

"She's still wired from earlier, right girl, and also drunk as hell," the security guard answers for her.

"And I'm so horny tonight," she adds.

"You're beautiful, those eyes, those ice eyes. Are they made of ice?"

Time passes, did some time just pass? She is sitting on top of me on the ground, those eyes, and she is wearing almost nothing, a mesh shirt with big, soft, firm tits busting out of it. Porn star blonde hair frames her model face. I'm cracking her up, and we are hypnotized, completely enraptured.

"Both of you are so hot," I say to her double image.

"Bro, she is only one girl. ... I love this guy too, Lucy. What is your book gonna be called again?"

"What, Al?" Wait, I know this cop's name. How?

"Am I in trouble?"

"No, Van, we like you, she fucking loves you, relax, I have been just as messed up as you, plentya times, bro. You are amongst friends, well and Chico over there. He don't say much of shit, so you ain't our friend, Chico. Just kidding, fat fucker. We are all good. You are making the night fun; we are working right now."

"I am not," says Lucy.

"Do you work?"

"No way. I act."

"Bro, she is just rich and hot and acts."

She is sitting on top of me, on the pavement of this parking island, saying, Van, honey, can I kiss you a little? Do you like that? Do you like the way my lips feel?"

"Yeah," I moan.

"How hot do you think I am, really hot or just hot?"

"I don't know, hot, just hot." I want to see what this answer will do. I'm lying. She is very hot.

"Hold on then, wait, then tell me."

"Holy shit, bro, she is taking off her shirt for you."

"Yes...four titties in my face. Yes."

"Suck on 'em, bro." Al says.

She says, "Go ahead, lick them, ooh...yeah. Van, honey, how hot am I now?"

"So fucking hot."

And then things are somehow even more cloudy in my mind. Then everything seems too fantasy between the two of us. Then she is gone.

She tried to take me to her apartment I'm pretty sure, but I fell over following her. The security guard, Alejandro, my new friend, decided that I could not probably even fuck her for a while even if I made it up there, and she has an audition in a few hours. She is gone, and I'm too far gone.

I spend the rest of the night walking around LA with Al while he takes breaks and Chico guards the gate. We smoke bowls out of a big glass pipe. We must look funny, a young, big Mexican security guard and a wasted whiteboy writer, smoking bowls and walking at 5:00 a.m.

He tells me that he also works security at Will Smith's house in Malibu, and he can find us some pot before he goes to that job at 2:00 p.m. today if we are interested. He likes my book ideas.

I miss Lucy's voice and tits and eyes...and extra tits, but I do like Al. He has great energy and is cool to talk with, and when he gets off work at daybreak I get his number in case Cris needs to find weed still.

I walk back toward Dave's to sleep for a couple hours. I'm coming down. I find the building with the big blue box on top of it, that means I'm near. I see the apartment next and am so relieved and exhausted.

I knock on the window and Cris lets me right in. He says, "Hey, buddy...love you, buddy...hope you had fun, buddy."

I immediately lay down and fall asleep.

UP THE 5 (DRIVE 4):
(-Los Angeles/-Highway 5/-San Luis Obispo)

As I wake up the next morning, Cris and Dave are also in the living room and talking about me.

Dave is saying, "...crazy but he is going to make it huge if he stays off the stuff. Sometimes you have to be at least half-crazy to get to the top; it's just so much more natural that way."

"Who's crazy?" I ask.

"Get up and let's get out of dodge," Cris says to me. "We did all we could do last night, I'm pretty sure."

As we get in his car to go have coffee, he is singing the Nine Inch Nails' song "Starfucker."

"Yeah, I sung that all last trip," I say. His face is hurt, like I shoot everything of his down. What I meant was "great, another shared experience," but he took it the wrong way. I may have expressed it weakly because I'm so fuzzy-headed.

We follow Dave in his Bronco, and we all stop at a nearby coffeehouse for coffees on Dave. He even bought us something on the way out. Dave is still my best friend even though he lives across the country. He and Cris are both such good guys; glad I still have friends.

The caffeine works just long enough to keep me conscious while we leave town.

I say: "Bye, LA, bye, stars, bye, starfuckers. Cris, I may need to sleep for a while if you don't care."

He answers: "Crash out, man. No problem."

"Remind me to tell you about these two Lucy's when I wake up."

"Okay, man, in the sky with diamonds I'm sure, get some rest...you crazy wannabe star, roll head."

I won the LA game against Cris. I laugh aloud and think in voice-over narration as I start to drift off: "The VAN had won. Crispin finally admitted LA was fun, and then they were back on the road in California."

This is the fourth, let's see: one, two, three...yeah fourth major drive I have taken on this trip. This is a real Cali road trip.

We really did LA up huge last night. Glad I came

through that whole experience okay. I was way, way too high, but I'm really happy for Crispin that we had fun, finally.

I personally want more LA now, the right way, but I'm also glad to be heading north, glad to have had a good taste. I'll be back next year.

Dreaming on Highway 5, dreaming of a better future life, I drift off to sleep.

I wake up to Cris sexy-talking into the phone.

"Who was that?" I ask after he hangs up.

"Ole girl again, from Atlanta. Crazy psychic bitch knew I was thinking about her. Every single time I think of her, she calls me."

"Madeline and I were like that," I say. "She had radar when I was in big trouble with the drugs."

"Right. Anyway, she wants me to fly home right away, to skip any other travel plans I may have and get on an airplane right away and get on that big ass of hers. She ignored me last time I saw her, crazy bitch."

"Maybe she's not such a great idea if she ignored you and is just pulling your strings for fun."

"She was with her friends in Athens. I went up there to see a show, my last night out in Athens before heading west. I was with Jenny having Thai food at a nice little place, and I see her through the window. I leave Jenny just sitting there and go outside, and she fucking acts like she can't hear me, doesn't recognize me. I knew her friend that she was with, from her. I almost pushed her in front of a bus."

"Very healthy relationship. Glad you didn't kill her. What about Jenny?"

"She is the only person I really miss from Atlanta."

"Thanks."

"You don't count."

"Thanks again."

"Jenny and I met up fairly recently. She flew to San Fran and we had a weekend together. That was the last time I got laid."

"Don't let sex rule your decisions."

"You are one to talk."

"Yeah, I fucked up. I had an affair. I got into drugs and obsessed over tits and sex so much that I went out and had an affair. When I give you advice, it comes from experience."

"Lighten up. I just want some ass."

"All right. I just want to see you start to take care of yourself and leaving nice, normal Jenny sitting alone in a restaurant to go throw your ex ho in front of a bus doesn't sound too good."

"What about you?"

"What about me?"

"You still call Ansley. She makes me sick. Y'all make me sick."

"Me too. We ruined each other together. I started calling her again because we had no closure. I fell in love with her. I called it off. She begged me not to. We are done, but I had some loose ends with her that needed to be discussed."

"I think that would be good if you were done with her."

"Madeline would hate it if Ansley and I ended up together, so for that reason alone, I don't want it to happen. I will have to have peace with Madeline on some level to have a happy life. Plus, until recently Ans and I hadn't spoken in many months."

"Good. Go back to that. And you're right about that needing peace with your baby momma, bro."

"I know," I say quietly.

We stay quiet for a long, long time listening to each other's thoughts silently, while I admire California's often rural landscape.

Cris asks if I want to get high, and I say, "I'll pass today. I just need food...and I'm totally out of money."

"I'll buy you something, I guess. I guess I have to."

"You don't have to do anything for me, Crispin."

"You have to eat."

"Worry about yourself instead if that makes you happy," I say in a light, Zen-like tone.

"I didn't spend much money in LA, not compared to what I could have...and I never ran out of weed," he says.

"Great," I say. "Good for you, buddy."

We stop in lovely San Luis Obispo and have a pleasant lunch with great service. San Sushi Obispo has a great name. The town itself has a good name, but seriously, how can we resist sushi in San Luis Obispo...at San Sushi Obispo?

We don't, and the server earns the tip. We appreciate good service as we are both foodies from way back, both worked in the restaurant industry and always eat out.

I thank the waiter for his excellent service and tell him we are traveling and I'm writing about it. I ask if he likes it here.

He tells us: "I live near here in Cambria, exactly halfway from Los Angeles and San Francisco. Middle of the Cali Coast and basically the unspoiled middle of nowhere. But it's boring as fuck after about a day unless you're in the water. I want to move. I'm thinking of going to San Francisco."

"You should," I say, silently singing to myself: "Be sure to wear a flower in your hair."

The strong draw of the California counterculture, native Californians feel it, perhaps even stronger than the rest of America does.

"Are you Anti-LA?" I ask.

"Not really because I love to shop and party in clubs there, but most of my friends are. San Fran is more of an art scene and LA is, I guess, more commercial. I can do this anywhere."

"Did it for years," I say to the smiling server as he departs.

Cris says to me, "Remember how you earned it when you were working at Vino Studio?...I remember one time you said, 'Everything's excellent?' to this table. I was having a drink nearby. That was the ultimate way to phrase a rhetorical question."

"You loved that place," I say through my last sip of dry Japanese beer.

"Totally! Okay, overall how was your sushi, Van?"

"San Rhetorical," I say.

"Ditto," Cris says in a tone indicating closure.

"Everything's ditto?" I ask in the same tone he used for my "Everything's excellent" quote.

He scowls and says: "You always one up. Why do you always have to one up?"

"Sorry," I quietly say, feeling humbled and too off for

a scolding.

Back in the car, I tell Cris about my ecstasy-fueled hallucinations from last night. Then I tell him about Lucy's tits.

He is fairly amused by my story and does an impression of the cop from Smokey and the Bandit, saying, "Nice Lady. ... Thanka Kindly, nice lady. You shoulda said that to her when she took off her top."

GOD BLESS THIS BOOK:
(-Highway 5/-Santa Cruz)

Crispin's mom just called and cancelled as we continued our northerly climb, still in sunny SoCal. His stepfather had a cosmetic surgical procedure. They aren't even together as a couple anymore, but apparently he needs her help with his recovery.

Cris is bummed. I'm bummed. San Francisco and the wine country are out for us. Well, there was some San Francisco - we had a damn tostada - but we wanted to do it up huge.

Instead, we near the NorCal border with no specific plan of action. Zooming north, our ascent has no other real direction. We stop at Johnny's spot for the night and to pick up Chauncey. The Braves are playing the Giants in a day game tomorrow in San Fran, so we decide that we will all go do that.

Suddenly, San Francisco is back on the agenda again. A day game in The City will be perfect enough, come to think of it. An evening in San Fran afterward sounds nice, even if it's just me and my buddy in a restaurant or bar. I don't care much that Johnny is already wavering; he said yes then started to waffle right away.

I'm so exhausted from last night that I plan to crash early. Barely conscious at all today, endorphin depleted from abusing drugs. It's getting beyond old to still be doing this to myself.

Trying to think up: tomorrow, the game, the ballpark. The Braves and Giants, Barry Bonds, views of The City by day, The City by night. It glows and twinkles in my mind.

I'd like to check out more stadiums...and cities. I love culture and urbanity. Baseball is Americana, just as college football defines the South. And cities are the pulse of America.

Cris gets Rick on the phone to confirm; I'd asked if he was working this game what seems like months ago, on the way to trim. Cris tells me we may even all hit a party in "Bezerkely" after the game.

When I wake and walk to the living room, it is halfway

192

through the game. The game is on TV. Cancel everything. They decided not to go, without my input, while I slept and didn't even wake me to watch the game on TV. I'd told Cris to wake me. I'm angry and depressed from taking hard drugs and want the fuck out of here.

Thankfully, we soon leave, and I'm thinking: We aren't going: A. To Napa, B. to ballgame, C. to San Fran, at all, and D. Is youth over for me? It should be. Is childhood over, prolonged childhood, or whatever you call the state of existence that young men enter in this day and age in America, in the Western World, after childhood and the teenage years, after the early twenties, when they grow up? Post-College for some, instead of college for others. What are these years when women grow up and men should grow up or are almost forced to, often unwittingly? It's a strange time in life, a man in your thirties in the post-modern world. I need to take control of my life and become a better parent and person. I need to get closer to God. God, help me to grow and change. I feel close to you, God, right now, in this car. Please help me.

Crispin's ex that has been calling for days, from Atlanta, is this totally hot, big round butt on a skinny everywhere else blonde woman. Half-Swedish and half-American Indian, long hair in braids hot, works at a porn shop when she works at all, hot. That freak keeps calling. Plus, he wants his new motorcycle, his Harley, which is on hold for him in the ATL. He wants his fucking mommy is what he wants. What the fuck!

I tell him he can do whatever he wants. Not to worry about me. I want my personal adventure to take a cool twist, and I'm honestly ready to be away from Crispin for a day or two, at least. As long as I have some work, all is fine. Fine enough.

When this trip is done, I want to get my life going again. I want to get healthy...and clean. I can't be clean with Cris and I on a party trip.

Suddenly, Cris comes up with a new plan and makes a call. We are heading back to Humboldt, back to work, via my old roommate John Connelly's place in San Jose.

Still in the car, I pray again: God, please help me to be a better person and parent. God bless my children. God bless my family. God bless my friends. God bless me. God, bless my wife. God bless California. God bless America. And God bless this book.

"I can't wait to check out San Jose," I say, trying to sound so chipper that I could play third base for the Braves. I'm actually still disappointed, so I come down a notch to reality and say, "At least that should be something to do. It's great to be around Pook."

"I can't wait for that part either. I miss that ole boy, when I think about it," Crispin says.

"He's good people."

"Definitely."

"He'll fuckin' steal a bud from your bag, but he is still a great guy."

"So will you. What do you mean?"

"He used to do this move, where he would say 'Let me check out that bag,' and he would pilfer a bud out of the bag. Let's see your bag."

"It's in the console. What's in San Jose, Van?"

"Silicon Valley, dude, all that computer stuff. The tech money."

"That's right. I knew that. I forget...stuff."

"You smoke a little too much herbals. Anyway, nobody smokes more than John did. Here was the move. He would roll a bud out like this...then not buy the bag."

"You're fucking kidding me."

"He was one shisety mofo back then. His creditors were the reason he moved out of Chase Street. To escape them, he left the best party house in Athens at the time. We had an appliance smashing party. Who does that? Stipe was there to like totally post-LA namedrop one last time. Got that out of my system. People change. Now, Pook rarely even smokes."

"No! Everyone is quitting this and that."

"We are finally growing up, Cris."

We are both real quiet and introspective after that for a long, long time. Two friends rolling away from our sorted pasts and into our unknown futures. This phase of my life is almost over, and I start to think and act differently from here on out.

I'm drifting off, half asleep thinking, praying: God bless this book.

SAN ANYTHING:
(-San Jose/-Santa Maria)

California's original capital, San Jose. Silicon Valley. Home to a technology boom that exploded the American economy roaring upward. This place has money. Tech Boom money created from thought. This is the Tech Age, and we've barely scratched the surface of how much computer technology will impact our work and everyday lives. The tech geeks were right.

The tech bubble formed and swelled to an unbelievable crescendo, then burst. But it is constantly reforming. The fallacy of Y2K, the tragedy of 9-11 and the harsh realities of war have hurt us as a country.

The American economy is vitally robust in places where innovation is for sale, like San Jose, Austin and Atlanta. This is a real boom town I expect to feel...yet I'm here low on energy. The grind of the road and the drugs have taken a major toll. My emotions have pinged all over the state. Right as I start to get another wind and cheer up we reach town, finding John Connelly's house without even getting lost, his directions were that succinct.

John greets us warmly, and we enter. We meet his roomie, a much older local guy in his late fifties, I would guess. He is the homeowner, no wife anymore, kids moved out. John rents a small room. They have a pool that reminds me of a 1974 movie set, very Boogie Nights.

An insurance adjuster by day, John rents a small room here that doubles as a studio where he makes electronic music. His passions also include overeating and collecting obscure toys, the former resulting in his increasingly large size. He has been a culturaphile as long as I've known him and was the urban music show DJ and program director for our college radio station.

We listen to the fresh beats John made in his home studio this week then head out. As we pile in Crispin's car, John tells me he is thinking of finding a hot female singer and forming a full band.

It seems a little slow out, a weeknight in a working town. The same boring nondescript buildings I saw before.

Do computer people not like architecture as much as they should? They're probably just like, "Give me any box so I may perform my work tasks adequately."

We roll to the center of the city and park and see a huge group of Asians hanging together on the sidewalk, giddy-talking, laughing, maybe fifty girls and thirty guys. So many thick Asian girls our heads spin.

"They make them like that here?" I ask John after we walk through their crowd in amazed wonder.

"It's pretty awesome," he retorts.

"Pretty, awesome," Crispin chimes.

My computer geek friend, Roger, calls me on Crispin's phone.

I say: "Good to hear you, too, Roger...If I am back down there...I'd like to get back...No he hated it...Yeah...I don't know yet...Maybe...Me too...Cool...That would be good...You did...Track me down through Dave...Don't worry about that. Roger, it's done...You wanna talk with Pook?... Okay, bye."

"How is he?" Crispin asks me.

"Sounds surprisingly non-depressed, which is really good for him. He got your number from Dave. Sorry about that."

"Fuck it. He's cool. You didn't sound thrilled to hear from him."

"We had a huge falling out in Charleston on a trip, and I thought we may be done as good friends, sadly. It was good to hear from him. I was just...surprised he made such an effort to reach me. He's coming to Downtown LA for a computer animation convention soon."

"He didn't even want to talk to me?" John asks.

"He was like, 'Nah that's okay,'" I say.

John grimaces for a few seconds then says, "Fuck Roger then. What have I ever done to him? We were roomies before you and I."

We eat turkey burgers outside on a patio, and the breeze feels nice, the night air is nice. I appreciate that it seems community oriented here; they show free outdoor movies on weekends in the summer.

I'm thinking the best ideas happen in California: Napa is wine. I came up with an idea in Humboldt, but Humboldt and Mendocino, the Emerald Triangle means the finest weed, which is nature and nurture. And San Fran is music, subculture and art, the creative class. LA is The Industry. TV and movies are nothing more than complex ideas and inventions. San Jose is computers. Santa Cruz is definitely farming, which is based on invention and machine, but it's also skating - which is an invented and inventive sport. This state is about global innovation.

Even out in the suburbs, where my cousins live in Orange County, there's Huntington Beach, which is Surf City USA. Even snowskiing and snowboarding happen in Cali. Leisure pursuits are big business in America, and America gets many of its leisure pursuits from California.

We go to three distinct San Jose bars. First, a typical hole in the wall with a business crowd drinking the workday blues away in the land of venture capital, second, a cheese bar with the usual assortment of mainstream middle California posers and average folks playing pool. Then, the last bar is an artsy rocker bar. It is John's regular hangout.

The people I know from Athens all love this type of bar because it reminds us of the dives we frequented then, during the early '90s, the early days of the Georgia Bar before there were tons of alternative hangouts downtown. The hip crowd, the alternative artist and culture knowing crowd was there. John calls this place Georgia Bar West.

After a drink, I go to the bathroom and notice something powdery on the toilet paper dispenser. I first wonder if it is blow and get an urge in my stomach. It's the remnants of where some meth was crunched up. I am not surprised, since I know a horrible meth epidemic is sweeping through America.

"I found some crunch up," I say to Crispin after leaving the bathroom.

"Did you buy it?" he asks.

"No," I say. "I hate it and just found a very little bit. I'm broke."

"Oh yeah...don't remind me. Just kidding, dude. Of course, I gotcha. I'll buy you another. Stick with the seven and seven, the fourteen?"

"That last one was way strong."

"Another fifteen, then?"

"A beer. A Hoegaarden, please. A 'Ho.' That was a

seventeen."

"You used to like them like that, Van."

"I'm thirsty. It made me thirsty."

"Could have been the crush up you found. I'm getting you a fifteen and a water, pussy."

"Fine. There are some tweaker bitches here, big shock, right?"

"I had noticed that, Van. You only confirmed what I already knew."

"Where's Pook by the way?"

"Talking to some guy over there," he says, pointing.

"Are you moneying these two for us," I say gesturing to a couple of cute rocker girls nearby, one I saw glancing at Cris.

"I...guess. They may be shmoovin' on me."

"I think they are. That one keeps peeping."

"I know. I'm peeping right back...the brunette?"

"Yeah. I'm gonna holler at Pookster. Hang here or move in."

"Godspeed, lad."

I walk over and John is talking to his landlord's son. We are introduced. He is a pro skater. I want to start skating again.

"I like your dad," John is saying to him, while I listen in and smile.

"It is different for you, I'm sure," the skater son answers. He is maybe twenty-five years old. "I couldn't live with him anymore, but he is okay...probably a good roommate actually."

"He is a good housemate," John says in his easily excited gregarious baritone of a voice. "I'm surprised you weren't at the cookout longer on the Fourth."

This makes me think of my dad. I love him, and he is a good hang, might make a good housemate even, just not for me. I could be at a cookout with him and be happy. We just have too much baggage. I have too many unrealized expectations for the poor guy, just like this dude does for his dad. I want my sons to think of me in a good light.

My dad hated his dad basically. He might not admit it. The great aviator, the inventor, the leader, my grandfather died when my dad was maybe sixteen, in a boating accident, and my dad never recovered. They never

198

made amends. I hope this dude and his dad do.

His dad seemed like a real nice guy, and the place was very homey, a homage to comfort, to a suburban home life. He was probably just too 1950s, too 1960s, pre-1969, for this skater dude. My dad was maybe a bit too 1970s, post-1969, for me.

I blame my dad for too much. He is a genuinely nice man, in reality. He has a big heart, but I wanted consistency, dependability. The very things I've had recent trouble with myself. My dad was just not very mature. And I'm not either. He rebelled against his dad and that subconscious, ingrained 1950's guilt that always seems underlying in many of the old hippies I know from my folks.

Too like how my father was and is, I need to grow up.

Skater Dude's dad is probably too mature for him. Much older than his son, they probably do not connect on much. My dad didn't connect with his old man as much as he wished, but he loved him.

What kind of father do I want to be? I want to be fun, not stuffy, but I also want to be reliable. Most divorced dads are not the rock that their children need.

I really like Skater Dude and am glad to have met him. He grew up here. He is genuine and friendly. And he is way Cali.

We are getting vibed hard now, especially Crispin. This is his turf. This type of bar is all his. He owns this shit, his type of girls.

But suddenly, John decides aloud we need to leave. He has to work in the morning, so we leave too soon for anything, even conversation, to develop. Just a bunch of alluring, sexy stares. I may not have had it in me to be frontman with the ladies tonight anyway, on our friend night.

It's already been such a long summer for me. That I feel.

We go back to John's where he and I talk and listen to more beats, while Cris goes straight to bed. John asks about the development of my travels since he picked me up from the airport, back when I first entered California on the Fourth of July.

I say, "This is a book, John. Tonight was a chapter."

He says, "I got that. Sorry nothing much happened."

"That's okay. Stuff happened: your good beats, us talking, friends hanging out, turkey burgers in the breeze, thick Asian girls in clusters. It's like reality TV: the mundane is just part of travel...and life."

"What are you planning to call it?"

"Golden State Genius. I just decided recently. I smoked some bud called genius, and that's when I first got the idea for the book."

"I like that. You are going to do really well with these books. Don't forget me when it's time to celebrate."

"Never!"

"What went down in LA?"

"Now you with the same question I had for you about your crazy histrionics from last year. That's exactly what I asked you the last time I saw you, at SFO when we were circling the airport. Remember?"

"We all make mistakes, Vanity Plate. How was it down there?"

"L-A for us was...an up-and-down experience. Some fun but lots of driving around and way too much car time. Dave was pretty busy but cool, of course. Venice Beach, Hollywood, the Strip, good restaurants, bars...the usual. We relapsed on blow, which totally sucked. But we went to some fun places and met some people. We did Basquiat; great show."

"I like him."

"I figured you did."

"We did X the last night at Hotel Deleanor."

"With Dave?"

"Nah. Me and Cris and some others."

"What a rockstar road trip for you guys. Dave wasn't there?"

"He got us in. He was there. He doesn't roll, but he was there."

"You stars, you. Chicks hot?"

"It was LA. We were with Dave."

"Right. Good X?"

"I hadn't done that shit in years and yet took two. That's why I'm so tired and numb, sad actually. I have been sad for a long time, really."

"Endorphin depletion. Plus, what you've been going through. It must be tough."

"Yeah," I say, barely audible.

"The lack of endorphins alone, Van. I did sextasy and drove to TJ and screwed like three hot hookers all night long...alone."

"Wow. Crazy fuck. That a true story? What even is sextasy?"

"X and Viagra blended."

"Holy shit."

"In reality, I'd be done for two weeks if I tried it."

"I bet."

"You real sad about your wife, Van?" he asks quietly.

"Of course. And I miss my sons and hate myself right now."

"Stop hating yourself first."

"I'm trying."

"I love you, man, if that matters at all."

"Of course...just...sad."

"Can I hug you right now?"

"Yeah," I manage to say before the flood of tears comes.

John and I plan to meet back up if I come through this way again, or if I go back to LA he may come down. My plans are so indefinite, and I'm glad to have seen him twice already this summer; it'd been years.

I hit the hay soon. John has his work, and Cris and I will ascend into the lovely California mountains tomorrow. It'll be good to see them. Too bad we didn't make time to see more California nature, like the Redwoods or Yosemite, or even the Salton Sea.

We all wake up and leave early. Crispin and I pass through Vallejo. My cool homegirl back in ATL is from there. Weird that this reminds me of where I lived in Louisiana in seventh grade, looks like the road out to Big Lake from Lake Charles.

My thoughts are looping. Travel makes me reflective, and I remember so many wonderful snippets from Athens, from Marietta, from my childhood. I think about my problems, about putting them behind me. I'm so shot out from the drugs yet trying to think positively.

201

We make a final stop in cute little Santa Maria. In an otherwise relaxed Santa Maria restaurant over a plate of pancakes, Cris admonishes me for spending all my money in LA.

I just shrug and say, "I thought it was cool at the time to hand out those rolls to you guys."

"It was cool," Cris says. "I thought it was super cool at the time!"

Out of necessity, Cris grabs the check. And we walk around the little town together. I recall my original ride, Rick the artist, telling me Santa Maria was lame, but he lives in The City. I like it here. There is a small-town almost collegey art vibe, and it feels a bit like a miniature one-off of the Bay, that great center of American energy.

"Pretty cool here," I say. "Definitely not SoCal. What do you think?"

Cris says, "San or Santa anything is pretty cool."

I chuckle and say, "True."

Cris says, "I'm still pissed off that didn't work out for us this time around like I thought. The City was not really in the cards for us."

I just nod in agreement. I'm not pissed off anymore, just sort of lightly bumming San Fran is out. That's a good one: "San Fran is out." I like to make up slogans and that one would go over huge in the Castro District. My slogan for Oregon is perfect: "Oregon, It's above California."
"Copyright," I softly mumble to myself.

Too bad Portland is out. I would love to be in the Northwest now since I have a case of the Mondays and it's all of the sudden lightly drizzling. I hear the grungey sadness of Nirvana playing in my mind.

Back in the car, I'm silently reflecting as we slowly approach Humboldt County. The big Road Trip coming to a close was so Hollywood, such a Hollywood movie. That works for me because Hollywood is one of our mascots, America.

And California is our emblem. California and NYC. And Texas.

Interesting that California and Texas are both Republics. California has always been a land all its own, a frontier land of freedom, the edge of the Western World. Texas was a country; therefore, part of my national heritage

202

is Texan, part is multinational Euro-Mutt, part is Southern.

I'm 100% American, and despite our flaws I love the United States.

And Glory to Ol' Georgia, my longtime home and largest state east of the mighty Mississippi River. Wishing I was back home in good old Georgia now, sleeping in a comfortable bed. I'm wiped out. It'd be cool if Georgia had been a Republic, too. We were pretty strongly independent before the Civil War and all. Just too old of a state, I guess.

ACT III: Golden State Genius

TRIMMIN' AGAIN:
(-Humboldt)

Crispin and Chauncey and I cross over into Humboldt County, back in Weed World. A short time later our big road trip together is officially over.

We get to Pete's just past time to trim much. The weed I cut down was hung to cure, and they've been trimming it for the past few days. The Goat and Stan wouldn't help, so Pete has hired a local girl and he and Jena are also working at it. I decide to join in with what's left and for two hours I do the exact same type of indoor trimming I first did up on the mountain, while Cris quietly decompresses from driving and Chauncey hangs with Pete's dogs.

When Pete's work is done, we leave and I'm no longer entirely broke. In the car I'm thinking, that trimmer girl was sort of cute; she kept suggestively staring at me and was definitely cute for Humboldt. But I've recently been to Los Angeles, Santa Barbara and Santa Cruz, and maybe her look didn't exactly compare favorably to the fashionable SoCal lovelies. She was one of the cute ones but Crispin may be right about some of these girls lack of refinement.

He and I drive out by the old trim shack and quietly climb up the mountain and enter. I get the purple Adidas bag I left behind with my remaining T-shirts to sling. I'd forgotten it there I was so out of it. I should have brought them to LA, but we left so stoned and suddenly. My Rockstar hat is here, covered in dog hair. Cris says it turned up after the cleaning. The place is stripped down. None of the signs of activity from before remain, just a humble mountain home with no driveway, six hours north of the Bay Area by car. We're up here.

We sit awhile and rest up, then I decide to give Cris the very last fly-wear sticker I have, and he sticks it on the fridge. He will be back. I won't.

I have only a few fly-wear shirts left, and Cris already has one in each color. I wish I could pay him back more but have nothing for him.

We depart and when I say a final contemplative farewell to the place, it's with a sense that I will be nostalgic about this shack someday.

We walk down the mountain and drive to the post office. We are, I sense, saying bye to each other, Huck Finn and Tom Sawyer going their separate ways after an adventure on the Mighty Mississippi. We don't put it into words, but it's there in the air, and it's mostly brotherly love. But, a road trip across the country feels more unlikely than ever, because we've grown apart.

Outside in the car, Cris tells me he has decided to lend me only five hundred bucks, to send home to my soon-to-be ex-wife and children. This is a big blow to me and to our friendship. I try not to explode at him, but I'm fuming. I just won't speak to him. If I'd said a thousand, I'd definitely give him a thousand. The money I spent was when we were adventuring together, so I just don't get it. I don't get him at all anymore. Fuck him.

He told me he would lend me a grand all along, then only gave me five hundred dollars and even had the nerve to say I would owe him interest because: "That's how they do it out here."

I could care less how they do it in Humboldt. I came to see Crispin from Georgia, because he told me it would be golden out here. I thought he was my good buddy and our friendship still meant something. Plus, I recently called my ex and told her I was mailing her a grand. The loan was originally his idea, so we wouldn't have anything to worry about while we traveled. And I've bought him literally thousands of dollars in meals and drinks over the years and never asked for repayment, much less interest, so I'm extra disappointed in his sudden pettiness.

I ask myself: Was it even worth five hundred dollars to listen to him bitch and moan? I could have traveled to Los Angeles alone. I came out here broke; I'm basically broke again. Sorry I had to give Crispin drugs to get him to fucking smile and act like a true friend.

Then without speaking any of it to him, I realize my anger is way out of control. I'm still strung out on drugs. I'm disappointed in us both.

Cris unceremoniously drops me off at DJ's. He found out from Pete that DJ's crop is ready and called ahead to see if I could come right over. At least he did that for me, I guess. I'm glad to be away from his attitude. I'm going to focus on myself, and there is no need for a long goodbye.

I'm suddenly not so mad anymore, but I'm just not all that down with this whole mountain weed scene. I'd have rather stayed in LA, and I just want to make enough money to get a flight back to ATL and get out.

Sitting on a wooden chair alone in the kitchen of DJ's remote mountain house, another hot wave of anger hits me. I wonder if I'll ever see Cris again. We left everything ambiguous. First we were going to The City big and Napa and planning to drive across the country. That fell through, but we were still supposedly cool. Then he pulls that move. He acted like he didn't trust me or that I was going to spend the money on drugs. How the fuck was I going to spend the money he promised me when it was going to be a fucking money order? Fucker.

I felt sort of uncomfortable when Pete and I briefly talked a little about LA earlier. Cris was coming in and out of the room, and I didn't want to say anything about his omnipresent moodiness on the road trip. I ended up censoring much of the whole story.

I also told Pete that I plan to go through Santa Cruz, maybe, if I go back to LA, because I may ride back down to LA with a friend of Sasha's making the trip down from Santa Cruz. We could do that professional consulting workshop for Grow Star. I could help him.

It's trim time again, so we walk out to a separate building that is DJ's trim shack. I sit at a table and start. I'm working with DJ, his girlfriend, Audrey, and a friend/subordinate worker, Shawn.

Shawn has strong charisma, claims to have a family connection to the Kennedys, hails from Massachusetts and is maybe ten years younger than I am. He and I talk football, food, guy stuff. We hit it off. He was here when Cris and I stopped by before, and I'd immediately liked him. It's refreshing to be around someone with a positive attitude and time to talk. I like this guy.

Actually, they are all pretty cool. Audrey is a sweet,

reserved, pretty local college girl. And I've decided that DJ has become a cool maverick weed lord, a somewhat introverted loner, somewhat outlaw. He has on a skull belt buckle and always had a good fashion sense when I'd see him in Athens, a bit Jim Morrison-like. The two of them are mostly quiet, but when we do talk there's a sense of maturity and friendly commonality to our conversations. Shawn buys one of my shirts and we click. It's fun.

So, many miles from it Shawn and I talk a lot about home: Boston and Atlanta. We are decidedly East Coasters, but I say, "Atlanta really isn't even on the coast. It's in a coastal state and relatively near the Gulf and the Atlantic, but ATL is no ocean town. It's a virtual city, like Vegas or Orlando...No part was there first. It was created out of nothing, land, ideas and resources, an invention...A transportation hub before it even incorporated, what could be more virtual?"

Shawn says, "Boston is more provincial and stagnant, more old Beantown than boomtown."

I say, "Atlanta probably has more in common with say Dallas than any old port city. There's nothing geographically containing it, unlike the major city it is becoming: a Chicago, a New York, or a Los Angeles."

I feel LA pull me to it like a magnet, La Mag-Neat. What is LA?

I get back to my ramble: "If you just stick to the capitals in the East Coast, you can have a blast. NYC is the capital of the whole world and DC is the US capital. Your Boston is of New England as Atlanta is of the South. Miami is practically the capital of Latin America, although that may be Mexico City to some. And all five of those places are also the capitals of other things, like Miami is the capital of Cuban cuisine, and New York is the fashion capital, and Atlanta is the strip club capital and DC is the crime capital. Wait a minute...that may be Detroit."

Talking to Shawn, answering his questions for a couple of days, really got me thinking about Georgia being a coastal state and about big cities and my life back home. The ATL was becoming something greater than it had been, like a butterfly. Urban dreamers mixed with the old-fashioned locals, migrant Southerners, foreigners and carpetbaggers moving to the Sunbelt and boom. I need to blossom and shine and boom. I need to grow.

When I get back, Georgia needs to welcome me with open arms...if not legs. Ha ha. Things need to go well, and really does a divorce and starting over ever go all that well for anybody? One can be hopeful. I miss home, yet part of me dreads Atlanta because I made such a nasty mess of my life there.

Cris ends up leaving California without ever even saying a proper goodbye. Our friendship is greatly lessened and may be over. A message is on DJ's phone saying he left and hopes everything works out for me. Fuck him. I mean, God bless him. I love that dude.

I need enough money to get a one-way flight home. I'll Greyhound to a real airport town first. I may still go up to Portland. I can find a cheap flight, hopefully, from there or LA or Diego or Seattle or Vegas. Never been to Las Vegas. Not up for gambling before college football season starts, but if I found a cheaper flight from there I could at least see the bright lights. At least I'm fluent in American travel, that helps.

Dude I've known a few years named Numero comes by one day. He's the only crossover member of both indoor trim scenes. He and I were at both and just as at the last trim, his appearance and work effort are quite brief but enjoyable enough.

He had some of the same problems that I had, and he escaped to this wilderness to get better, and he did. Nature heals; isolation heals.

He got out or someone got him out and saved him, and he's fine, same sardonic wit, same weird sense of humor. He always had this strong desire for justice and suspicion of imminent injustice, and if he felt some girl, some person, some friend, was treating him unjustly, he had always expressed it. Maybe he felt the world was unjust or whatever, but he definitely slipped. He had some smaller slip-ups first over a several year period, then hit rock bottom. But he got out.

A change can be good. That's why I had to get away, even if it was not for very long. I had to leave. He seems fine, like the old Numero that I first met in Athens. I'm on my way up from a bottom.

Three solid working days later, we are done. DJ picks up and pays for burgers for all of us to celebrate the last day of the trim scene, and we have a strong sense of camaraderie as we eat together.

I never knew DJ real well before, but we always gave each other a good vibe and respected each other's heat. I like him, although he is even more of a recluse than the other growers I met. He's all about just him, his girlfriend and his crop. Only one guy works for him at a time usually, and he is very selective about how that person acts. Cris worked with him for a while, before they mutually decided it was best for him to work elsewhere. Cris went to Smoothboy, and DJ got Shawn. DJ is a boss; Cris hates bosses.

Working for him was fine. It was back to the fine trimming, the table trim. And now that that tedium is over I'm not broke. I have some money, nowhere to go. Exhausted. Can't decide. Decide to decide tomorrow. DJ will let me stay at his place in town, for the night.

I ride into town with Shawn in his jeep. We hang out at his place and watch TV and smoke a bowl with his roommate. Down off the mountain, and I'm finally all done trimming. I've had about enough of it. I was glad to work, and I'm glad it's over. Shawn's my homeboy now.

The roommate strikes me as one particular type of college kid I remember from Athens, mildly alternative, somewhat hip, lazy, disinterested and self-involved yet basically friendly. Not much different than many of the college dudes I have known over the years, he's in Humboldt "for school." He buys a shirt.

Their place is surprisingly cute, pretty nice for two dudes. I guess Shawn's weed money helps pay for a good place to live. Shawn may get family money, too. This other guy may work, but he definitely gets money from home. I can tell just from seeing him, his clothes and the place. This typical trust fund college burnout doesn't work enough to pay for half of this place. It's cozy and fancily decorated. The places I have been to in Humboldt were all so sparse, except for JimDawg's.

Smoothboy's sister's place had a little style, too, actually. Maybe, most of the in-town places are somewhat nice. It is the trim houses, or not much more than trim houses, that are so sparsely pared down.

I wonder if they grow weed here. You could probably get raided much easier in-town. It may be similar to getting busted in any other city, except they wouldn't prosecute hard. The laws wouldn't be as harsh.

I imagine being paranoid here, seeing movement through the boards of the fence and thinking the cops are coming. I can almost feel the old fear, as if I was really high on blow.

I could see hanging out with Shawn back home, watching a game and drinking a beer. He's an every man, a football-fan-type-of-a-guy that would hang around with my old friends in Marietta, the type of dude that other dudes enjoy on that basic level.

Dave is a true guy's guy like that. I enjoy that level of male bonding: talking football, watching a game and just being dudes. Not always having to out-culture each other or act so deep and experienced about everything.

Shawn gives me a ride to Pete's, because my bags are there. At least Crispin left my bags somewhere. The message on DJ's phone that said Cris was leaving by plane indicated my stuff would be here.

The door is open and no one is home. I see my bags in a pile and realize that now nothing is keeping me in Humboldt.

Cris was supposed to have left all of my stuff, but my Sonic Youth bag and all of "our" supplements are gone. He stole my fucking favorite bag. That bastard, I loved that bag. I know he coveted it because he told me, but I didn't think he would steal it. Some of those vitamins were mine too. Most were his but my Kava, I could really use the last of my Kava Kava to settle my ass down and keep me balanced. I'm pissed, and he didn't even care enough to say he was leaving to my face...figures.

Shawn and I go to Audrey's place. She is in the spare bedroom of her apartment, which is full of weed. It is another grow scene. I bet Shawn's was, in that case. I bet everybody here grows. She's working on her weed, then finishes and comes out and serves us chamomile tea.

We leave and Shawn drops me at DJ's in-town spot: DJ's Inn. He has a separate apartment, and I can stay tonight, and then I'll find somewhere else to go on my way home.

I'm left alone in the apartment and do my laundry. If I buy a plane ticket home from a major city with an advance purchase, it may not even be expensive. I have to get myself home. I'd prefer to return to SoCal and depart from there if at all possible, since Dave will take care of me, and I do have a free ride from Santa Cruz to LA if I want it.

A ticket home right away is a remote possibility, but that would be expensive without advance purchase and end my research trip. I need to finish this quest first. What am I looking for out of this journey? I needed to get out of town and did, and I've traveled some and worked some. Have I grown?

If Pete is ready, I could go straight to Santa Cruz and start working with his legit business there, earn some consulting money, and then I could head to LA and stay with Dave. I need to make phone calls.

I call Pete, but he isn't ready to pay me, because he has hit a small legal snag with his company and is waiting for money. That's out. I call Dave and get no answer and leave no message.

I try to call home to talk to my sons and to tell my ex I'll be home soon, back to Georgia. She doesn't answer, which is typical of her even when she's home.

I start to cry thinking about my divorce. Audrey walks in and catches me leaning against the dryer crying. She hugs me, and it feels good to be comforted by a nice woman.

She and I smoke and chat about family, about her relationship with DJ, about choosing to live in Humboldt for school. We decide I should probably wait to talk to my ex until after I have a definite plan.

She's a sweet person, genuinely nice and attractive. Her best feature is strong, incredibly sexy-looking legs. If Audrey wasn't with DJ, I might be inclined to ask her out. But she is, and I'm just lonely, not covetous. I've enjoyed her company, and she's the only girl I've met up here I would contemplate dating. A girlfriend is extra money to these weed growers - they put girls to work.

DJ returns home and I use his laptop to scan the net for deals. I'd love to soak up the sun and mostly lighthearted optimism of San Diego but don't see anything affordable. I search LA, San Francisco, Oakland, even Portland. The only cheap deal I see is when I expand the search: VEGAS. I've never been and briefly contemplate the Dr. Hunter S. Thompson type I am becoming. Those bright lights await me.

JimDawg comes by, and I don't have credit and first ask to use his credit card to buy a ticket home from Vegas and pay him cash. It's a super cheap flight, and I'm relieved to have found a ticket home. Even if it is from Vegas and even if it is a few weeks away from now.

DJ ends up aggreeing to complete the purchase for me after I've made my selection and entered my information. Vegas to home in a couple weeks on the first cheap flight with advance purchase, sounds fine. I'd rather leave sooner, but it'd have cost hundreds of dollars more.

I'm heading back to LA. I guess I will take another bus to Vegas from LA, unless someone wants to drive me. I don't want to be in Vegas long, but I want to see it. And I can hang with my good buddy Ramon, since he'll be there then. I need to get to Santa Cruz to get that ride to LA. Dave and I can talk things through, and I may just walk around and write about LA.

Then I'll see the Vegas Strip and old Downtown Vegas, where the Rat Pack ran around. Traveling alone, my fraternity of friends doesn't feel like a pack anymore. I will see Ramon in Vegas, but it's still just me. No Crispin, no Dave, no JimDawg. I have friends and family in this world. Yet, it is just lonely me again, and I will have to face my problems soon.

Some marijuana dealer dudes show up to buy DJ's weed, while Jim and I are in the other room using the computer. They're college-aged, bearded with short hair. Real friendly guys, from the small interaction we have after we finish. I sell them each shirts.

I'll figure out the rest of the logistics tomorrow. I have a basic plan, so I leave the date of my return to Georgia on my wife's answering machine and am brave enough to ask her to pick me up if at all possible.

We all smoke vaporized weed out of a balloon, and I'm gracious to DJ for what he has done to help me and thankful to have a free place to sleep tonight, though I do want to go out first.

JimDawg and I decide to go to the health food store

for some snacks and see the same dealer dudes in the store. I buy a Humboldt shirt at the store for my buddy Lazy T, back home. He asked me to pick him up a shirt while I was out here. Carrot juice helps me feel better.

Jim and I go to a bar in Arcata for an hour and then return to DJ's after having bourbon and a few beers. Jim plans to drop me off for the night, but it looks so quiet that we decide I should stay at Jim's place.

I should've thought to ask to stay there in the first place. Big picture, I hardly know DJ, and Jim and I are friends, so this makes sense. I feel like the rest of my trip is coming together. We can check the bus rates, and I can make my calls to LA from there, tomorrow.

So before I ever sleep a night in DJ's Inn, I gather my stuff and give DJ back his key. As we bid a farewell and depart, I can tell DJ is surprised and relieved that I'm not going to stay with him. He wanted a laborer not a squatter, and in reality I may need a day or two to get my plans super straight, as far as my triumphant return to Los Angeles goes. I'm so mentally tired and want to be sharp for sunny SoCal.

A FAMILY LIFE:
(-Humboldt)

Jim lives on a corner lot with fruit trees, in a nice neighborhood in Eureka. It reminds me of the place I lived in Orlando. He has a day job as an electrician and only grows bud for personal use within the legal limits specified by law. Via his medical marijuana card it is perfectly legal as far as the State of California is concerned.

JimDawg's girlfriend, Lana, was married once before and has a five-year-old son, Ian. The three of them overwhelm me with kindness and hospitality. For the first time on this whole trip, I feel like I'm a welcome visitor in someone's cozy home. I'd felt welcome elsewhere, but it was more like a youthful adventure or work instead of a family visit.

They cook for me and I have real talks with all of them. I adore Lana's son and miss my children desperately. I also realize I miss home life with my wife, the way things were before they went badly.

They have a nice relationship though, they seem to talk well, and my wife and I always had communication problems. We never had our act completely together as a couple like they do. We tried for years and loved each other for years. I failed. I'm a failure at marriage and adult life, but I'll improve. I want to start over and make it work, to begin anew.

You can't start over in life and have it be quite the same. I want to be a good father and man, and all else will take care of itself. I will live near where my kids live and be a good, stable father and person.

I'm so lonely. I know I have to finish this trip but wish I were back home. I spend hours alone in the guest bedroom, in comfort and think and cry and pray and plan. When I'm not in the room, I stay as cheery and friendly as possible and enjoy my hosts' company.

Lana and I become fast friends. I like her at least as much as anyone I've met out here, and she's from here. She mothers me some and I start to feel like my old healthier self for the first time in months. It's been a man's journey but misogyny is not what this book experience is about for

214

me. I'm relearning gender relations as less than opposites. Time passes. A few days pass. We joke away the hours; we talk away the days. This is the most inaction that I've had in a long while, and I enjoy it. Jim goes to work, Lana goes to work and Ian goes to school. I just hang, waiting to leave, waiting for my ride to be ready from Santa Cruz this weekend.

I think about the importance of family much of the time, and I miss my family so much that I almost wish I never came out to California. I was going so crazy that I had to leave.

Though I feel like an utter failure, I know that my life isn't over. I need to focus on improving me, getting all the way better.

Over a big pancake breakfast one morning, Ian puts his arm on top of mine and says, "Van, I really like you."

"I really like you a lot too, Ian," I say.

"I really like you and guess what, tomorrow I will have the most money I have ever had. After I get a few more dollars from Mom tomorrow I'll have twelve dollars; that will be the most I have ever saved."

"Here. Have a five. See how rich you are." Everyone at the table beams; I pushed his cumulative saving's total over his previous record, and the birthday money he gets will shatter the record. It's easily the single happiest I've been on the trip. Jim and Lana smile at me again.

"He wants to be a gardener when he grows up," Lana tells me later in the meal, rolling her eyes.

I say, "Product of his environment, I guess. He's a great kid."

"I know," she says.

"You and Jim are raising a really nice young man."

Jim makes a good stepfather and gets a kick out of Ian and I becoming friends. Ian plays organized t-ball and tells me all about it, and I tell him about my sons back home.

Jim and Lana give me a notebook to start writing my book in detail. It was hers, and they both thought it was a good idea to give it to me. I adorn it with a Humboldt skate shop sticker.

Jim and I'd stopped by there to buy wheels and trucks for the board. I chose trucks that look like they are made of polished wood. The yellow wheels that I bought are by a brand called Satori Movement; my son had asked me for yellow wheels. I was given a free Satori Movement sticker and told that the owner of Satori lives in Humboldt and is from Georgia. They use indigenous iconography mixed with modern objects. It's a fitting sticker for my notebook, a tribesman with a jam box representing to me voyaging, traveling, mixing California with Georgia.

I'm a postmodern man at a crossroads. I'm coming to realize that I love art to the level that I may not be okay without it. Art means so much to me...it almost feels like redemption and is now part of my identity.

"I hear you were a big stud back in Athens," Lana says to me in her kitchen one night after a family dinner of pasta.

"Let's just say I had a stretch," I answer. "I had three serious girlfriends over the two periods I lived there. Five of the six total years I lived there I was in a relationship."

"And that other year?"

"You got me."

"Was Jim a stud in Athens? I know Crispin was."

"Do you know how suggestive it is to be running around with a name like JimDawg? He had his own level of stud."

"Okay. Not sure what that means. That was a Van riddle."

"Right."

I know truthfully that the answer is not really, but I want to be diplomatic. Jim was a stud to me in his own way: he was cool.

"You know what, Lana?" I continue. "He's a guy that if a girl digs him, she really digs him because he marches to the beat of his own drummer. He may lack a little, say mainstream appeal because he's up here in the satori, the stratosphere. Chicks that dig him really dig him."

She just kissed him. Good, I think. That was good. There is nothing wrong with my buddy and nothing wrong with her loving him.

The next morning, Lana comes in while Jim and I are listening to her Missy Elliot album, by my request. I'm folding my clothes, and he's rolling a joint of the weed he grew.

"Having a girlfriend moment?" she asks.

Jim shines more than ever in my eyes, and I've always liked him.

That night, Sasha finally calls me back. Jim and I have just smoked the fabled Kush, and I'm too stoned to say much.

While she talks about her busy work schedule, I half-listen and think to myself, I'm going to quit smoking completely soon. But in Humboldt almost all there is to do is get high. I'm amazed how baked I've been this trip, and this weed is the absolute strongest I've ever smoked.

When Sasha stops talking, I say: "Had you not called back I would've just taken a bus to LA without much price difference."

But she encourages me to ride with her friend still. In no mental condition to argue, I just want to get off the phone and pass out.

"I will, then," I say.

"You should be Van," Sasha says.

"I am him," I say. "I made him up. No one calls me Vincent."

"I was listening to you in my car the other...the other night, and it was really good."

"What...my rapping?"

"Yes. When you were really drunk, I recorded you the other night in my car, and it was so good, and I...I really think you should be Van."

"In a movie?" These Hollywood types live in that lone fantasy.

"Of course in a movie."

"Dave's gonna play me."

I THINK I'M IN ARCATA:
(-Humboldt)

Blow makes me paranoid as hell. I hate it. I feel like this place is about to get raided. It's not.

What time is it? Almost 9:00, I've been up all night. Relapsing is becoming a fucking pattern. Relapse is often a part of recovery, I guess, but I must stop.

I'm at Paolo from the trim scene's house. I went out alone last night and scored blow at a bar. Then I ran into Paolo and another guy I'd met at Paolo's birthday party, and we snorted until the sun rose.

All that rest and recovery I got was for nothing, because I feel like shit. I should take a shower. Paolo may not wake up for hours, and I'm sweating bullets. I hate this feeling. If only I was sound asleep in Jim's cozy guest room.

Paolo's guest room is actually pretty comfy, but I'm not okay. I will be fine. I need to permanently stop using blow, and I haven't been able to completely shake it. Just never use the stuff again, and you'll be okay.

Ah, the water feels really good. I need a ride home. Maybe I should just go for a walk after this, to waste time. I can call Jim pretty soon, but not before 10:00 on a weekend morning. Poor guy gets up early every day during the workweek. He may want to sleep in a little. I could beat off again? First time I beat off this whole trip, and I did it with half-hard coke dick. The brain needs something to fixate on when high on blow, so I usually try thinking of beautiful bouncing breasts instead of cops crashing through the door.

I never used to get paranoid, and then once I started to get paranoid, I always got paranoid, every time I used. God was telling me not to use, and I was telling me not to use. I can't fathom using something you know you hate, but that is what I did tonight. Just be done with it. I've have been mostly clean for a few months, just get all the way clean.

Get on with your life. You have children. People care about you. There is more to life than this. There is so much more to life than this.

I'm still wired, and I need sleep. I hate this addiction.

I can't believe I used tonight, last night. It went so bad the one time I used in LA, but when cocaine reared its ugly head I was in...I bought some. I regret that.

The water feels great. Maybe I will stay and hide in this shower forever. But there is enough weed in the living room and scales and bags for the cops to take this place down, probably. I need to get out of here before something happens. And that may be it for the hot water.

"Fuck," I say. There is no towel. How am I going to dry off? The sheets of the bed down the hall, in the guest bedroom, I guess. What a high move to not check for a clean towel first. Fuck it. Paolo's sleeping, and no one else is here. He's bisexual anyway, so he probably won't mind me running down the hall nude if he does wake up and come out of his room. He said I had nice legs and would probably want to fuck around with me anyway, if I wanted to do that. I'll just move quickly.

"AAAAHHH!" Paolo's girlfriend screams, confronted by a shocked, nude, wired, paranoid, shriveled dick, soaking wet me.

"UUUGHHH!" I shout back, stunned, embarrassed and retreating to the bathroom. And she is down the hall. I hope she doesn't think I'm screwing her boyfriend and intentionally running around his place nude.

"I need...a towel, sorry!" I say through the wall.

I'm stuck in the bathroom, dripping wet, contemplating my next move, until her hand reaches in, delivering me a towel.

"Van?" she says.

"Yes," I say. "I'm sorry, Mika."

"Don't worry about it. ...I'm just pissed at Paolo. Here's a towel."

"Thank you," I say flaccidly.

I can hear her bitching him out for skipping class, again. She leaves. I towel off and go back to the guestroom and get dressed and quickly leave, saying, "I'm out," through Paolo's bedroom door.

I walk away thinking it would be convenient to be bisexual, though. You could always find somebody to love. I wish I were gay sometimes, just to avoid the constant emotional female drama I help to create in my relationships. Just bro out and still get laid. I love ladies.

This is a nice neighborhood. I like these little bright houses and there's pleasant and similar architecture throughout. This is a cute little place, but I'm not cute. This drug is so far from cute or funny anymore.

"Let this evening be over," I say aloud as I cross the edge of the neighborhood. The bright California daytime sun is out already.

I'm going to find a phone and call Jim. I could go back to Paolo's place and call. Nah, I'll find a phone.

I walk to a nearby coffeehouse on wheels, type of deal. I buy an ice cap and call JimDawg, explaining, "I'm at a coffeehouse on wheels. I crashed at Paolo's eventually then walked here. I think I'm in Arcata."

"Ha, ha, ha...you're in McKinleyville...if you crashed at Joey's."

"That's great. I don't even know what town I'm in."

"It's funny, Van. It's good book. Are you okay?"

"Yeah...fine. Hung over, strung out, but...fine, I guess. Nice lady let me use the phone."

"Surprised you didn't scare the crap out of her, looking all weird. You will be just fine, Van."

"Can you? Can you come get me?"

"I'm on my way. The coffee stand right near Paolo's, right?"

I chat with the coffeehouse woman while I wait. I only seem to scare her at most marginally, and she was nice to let me use her phone.

I have to stop relapsing. I don't enjoy using past the first two lines, and I always just want more and more, and then I freak out.

Please, God. Please let me be done with this shit. I hate blow, and I love you, God. I trust you, God. Please help me. Help me save myself from this still strong addiction.

I'm done with this stuff...I want to be done with this for good.

220

BIRTHDAY BASH:
(-Humboldt)

The following morning I wake up mostly recovered after a full marathon of sleep at Jim's. He and I have our daily coffee talk and then walk around his yard, checking for progress on his fruit plants.

"Van, I don't know if you really want to go, but Ian's party is today at his dad's place," Jim says in his deep monotone.

"Definitely," I quickly answer. "I wouldn't want to miss my little buddy's party. ...Plus, I want to see what some more real Humboldt people act like in a 'normal' setting."

Later, Jim and I listen to the Ween dude's side project album on the way over in the convertible, top down in the sun. Two friends on a fun zoom, and he has John Lennon-like round glasses on.

He says, "I love my new CD. Hahahahhaha..."

This feels like California, I think, glancing at my reflection in the rearview. Cool sunglasses are a must out here, and a breezy sunshine daydream is underway. I glance at Jim – he's feeling it.

We park a few short blocks from the party and walk. This is a cute enough, almost suburban-feeling neighborhood. The houses are one story and have large rooms, high ceilings. This reminds me of the Athens Boulevard District.

"Hey, thanks for coming to this party," Jim says to me as we approach the house party.

"It's cool, Jim," I say. "Wouldn't miss it." I notice an older rich-looking lady parked right outside the party in her Volvo, playing video games in her conditioned bubble and say, "What the fuck. Hey lady, you can't park there!"

"Right, right," Jim chuckles. "Move along, lady. Right, right. Haha."

We enter. Ian's Dad hugs me way too hard. As he is much shorter than I am, it is just awkward and makes me happy.

Kids play. Grown ups talk and eat. Hippie spread of almost normal party stuff is served. These parents are all super hippiefied, and the food is healthy versions of standard kiddy party fare.

We kick the soccer ball, and I dribble behind my front foot on my first touch. It is the only soccer move I know, but I like the game, the National Team, the World Cup.

We go inside and this mom is overly interested in Ian's dad. She loved the chocolate cake and is standing too close to him and close talking while making these funny little clucking noises with her mouth, which remind me of a noise my dad makes after eating. She has a big, intense horse smile, and he is smooth talking hippie game to her.

"Yeah. I used kamut…since wheat is a totally bunk grain," he says.

"Mmm-hmm, cluck," she replies, starry-eyed.

"I used half-sugar, half-sweetener, and you can make this, easy. You can make a great cake, and it is good for you."

"It's delicious."

"I know."

The nice dude I was outside kicking the soccer ball with, the huge pants hippie, and his wife and kid are sitting on the floor in front of me. And I am fairly amused.

"I love your hair," I say, briefly touching their daughter's bright golden mane.

"I'm gonna have dreads again soon," she says.

"Yeah. She had some wicked dreads," dread dad says, proudly. Dread mom just smiles as she pokes hard nipples at the whole room.

I look out and still see the Volvo lady, saving the fucking Princess. "What the F, Ron?" I say to Ian's dad. "Have you seen that car out front?"

"It's the cops," Ron answers. "They found you. They are coming to get you, man."

He doesn't know I have felt that way in the not too distant past.

"Right?" I say. "Have you noticed this woman, sitting in her Volvo out front, playing video games?"

"She is Billy's grandma; she won't come in and hang out because we aren't good enough for her," he says.

"She should be embarrassed," I say.

"She would be embarrassed …to be inside, I guess."

222

Here is this yuppie dressing, perfectly LA, perfectly Santa Barbara, in a shiny new silver Volvo, playing a video game, with the air conditioning cranked to keep her from sweating and the engine running lady. What's she doing this far from the California they see on the tube?

"No need to grace us with your presence," I finish aloud.

"Van is doing a book on his vacation, and he thought that she would be funny to write something about," Jim says to Ron.

"Is it about Humboldt?" Ron asks me.

"All of California, actually," I answer. I have been to LA, through San Fran and Santa Cruz...and San Jose, and I'm going back, to LA. I'm heading back down south tomorrow actually."

"Crazy," says Ron. He is starry-eyed.

"This is a good little party. Thanks for having me over."

"You are more than welcome, my friend."

"Will you play me something from your extensive reggae collection."

"Sure," he says.

"How about Black Uhuru?" I say.

"Of course."

"I was a big reggae fan, still like it."

He's a good guy; I got an impression from Jim and Lana that he was somewhat uncool, probably just typical ex-speak.

I can't imagine my future ex-wife, with a stepfather figure and me. Just me, lonely-old-pathetic-wretch-of-a-man me. Or worse, me with a rotating cast of loose women. My dad had too many women over the years, some of them nice. I imagine saying: "This is your stepmom this week boys ...hot right?" That would just be pathetic! Man up!

"If this was not a real parent party," Ron is saying, "we would be doin' major rips and havin' a funky good time."

"Oh, I know," I say. "I'm serious though. This is a good time."

"Glad you're having fun, relaxing."

I'm enjoying going at a slow pace today. I have been adventuring. Clearing my head today, attempting to, I was exhausted. And Jim and his family took me in and made me comfy. Lana treated me like a mom treats her wayward college sons. Traveling creates such a wayward feel.

An hour later, Jim and I walk to his car. I'm thinking, I like how Ron and Lana and Jim are all civil friends.

We enter the vehicle and depart the neighborhood and go toward the beach for a look, Jim and I cruising in his groovy old convertible.

We park and walk out to the water. Dark sand, decent waves, nice California sunshine, it's super-breezy.

I'm refreshed enough after a rest to make this journey. No. I'm not. I'm too sad. I miss my sons. This stop has been introspection into family.

I will always be my sons' father and will always love them. I can never have their mother back. I know that. I was too much of a fuckup to stay married. I messed that up. She did, too, but I really messed up.

I look out into the vastness of the ocean, and it soothes me some. I calm way down and pray: Bless me, Lord. Heal me, Lord. Let my worries wash away with the waves.

I walk out of earshot of Jim and say aloud to myself, "Let the water wash in and out and let my worries wash out and less of my worries come back each time."

ANOTHER CALIFORNIA ARTIST:
(-Humboldt/-The Bus/-Santa Cruz)

This trip is my rite of passage: I'm finally ready to become a grown up and won't be young again. I fully realize this on a warm, gusty NorCal night spent lounging around my friends' house and yard. In the guestroom, which almost feels like home now, I pull out the notebook they gave me. I start writing down detailed notes, for the first time.

Later, I clutch the notebook as I sit in a cushy chair on their little outdoor patio. I decide to read Jim and Lana the first bit of dialogue I wrote down for this book, it's of Lana's ex-husband talking about using kamut to make a cake.

Then I ramble: "I have done more actual writing with pOp 101, but this is about actual or so-called Californians. You and your son are, like the only real Californians I know who are from here, Lana. I really need to start taking more detailed notes. I'll start writing everything down from the time I get on that Greyhound bus in the morning."

I retreat to the guestroom soon and write a little more and am grateful. Jim and Lana have been so gracious, and I feel blessed, refreshed, invigorated - ready to get back on track.

I close my eyes and immediately sleep well and wake up and have some coffee. Two hundred dollars is on the kitchen counter. I'd asked to borrow a hundred from Jim, when I realized I had so much time before I was going to be able to get myself home.

Jim enters the room and says it's all for me, and suddenly my faith in friendship is fully restored. It feels that good to have help right now.

I give him two of my last three remaining shirts. We get in the convertible and drive to the bus station. I buy my ticket to Santa Cruz.

We stand outside in the cool but shiny-bright Northern California morning and reflect. I thank him for everything, especially for his family's hospitality. "Off to the surf town for a day, then on down to LA," I say.

I mention that I've been depressed, and he says I have a funny way of showing it. He encourages me to stay up and continue traveling and writing. He says he wishes he could come with me on my adventure.

I tell Jim that he has been with me on this journey.

We are quiet together for a few minutes, two old friends in the sunshine. I can feel a brotherly love, between us, and our love for life and humanity. I'm saying a permanent goodbye to Humboldt. I won't be back.

And then I'm alone again, a traveler of the soul off and drifting through the greatest country in the history of the world and the new millennium. A lone man with a notebook and a pen, a man under the sun traveling and writing, reporting back on big blue sky America.

(Random) Notes from the Bus:
Arcata: Reclining on the bus, I see a Eureka Harley billboard. Thoughts looping. That was an annoyed female voice I heard when I called Lisa. She seemed friendly at work in the Harley shop and when I called her the first time. Perhaps that was her sister that answered. I hope she's okay; she's an artist. Holy shit, I'm an artist. Me, I've always wanted to be an artist but can't paint or draw or sing or play any instruments or anything. Huge fan, though, an advocate. Is a writer an artist? Surely. Yes - Van, you are an artist now. This trip is about me finding my art.

Hopland: This is my 1-2-3, fourth time through Hopland. Every time I pass through I will mention the wine tasting at the high school. That will be funny. "Hopland: wine tasting high school," I murmur.

Willits: Ah yes, the home of the pregnant teen. Cute young girl sitting next to me gets on in Willits. Heading from home to the San Fran airport to fly to Portland. Nice belly piercing and she has a sense of style. She says, "Home is boring except for the weed, and Portland is like a little utopia. It's totally phat." I'm just glad she isn't visibly pregnant. She likes my T-shirt, saying, "That's a dank shirt." I tell her I designed it. It was funny when she commented out loud about the exposed hairy chest on an older woman: "Don't wear that shit then if you don't want me to say anything," she said to no one in particular, me I guess.

Oakland: Oakland has some pretty areas, with housing that looks almost like San Francisco. San Francisco is what everyone thinks of when they see row after row of these cute, pastel Victorian houses vertically stuffed into a city block.

San Francisco: Stoned with tattoo boy and Arkansas girl. I asked him if it hurt to get those tats on his face. He did it himself, fucking up the almost too handsome face that mom and dad gave him. I wonder what his grandparents think. Before that I kicked it in the Embarcadero area with some nice Oakland black dudes I overheard talking about Atlanta. I got them stoned on Train Wreck. The one that was Half-Chinese taught me the phrase "Cokeland" when I asked about the nickname "Oaksterdam." They also taught me about the Hyphy Movement. It's the West Coast's answer to the Dirty South/ATL crunk hip-hop scene. They have their own hip-hop, and they love to low speed cruise and then get out of their cars and run next to them while they move; it's called ghost riding whips. They said the police in SF are starting to crack down on weed, but in Oakland, "Nobody fucks with us for nothing. We ghost ride whips and they don't care." They were a little scared to smoke pot in public in San Francisco but openly did graffiti with no fear of arrest. Beautiful city, now I really remember from years ago. Pretty city.

Moving: The view of downtown San Francisco from the Bay Bridge gives me an almost dizzying rush. "This is spectacular." Buildings are right up to the edge of the water, shimmering in the sunlight, water and buildings sparkling at me with barely a discernible break between them, and it's a nice time of day to be out here on the water. Remembering: the Golden Gate Bridge leads to Napa and Marin. I loved seeing that bridge from Muir Beach. "Do you see how the water swirls like that?" asks the Arkansas girl. I was just looking at the same thing. Is she cute?

Oakland again: Why did we go from Oakland to SF, then back through Oakland? Maybe they don't want your white ass waiting around getting mugged, so they take you for a joyride. Arkansas girl looks hot in those jeans. I see her through the window smoking cigs with tattoo boy. Before I stop writing and get out to hang with them, she's back.

San Jose: Nondescript from afar, that think tank and money center. Those low, boring buildings yet it was a vibrant little city when we hung out there. Silicon Valley venture capital, lots of smart entrepreneurs and cash flow: idea energy. Like Cris and I said: "San or Santa anything."

Moving Again: Wish I had a ticket all the way to LA. Maybe I could snuggle with the Arkansas girl. She is wrapped in my pink/brown blanket now and is going to be stuck at the bus station for five hours in LA. I'd like to have breakfast with her. She has that distant look that I love: far away eyes. Maybe because she's so stoned. I found out on the last stop that her weed is good, and she's thick in all of my favorite places. I'm just lonely probably. Scratch that. I'm definitely lonely. She seems forlorn when I get off the bus, like she forgot to make out with me, or something.

Once I finally got to Pete's primary residence, which is on the beach in Santa Cruz, I was able to write about what had happened previously in Downtown Santa Cruz. I've morphed into a working artist:

Santa Cruz: No planning: I was scrambling, stranded looking through my bag for phone numbers and change and using a pay phone with no luck. I finally convinced Pete to come get me. What an imposition. Johnny's phone wasn't working and I'd only mentioned casually to him that I might need a ride and place to stay if I passed back through and had never confirmed that he would be picking me up. A security guard told me to "move off this property" after I used the pay phone and was waiting. So I moved five feet to the street corner, and a skater that had been passively watching nearby said, "Did he just ask you to move? That's so gay." I still look heterosexual which is good, but I look like a criminal of some sort apparently.

I called Sasha and then coordinated things with her friend Malia, my ride to LA. Calling them at midnight was rude, but my calls went well. Sasha and I are deep, everything is set and my ride seems cool.

I enjoyed a conversation that Pete and I had before

he went to bed. We discussed Crispin's breakdown in LA. He'd heard about it from Cris, and I reiterated the whole story with, according to Pete, very little deviation.

Pete said to me, "When you travel, there's usually a conflict that leads to an epiphany...

"That's what traveling is all about. Travel=Conflict=Epiphany."

I said, "Our trip was just way too much for Cris... after coming down off the mountain."

Now I lay alone in bed thinking: Maybe it was too much for me. I miss my family so much. Maybe I should meet a new woman soon and fall in love. Or eat more chocolate at least, chocolate sounds good. I should eat more of Pete's candy. Nah, I had enough and need some sleep.

MALIA BECOMES GENIUS (DRIVE 5):
(-Highway 5)

It's far too bright from the California sunshine to read the radio numbers to find a station. Malia turns the radio lights on; that helps; now I can read them.

We see a prisoner bus, lots of farmland, and then some burnt land. We drive away from Santa Cruz on Highway 5 and quickly enter the remote middle of California, so uninhabited compared to the coast. Looking like Humboldt again: hill country.

Eating tangy lime Tic-Tacs and driving into the intensifying heat, Malia asks me if I have any weed.

A few minutes later, I'm handing Malia a joint while saying, "This weed's called Train Wreck. It's the signature weed of Humboldt."

Malia lives in Santa Cruz, and since she and her female friends shave their armpits I decide that most girls having shaved armpits may equal the SoCal border. NorCal is the land of women with hairy armpits. I tell her this and she cracks up.

"Look at this drawing," I say. "This is what the cover of my book pOp 101 will look like."

"I like that," she says.

"This is like my fifth long car drive since I left Atlanta. Drive five. Fitting that we are on The 5."

Malia tells me of a heartbroken friend who has recently left some man in Colorado after almost marrying him. She headed to Montana alone and then was "not feeling" some dude she was staying with there either. Now she has a week at the beach in Santa Cruz with the girls for some sanity.

"That is so healing," I say. I laugh at myself, realizing I've been around hippies for too long.

The 5, the fertilizer, feeling alive, the soil...the warmth of an American summer wraps around me. Like many before me, I understand how the magnetic draw of California has pulled me West.

"We've got cherries," she says. "I even have a mango. It cost a dolla fitdy."

I repeat the "dolla fitdy" part. I'm writing everything

down, and I'm happy today is off to a fun start and no longer regretting the trip down to LA being split into two parts.

An unknown to me guy named Ron enters Malia's discussion. I eventually find out he is her business partner in radio promotions. They get calls from nightclub promoter homeboys, "Talkin' 'bout gettin' paid. How many dollas, what kinda dollas I gotta pay for five hundred peoples on a club guest list? I want some peoples up in here at my club in Gilroy. You bring me the peoples."

Malia is the business manager, so she says to the homies, "How are you paying? I need a credit card." They pay then call her back two days later saying, "I don't hear my mentions on the radio. I don't hear you get peoples in my club. I need peoples from Salinas and Monterrey up in my club. I need more peoples. You best start doin' my mentions on the regula. I better hear my mentions."

I laugh at her job description, and then we call Ron. She and I both do the impersonations on the phone for him. I go in and out of character and back in doing the "peoples in my club" routine, as he laughs.

Malia says, "Fuck, we lost him. The signal sucks out here. I'll call him back in a minute. You two would really get along. I call him my work husband."

"He seemed like he was really cool. Ready to smoke some more?"

"Sure, Van. We should smoke, and then I'll make another business call, and a little later we can stop and grab some fast food or something. Do you eat fast food?"

I answer, "Super Size Me."

"I haven't seen that yet, is that a yes?"

"Me neither, so that is a yes. I've heard you can't eat fast food after watching that, and my stepbrother just gave me a copy, so I better eat all the fast food I want before I get home and watch it. The fast food restaurants are different out here."

"Really? No Carl's in Atlanta?"

"No Carl's Jr. No Jack in the Box. I ate at Carl's Jr. Jr. the other day, the small Carl's Jr. That name's hilarious." I hand Malia a bowl and say, "This weed is called Genius; it's the inspiration for the book title. It is a mind race weed, and when I first smoked it was when I realized that this was going to be a book. They have a weed for every occasion, every mood up in Humboldt."

"I bet," she says, nodding.

"Some you smoke to come down and then sleep. Some are actually stimulants. My book is about California lifestyle inventiveness, which is genius, but when I first smoked Genius my mind was blown. Get ready for your mind to run wild."

"It already is. We've been talking some deep shit, but I'm ready."

"Should I put some kiff in it? Nah, I want you to experience it by itself. I don't have much of it left, and it is not exactly the strongest, but it is the most phenomenal crap I have ever smoked. So, get ready to become genius. You already are, but this chapter can be called 'Malia Becomes Genius.'"

"This book is fun. I feel like we're in a movie."

"You are, Malia. It'll be a movie too, someday."

"You can light that now."

We smoke without speaking until the band Modest Mouse comes on the radio.

"I like this song, Malia. I like them. I make up the words because I don't know what they're saying, but I saw them on Austin City Limits; I'm from there originally, by the way, but point being they were awesome, they're weird enough and still so catchy at times. A band has to be catchy for me to enjoy it the most. I've never owned anything by them, but I like their sound, their style of music."

"They're good. Holy shit, my mind is totally racing, Van."

"I told you. I know. I just said like fitdy sentences without taking a breath or breaking thought. This shit wild, girl. It's like hard drugs."

"Wow. You know: I wish I could set you up with somebody to get you through this divorce transition. My girl in Montana would be perfect for you. She's just like you. Same energy. You're both rebounding hard though, which is both perfect and dangerous. I should totally hook you up with her. She's supposed to be coming to LA soon. I would totally hook up with you of course, if I were single, if I weren't married. I'm not entirely happily married right now, and monogamy has been proven to be not the most natural arrangement for any animals, and she's so hot. She's pretty hot. We may all hook up. Just, um kidding. I don't want my husband to read that. She has huge tits."

"My absolute favorite."

"Oh shit! Sasha, she might be mad I'm talking to you like this, and I have to, I totally, respect her."

"I'm thinking she and I are platonic actually. I'm not sure, but that is what I'm thinking more and more. We are connected for sure, but I think we may end up being just friends. We are definitely friends. We made good friends last year when I was married, and I think we may have...gone too far as friends to hook up. I don't know about anyone like that anymore. I'm so confused."

The phone rings. "Is that Ron?" I ask.

She shakes her head no, smiling. "It's her."

"Sasha?"

"No, Krista. The one with the tits," she whispers.

"How did she know we were thinking about her?"

The friend with the tits is on the phone, and Malia jokes to her that I'm Malia's new boyfriend. "My new boyfriend is riding with me. No, wait he is your new boyfriend, Krista."

She forgot Sasha again, and she whispers, "Sasha," to me. "He is all of our boyfriend."

Malia is listening mostly. I can't hear the other end but write her side of the conversation, while my thumb and index finger throb.

"Oh God."

"Right, right."

"Wow."

"Right."

She clicks her tongue.

"No. No!"

"Oh my gosh."

"Right."

"Wow."

"Great."

"Now whataya, are you gonna get a rental car?"

There is a long period of silence while she listens.

"No, that's totally Sasha's deal. You should call her. Where are you staying in LA?"

"He's so funny and is writing this book that's so much fun."

"I'm sure it will get published. He's brilliant."

"Divorced. Getting divorced. I know. That's what I told him."

"Great personality and hot."

"The two of you? Maybe."

I say, "Tell her she's in my book. I want to write about her."

I instantly wonder if that was too much. Testing the water again, which often gets me scalded or stung by a jellyfish. I don't have any concept of how a single adult acts around the opposite sex anymore. Honesty hasn't always been my best policy; too much Freudian disclosure. I've never even tried to fake like I was appropriate, and I'm full of anxiety and lonely.

"She heard you. He's writing you into the book, girl."

"Okay, you ready? Her home is 323- something and her cell is 310-something."

"Right my, but it's not my place to say that, and..." I notice that her voice suddenly becomes very monotone and flat. "Okay, okay, awesome, oh, okay, okay, okay, awesome."

"Yeah!" she says in an excited tone that contrasts the monotone tenor so much that I'm curious what Krista said.

"She said to tell you there's going to be an illustrated version of the book after we all hang out."

"Oh my God, woo, I'm aroused." Maybe I will meet someone.

Malia continues with details about Sasha's dinner party, plans for going out, shopping. I no longer follow and stop writing what she says.

"I'm in love again," I say after Malia hangs up. "Or I've officially lost my mind."

Malia says, "You're just on the rebound. I've been there, and you're doing fine."

"I haven't been single in a long, long time. It doesn't... feel right."

"You'll do fine. She really wants to meet you. She has huge tits and is dark and intense and spontaneous. She's part Hawaiian, totally tan and tiny except for the boobs."

"Tiny isn't generally my thing. No offense." Malia is

234

tiny with basically no tits, and I want her to understand that she is not entirely not my type because her personality seems so wonderful that I could probably get past the not my type issue with a woman like her. Even though she is married, I want her to feel included in my amorousness, which is ridiculous.

I say, "I don't, well I usually don't preclude based on body type alone, but I generally go for sturdy, curvy girls."

"That's funny. I feel bad about not inviting Krista to stay at Sasha's house. She's just totally spontaneous and hasn't even spoken to Sasha yet, and she'll be in LA tomorrow."

That sounds familiar to me. Why?

I say, "I just had a realization that I haven't called anyone in LA, other than Sasha, in a few days."

"That's okay though, Van. Isn't it? Dave knows you are coming. That's good actually. Write that in your book."

"I just did."

"Sasha is totally into her space, her privacy," she says.

"Wow," I say. "I was just thinking that Sasha is a lot like my wife."

"That's...interesting?"

"I know. It just occurred to me."

"You're like me in many ways," she says. She describes her flighty often over-productive and intense yet unfocused life.

"You have ADHD," I tell her. "I just read a book that says most of the good ideas in the world come from ADHD people. Attention Deficit Hyperactive Disorder."

A few minutes pass, and then Malia calls Sasha and leaves a long message about the possibility of Krista staying at Sasha's house.

Sasha is intense, and I don't want more tough love now. My wife and Sasha have many qualities in common, especially space. They need their emotional space to be private at all times. Maybe I'll meet Krista.

Malia tells me that Ron's a player. They have fun. Her husband, her marriage is work, and her relationship at work is natural. There's a connection between them that is latently sexually charged, but it's platonic. "We are like brother and sister," she says.

235

"Sounds more like kissing cousins," I say.

She cracks up in agreement then continues, "My husband is the opposite of a jealous guy. He's so confident, I guess, or disinterested."

"I rarely get jealous either," I say, questioning my real confidence.

I'm so comfortable with her that I decide to try to explain to Malia about the self-awareness box moment at Pete's mountain house in detail, to change the subject to something more appropriate.

I finish by saying, "…All of the sudden I realize it's a book, and then I'm like this is a book about now. I told the guy I was working for that I had to go write something down and dropped my scissors. Picture this: I have on shorts only, and I'm covered from head to toe in resin from trimming weed in some green house. And I'm, I have weed leaves stuck to me everywhere. And it was all, well not all, but it was partially because I smoked Genius."

"Wow," she says.

I say, "I don't think I should smoke anymore today." We are quiet for a half an hour or so. Then Malia says, "Oh my God. In the middle of fuckin' nowhere, Taste of India House Restaurant: To Go Food Available. Check that out." She's motioning to a covered wagon with a banner for a restaurant draped over it, in the middle of miles of empty fields bowled by mountains.

"We're probably almost in Button Willow," she says.

TIMELINE:
(-Highway 5)

On the road in what still looks like the middle of nowhere I say, "I really loved the people I was staying with last in Humboldt."

"You were staying with friends, right?" Malia asks.

"Yeah, my buddy, Jim. JimDawg we call him. He lives with his girlfriend and her son from a previous. They were all special to me."

"How old is her kid?" she asks.

"He's five, super sharp, sweet little guy. Made me miss my family even more than I already am."

"That's understandable, Van."

"I was just thinking of old JimDawg because he had decided that I would write about you. I was tired and missing my sons. And he was like, 'It ends in Vegas. You have a plane ticket home from Vegas, so it ends in Vegas.' I said I figured it did, and I was just a little bit bummed maybe about my friend Crispin bailing on our road trip. He and I were supposed to be driving home together after his mom came out to the Bay Area to meet us, San Fran and Napa, but she canceled, so he flew home. I can't stand his complaining anyway. I don't have much of a threshold for negative people anymore, and he bitched and moaned like a brat the whole time we were together. Part of me was extremely relieved to not listen to him anymore. He and I were in LA together last, and he actually tried to have a bad time."

"Why?"

"He'd been on a mountain for a third of a year, so it was a bit much. The paranoia and seclusion up there has turned all the growers into a bunch of complainers. Dave and I forced him to have some fun. Eventually, he was all 'We love it.' Anyway, JimDawg was like 'Vegas, Malia. You have huge plans. Don't get down. Stay up, Van, stay up.' I plan to go to the Italian Riviera for the first time after I make it big, so I said 'Riviera, Malia, Vegas.' Then I changed it to 'Timeline: Malia, Vegas, Riviera.' I felt excited as I said bye to Jim; one comment by one friend can swing my whole mood."

"That's something else. Friends really matter," she says.

"Where are you from anyway, Malia?"

"California, baby."

"The only true California girls that I have met and bonded with so far are you and Jim's wife, and I like both of y'all very much. Almost everyone else is from somewhere else. Same deal in Atlanta: everyone moves there, mainly from somewhere else in the South or the Midwest or the Northeast. People move to California from all over."

"You really mean all over when you are talking about Cali migration patterns," she says.

"It's like New York…almost," I say.

We are quiet for a half an hour or so, then perk up when we notice that we are entering a developed area.

"All right, you're Sasha's best friend, and you don't even know where she was born," I say, feeling like picking on Californians all of the sudden. "How Californian of you. Just kidding, but you should know."

"I totally know. I just can't…we have to find out where Sasha was born," she says. "I missed the rest stop. I have to pee! Should we stop at Wendy's?"

"Jack in the Box. Let's stop at Jack in the Crack. This'll be my first Jack experience by the way, never been jacked before. Well I've been jacked, and jacked of course, but never been to 'Crack in the Box.'"

I think all at once about hand jobs, the hot flash sound and sickly sweet smell of burning crack and about being jacked in New Orleans. Dude mugged me in the bathroom of a frozen drink bar on Bourbon Street before lunch on a weekday, when I was there for a convention.

Malia's cell phone ringing breaks me from my memories. It's Sasha. Malia finds out Sasha was born in Inglewood. They talk for a few minutes while I head inside, singing "California Love" by Dr. Dre.

Back in the car after lunch, I'm feeling somewhat sobered up and upbeat about heading to Los Angeles, thinking a line drawn across the country from ATL on a map would come close to LA. Regional centers.

Heading down, we meander further into Southern California and seem to grow fonder of one another by the mile. We are practically best friends by the time we stop

238

along the way to pick up Malia's teenage daughter from a summer camp for gifted students.

And then the three of us descend the final leg of the journey.

Zoning out as the miles pass by, I come out of a half-sleep.

"I was voted Senior Class Beach Bum," Malia is saying.

"That was a superlative?" I ask.

The schools here are different from others around the nation in that they are so impacted by Hollywood and the beach and subculture and the lack of seasonal weather. They have to compete with so much other activity. California is always different and the same. Here they have senior superlatives like other American schools, but the superlatives encompass such Zen notions as Beach Bumism. Californians are spiritualists, freedom seekers, recreation lovers, and they express it.

I say: "I didn't win a Senior Superlative at my school, but I did have the largest graduation party...in the history of the county."

"No way," Malia says. "That's way more important as far as cred at your school."

I ramble, "Yeah. I did it right after I graduated so all the cred was out of school. But I remember Dave and I and one of our other friends were treated like rock stars that first summer out of school...because of the party. We rented these horse fields near where my parents lived and you had to drive to my house to see the sign that said: 'Go to Horse Country.' When the cops eventually found us at Horse Country, they busted it. But there was so much traffic that we just walked home through the woods to my mom's house with all these girls and some money because we had even had some dudes charge for parking for us and got a cut. Then we all went to Waffle House."

Malia says, "I've heard that's good."

"It is, the hashbrowns. By the way, what do you want your name to be in the book, Malia?" I ask.

"No," she says. "I mean...Gemma! I want it to be Gemma."

"I thought you were too nice a lady for the name

239

'No.'"

Malia's daughter Leana says, "That's a cool name, Mom."

"What will your name be, Leana? Maybe you should go by your real name because I like it so much, and you have some real star qualities."

"May-be," she answers confidently, happy about the compliment. "I may think of one and tell you, Van."

"By all means please do, young lady, if one occurs to you. Malia, you do know that Gemma is a doll, correct?" I ask.

"Yeah. Is that bad? To have a doll's name?" she asks.

"No. I was just making sure that you knew," I explain, while truly contemplating the question for a fleeting instant. Is a doll's name bad? Probably not, if she likes it. Maybe a little cheesy. Gemma it will be.

"I did," she says. "I knew that, but I still like it."

We stop talking for a while; we all sort of settle down and rest in our own worlds. I'm coaching myself up: I want to stay on the whole time that I'm down here this time, investigating the essence of Los Angeles. What are you, LA? I'll write about the people that I met in LA before and liked. Maybe I'll follow them around and do a chapter with each of them. And I'll write about Dave's world. He will let me in on more if I'm partially writing this about him. He's perfect for this. So am I.

The mainly non-stop traveling part of my adventure is almost over, and I'm ready to bunker down and taste the egg orange yolk sunsets of Hollywood life for a while.

"Are we in LA, already?" I ask the girls.

"Kind of," Gemma answers.

"This is Metro LA for sure," I say.

I announce: "I'm going to write this book first. I'll write about Cali while it's fresh in my mind. I don't want to lose any perspective. I can write about Atlanta after, in a couple years, I guess. I won't-be-forgetting-no ATL."

"This book career is really evolving," Malia says. "I'm excited."

"Thank you," I say.

Painted past, eyes toward the golden future yet this feels almost all brand new to me, yet I feel like I'm really

240

back, like my sister and I talked about before this trip. I'm… almost back to feeling like my old self. I fucked up, but I love my children and family and friends very much and want to do better. I'm a good guy.

I'm back. Not just in LA, I'm back to my old self. No, I'm my new self. I'm not some cocaine junkie. I'm right here not Baja California in some coked up mess. Or hearing fucking sirens in my head hours after they stopped in Atlanta. I'm right here. "I'm gonna be alright."

I'm a generous and good person that made big mistakes. This process has helped me. God forgives me, and I have a bright future.

I say, "I bid a fond farewell to all parts of California north of Los Angeles. Hello, Los Angeles."

And I'm back. The VAN is back in Los Angeles. There is the sign.

"That is the county line," I say. "We've crossed over into Los Angeles County."

MY CALIFORNIA SUMMER:
(-Los Angeles)

Spin big wheel, spin. Summer breeze off the Pacific starts to shift from perfectly pleasant to a bit too cool for my thin Southern blood, as the sun finally sets. It's been a long, bright day in Los Angeles where I recall sprawling laughter LA as a joke amongst friends, all egg white yolk with patio sunrise omelette breakfast and less than caviar dreams. I feel accomplished after having written for several hours.

I close my notebook and eyes and pray for a few minutes. When I come out of deep prayer, the Ferris wheel is in full bloom against the night sky and I can faintly hear the surf. I'm more fully aware of the surrounding world than I've been for at least the past few hours, maybe all summer. I'm more at peace with myself than I've been in much longer. This is weird and dope, LA is weird and dope.

I walk back to the bus stop and crack my notebook back open and without pause write about Humboldt and San Francisco and the open California freeway until the bus arrives.

Zooming on a comfortable Metro bus back to LA proper while my pen and paper form a closer symbiotic relationship, I realize I've found a safe outlet for my high-speed chugging engine of a mind.

Santa Monica behind me, and Los Angeles is still ahead of me for a few more days before Vegas. Las Vegas lights for a couple of days and then home to Atlanta, where I'm decoupling. The prospect of divorce looms over me. But my troubled past is behind me now. I hope.

The next day, I'm at Dave's apartment. We're going out to Deleanor Hotel later tonight to celebrate the end of my trip, but we haven't started primping yet. Dave is back in his bedroom talking on the phone to work folks. I'm on the comfy couch with my trusty notepad in hand. The words are flowing off the pen.

Dave walks into the living room and says to me: "So, do you like it here now?"

"Of course," I say. "Now that I'm here relaxing at the

apartment and living a writer's life. I almost feel like a local. I like this area of town."

"You figure LA and California out by writing about it?"

"I'm still working on that, but I think so. I've found myself again. Great idea to stop smoking pot; I realize I was just burying the pain."

"You better?"

"A little bit. Actually, I'm much better. I'm healing through the process. Good to stay more still now after so much travel."

"You could've gone all the way across the country, as many miles as you've logged."

"But this was just a California summer."

"How does it end?"

"I'm going out through Vegas, Dave."

"Right," he says. "But I mean the book."

"I don't know yet. I guess it ends when I get home."

"You could write the whole book and finish it and in the end it says he gets his wife back. Then you could bring it to her when you get back and show it to her, and she'd take you back."

"That's awesome. But do you really think she would?"

"We spoke on the phone. I know she would if you were better."

"Not sure if I'm there yet, plus I can't finish a whole book in the next few days. Writing a good book takes some years of hard work. Neat idea, though, maybe it ends when I leave Cali or when I leave Vegas."

"I don't think this is about Vegas," Dave says.

"It's about finding yourself through travel," I say.

"Traveling California. You should just enjoy Vegas, Van. See the lights. You'll have enough material by the end of the weekend."

"I may already, and we are going out. ... Thanks for everything."

"You're welcome. When you leave California it's a blank slate for you, a new life, the start of the rest of your life. When you leave California should just be a blank chapter."

"At the state line?"

243

"Yeah, what's next? Vegas. So 'Vegas Genius' is a blank chapter."

"I want to write the whole time I'm in Vegas."

"Do it. You can make it as a writer if you work at it. But when you cross the state line, have it say 'The End' and have the three dots."

"Ellipses."

"Right and then it's a new blank chapter. Or it could be blank except you say: 'This all really happened.'"

Dave has to call his agent, so I go for a walk. Alone in the neighborhood, I'm thinking not many people walk in LA outside of the local beaches.

In San Francisco everybody walks, but that's The City, not this city. That's the subculture, subterranean white city of Kerouacian acclaim: the Barbary Coast, Gold Rush and Summer of Love city.

I walk an alley next and decide LA is "Alleytown," running behind nearly every street is an alley full of the real street culture. I see stickers of otherworldly art pieces, of aliens and UFOs, of obscure bands with unusual names and offbeat fashion lines. Spray-painted images of cameras flashing, which is appropriate for Tinsel Town, people from all over the country and world, conveying what it means to them to live in Los Angeles, through their street art.

I walk back to the street and the Spanish-influenced architecture of the houses strikes me: the tile roofs and stone structures. The semi-tropical, semi-desert vegetation, the lushness and beauty of small yards and nice homes – this too is LA. I notice a big cactus, citrus trees, palm trees, flowers and blooming trees, and the METRO bus zooms by.

I think of watching the helicopters fly around Downtown LA from friend's hotel room last week. It looks like he will get a job out here, and I hope he doesn't stay so depressed. I'm spacing out when I see an oblivious, gorgeous blonde driving twenty-file miles per hour over the speed limit, cell phone to her ear, only interested in her bubble, her reality. Something tells me she's an industry type. Random recall of hanging with Hugh Jackman one of the two years I worked Comic-Con in San Diego. He was in full Wolverine regalia and recognizing our glad-to-be-working-in-SoCal energy. I was Andy Lee's entourage and we were with the Heavy Metal comic book guys at a wide-open back table area, and Andy Lee fake blood tipped Wolverine's claws. Hugh was a good guy. I though was an antihero of sorts, sort of half-there, partying way too much and slinging Andy's shirts under the name of my fashion brand. Slipping from my old roommate's place in Pacific Beach to downtown San Diego to Tijuana and generally reveling as much as humanly possible.

The importance of the entertainment industry makes Los Angeles different from the rest of the state and country. Think of LA compared with some other major US cities I know well: LA is a huge melting pot like New York and Chicago. LA has nice weather like San Diego. LA has tropical vegetation and skin on display like Miami. LA is a regional headquarters like Atlanta. LA has an overabundance of pretty women like Dallas. LA is a giant sprawl like Houston. LA is a cultural center like San Francisco. LA has self-importance like DC. But what ultimately defines LA for me is that Los Angeles is the land of the dream, the home to Hollywood. Much more than an area of town, when the world says "Hollywood," they mean LA and that means the industry.

Singing "Hooray for Hollywood" through a smile walking back inside the apartment where Dave intently watches an old Bogart film – doing his acting research. I think of my good Latin friends, Rico is moving from Georgia and Alejandro and I won't be seeing each other regularly like we have, since the trip is ending. Alex calls his car Wolverine and Rico's we called 2 Fast, 2 Furious when the muffler got shot. They'd like each other.

I borrow Dave's phone and call Rico back home. He will be moving to Florida soon, and I want to catch him up since we won't be able to speak in person upon my return. I tell him about Humboldt and trimming and about the big road trip and the quicker trip I made back here to LA. I tell him I'm finally feeling sane again and have been living healthy in LA, and that "I might've have even moved to Cali if I didn't have kids."

He asks what I've been doing in LA for the past few weeks. I tell him I stayed in downtown LA with a friend and I stayed out in Venice Beach with a cool reality TV show carpenter that I know from Athens. How I'm going to hang out with the American Indian dude from Dave's building today and that Dave and I saw Mickey Rourke. I explain that I've hung out again with many of the people I first met on the big road trip with Crispin and really seen how they live in LA and how Dave showed me his life. "These characters looped back into my life as I looped back through the places I'd visited again. Organic."

He asks if I'm staying off blow. I say I relapsed but have been off the stuff for a few weeks and that Dave's been coaching me up on making a new life for myself.

I say, "I've decided to become a professional writer, writing a book about this trip. Thanks for being the first person to read my creative writing back home and encourage me."

He tells me he told his boss all about me at a residential concierge firm where he's been working and that they want to hire me to help with company growth. If I want to get a paying job set up before I even get home I should call him right away. He's expecting me to call him from a random California number and knows I'm traveling without a phone.

So I say bye and hang up and call Rico's boss and leave a message. He calls right back and says he wants me to start as soon as I return.

HOLLYWOOD DAZE:
(-Los Angeles)

Dave leaves to workout with his personal trainer while I interview the full-blooded American Indian named Wolf, a personal trainer, in his upstairs apartment. Dave had me sell my remaining assortment of weed to Wolf's client over a week ago so I could sober up, and Wolf gives me a nugget of the Genius pot that he put aside for me. He's a cool guy to know.

I go back downstairs after a lengthy interview and get high and think about Daniel Lonewolf's life at UCLA and then here, working out of his apartment in inner-city Los Angeles as a personal trainer dedicated to fitness, living with two real Wolves. The shallowness he too often sees in the women here was an expression of sadness.

Then I think about the first week I was back down in LA. Sasha chastised me for hitting on her friend and the friend blew me off after we made tentative plans, so I decided to focus on friendship and stop trying to be a cad or get laid. Wolf is a real friend now.

I start to write about walking the streets of Hollywood with my young friend Alejandro Victor, the Mexican security guard whom I met on the first trip down. Dave suddenly storms into the apartment looking frantic and says, "I need you to get some cooler clothes on real quick. Why are you high? Wolf doesn't smoke."

I say, "He gave me a bud of genius he'd saved. Have half."

"Later. Get dressed."

"We going out for the night already?"

"No. Just do it, Van."

In the Bronco, Dave tells me: "My bangin' actress neighbor and her friend are walking to Luna Park for a drink. We're going to meet them."

We park, and as we enter Dave says, "Just do exactly as I say."

Dave positions us in sight but away from them and tells me not to look at them. He orders us vodka drinks and tells me to stand up straight and messes up my hair. He waves to them and says, "Now."

We walk over and pair off, and Katie is a dream. From Kentucky, she majored in Speech Communication at a SEC school like I did. She is out here for graduate school, and we talk about the earnest South versus the vapidity of LA. She is aggressive and smart and has great facial expressions and the right amount of curves. And she makes it obvious that she's interested in not only my book but also me as a man. So I ask her to come see me the following night, one of my last in California.

Dave steps in, and I introduce them. He asks if we've made plans to meet and I say we did. He puts her number in his phone for me and we bid farewell and leave.

Dave's neighbor had a boyfriend, but he's proud of me for charming Katie and says, "See how easy it is to make a connection with someone cool out here when you try. We make a great team. You sure you don't want to move out here and partner up with me and run game. You and that girl might fall in love. My agent said he'd take you on if you start working out more and get your teeth whitened brighter, and you can work at the restaurant and write for Hollywood."

We roll through LA quietly in the Bronco for thirty seconds.

"I'll pass," I say. "Thanks for all that, but Georgia is home."

That night at the Deleanor Hotel's pool bar in Hollywood, Dave and I get the star treatment again on the way in and enter through the kitchen. An actor friend of Dave's having his twenty-third birthday party tonight has a long table reserved for all of us.

The shimmer of the lights bounces off the pool and illuminates pretty faces, as the chatter around the table reveals the professions of these well-dressed beautiful people: Dave's buddy Cyril has brought along a mohawked African teammate from the LA Galaxy soccer team. A big girl who owns a fashion house and works for a record label is seated directly across from me. The birthday boy is getting his first listing as producer on his latest film project, which starts shooting next week in Vancouver. His proud entertainment lawyer mom's on hand but has to leave early to be at her office for a meeting in the morning. A video documentary maker has a new project on the homeless just getting the green light. And two, obvious-in-their-beauty, youthful, brunette female models are talking about the casting couch, trying to screw for television roles. One of them is making eyes at Dave, and he is enjoying it.

I go to the bathroom and a radiantly gorgeous, blonde woman approaches me knowingly on the way back to the table. She says, "I saw you went to the bathroom and are with my friends. Those model girls and I kick it and work together sometimes. You got any coke?"

I say, "No. I was using the bathroom for traditional reasons, but maybe we can find you something."

"If you do, I'd love to party with you...perhaps all night."

Back at the table in Dave's ear: "Dude, you have to find me some blow with the quickness."

Dave quietly asks, "Why are you jonesing? We're having a good time, and I thought you shook it. You've been doing so good."

"It's for her," I say, motioning to the blonde as she joins her fellow models and our group. "She wants us all to party."

Two hours later, some of us are back at her boyfriend's apartment. He lives in the complex where I first met Alejandro. I'm disappointed that the boyfriend is in the picture but am enjoying the company of the crowd. Dave gave me a condom, and the energy of the room indicates I may end up using it tonight.

Cyril and I are on the couch chatting; I'm telling him my nicknames for the three girls. "The blonde is Canadian, so Miss Canada. Tall beautiful girl I call Mexican Amazon. And that Robin brat I call Snotty Hottie."

"Perfect," Cyril says. "I'm so glad we're getting to hang again, man."

"Right. We're both best friends with Dave, so we're already friends."

"Hi, Miss Canada," I say to her as she exits the crowded bathroom and plops down on the floor in front of us to chop lines on a CD case.

She says, "I like that. My boyfriend designed this CD cover, maybe I should use a different one."

She gets up and transfers a small pile of coke from one cover to another and gets back down on her stomach and spreads her legs. She has on a mini-skirt with no panties, revealing one of the nicest asses I've ever seen.

She snorts a line and rhetorically asks, "You guys like the view?"

Snotty Hottie enters the living room, where our attention is clearly on Miss Canada and our conversation.

"You guys are fags," Snotty Hottie says. "You hardly even notice the rest of us, and we are all hot."

I explain, "We are just getting to know each other better. We are both best friends with Dave, so we're bullshitting."

"Best friends are bullshit. You should pay more attention to me."

"Okay," I say, surprised at this blatant statement of neediness.

"Can I make out with you guys then?" she asks.

"Sure," says Cyril.

"You first, Van, you faggot."

I say, "Okay." I don't really want to kiss her, but I like where this could lead. I want to have sex with Miss Canada, and it would take an all out orgy for that to happen.

Snotty Hottie hops into my lap and sticks her tongue down my throat, while I go through the motions.

She moves to Cyril's lap next. They make out for a few minutes.

Snotty Hottie says to me, "I wasn't feeling it when we kissed."

"That's because I don't like you much," I say.

"Can I have another chance?" she asks.

"Sure," I say. She's sexy-looking and I try to make it hot for her this time.

"That was way better," she says.

"I tried that time," I explain.

Cyril says to me, "You know many girls like this in Atlanta? I want to visit the South with Dave."

"I'll give you the key to the city," I say.

Snotty Hottie says from my lap, "You are only interested in boy talk...and her ass. Girl, your ass and pretty pink are all hanging out. Better cover up before your boy gets back from the beer run."

"He does what I tell him," Miss Canada casually replies. "Besides… they love the view."

"We really do," I say.

I go to the bathroom to do a line with the Mexican Amazon and Snotty Hottie. They give me one tiny bump, which I make fun of as I leave the bathroom to sit back down by Cyril and stare at Miss Canada.

Her legs close as her boyfriend enters with a huge hip-hop-looking white comedian named Big Mike. Dave enters the room from the patio and hugs Big Mike and then takes Snottie Hotty by the hand and escorts her to a bedroom, saying to her, "You need to chill with me for a hot second."

Mexican Amazon follows them into the room and closes the door.

Big Mike asks me to chug beer with him in the kitchen. I do. We talk about fathers and how proud his dad was when Mike started doing stuff with his comedy. He saw the pride in his dad's eyes. We chug to dads. Then we chug another beer. Big Mike is big. I'm not, and I know how to chug but I'm getting drunk too fast and hard.

We chug another beer to our families. I like Big Mike and tell him so, and we chug another beer to friends.

Snotty Hottie enters the kitchen looking flushed and says to me, "You like men."

I reply, "I just don't like bitches."

"I'm a bitch. That's true."

"You really are. Are you not?"

"You can't call me a bitch or I'll tell Dave."

"Go ahead, like I'm fucking scared of David."

"You should be. He likes me."

"I don't see how."

Big Mike slips out of the room, chuckling.

"How much money do you have?" she asks me as she sticks her hand down my pocket.

"None. Dave has me covered."

"That's so uncool not to have money."

"Being a materialistic bitch is uncool."

"Where is your phone and money?" she says, sticking her hand down my other pocket. I have a condom in there.

"Gross!" she yells.

251

I say, "You are the definition of gross. Kissing you was disgusting."

Dave peeks into the room and calmly tells us to chill out.

"Give me another bump," I say to Snotty Hottie.

"Give me more money," she says.

"Why? I gave you twenty bucks for a bump already. Great deal."

"I need more money to get more blow."

"You're a scam artist."

"You shouldn't talk to me anymore."

"Every time I move, you follow me."

"I thought I liked you, Van."

"Sorry I don't like you. Give me a bump"

"I'll give you a bump if I can slap you."

I'm aroused by this idea and say, "Go for it."

She slaps me hard in the face, which turns me on a little.

"You don't get another bump until later, but that made me wet," she says. "Did that turn you on at all?"

"Yes. But you disgust me. Just give me a bump."

"I will if I can slap you again. I think I'm into you."

"Give me a fucking bump, bitch."

Dave enters saying, "Don't call her a bitch."

"Don't be a bitch, Dave," I say. "Bitch ripped me off."

I'm drunk, horny, jonesing and now angry.

Dave pauses then says, "Bro, I'm not bitching at you. I gave you the twenty bucks. Let's get you home. Everyone is leaving or went to bed and you two are freaking out together. You and Mike had a few too many chugs, Van."

"Probably. I'm fine. I'm leaving. Where's the key?"

"I'll drive you."

"I'll walk. I'd rather walk anyway; it's only up the block."

"Please let me drive you. I love you, buddy."

"Okay, D."

Dave tells me in the Bronco that he's dropping me off and going to fuck those two, and I could have come if I didn't dislike the one so much.

I get out in front of the apartment and say, "Only bitches date bitches."

He says, "It's not a date. It's only a fuck. They're

hot."

Even in my drunken state, the selfishness of being with wanton women you don't genuinely like is off-putting to me.

Dave tries to hand me the key to his apartment, but I say, "Fuck it. I don't want anything from someone who wants to hang out with a bitch that acts like that."

And I walk off alone into the cooling Los Angeles night.

BAKED SUNRISE:
(-Los Angeles)

I tried telling myself to stay asleep and ignore the fly eating at my sweetly liquored sweat, to stay melted into comfortable couch cushiness. Blazing late morning SoCal sunshine had a better idea: wake up and face reality.

Today's hustle and bustle noisily chimed around me as I realized I was sticking to the pleather junk couch on the street outside Dave's apartment. I'd slept here. I walked toward the coffeehouse, for the first time in full understanding of why so many people despise Los Angeles.

The couch was pretty comfy except for the fact that it was previously covered in duct tape, which is partially removed, leaving a black sticky resin all over me. I'm still wearing club clothes.

I enter the hip local coffeehouse and grab an artist's statement sheet for paintings on display. I read it and flip it over and start writing.

"Rough night?" asks the coffeehouse dude.

I chuckle and answer, "Yeah. Pretty obvious, huh?"

"What can I bring to make you feel a little better?"

"Definitely a machiatto, I have a few singles saved specifically for that." I reach in my back pocket and pull out the little money I have left.

"You probably need something to eat, too. What are you writing?"

"A book."

"I'll get you a whole grain bagel and some fruit. It'll help you write."

He returns with my little machiatto. I down it, and he hands me another one.

"On me," he says. "All of it. Let's hear it. I write too."

"I was writing about this materialistic bitch that I met. My best friend and I and some of his mates were hanging out with these models."

"Never judge your value on anything that a model does or says."

"Just use them for a fuck?"

"Not even that. They're pretty to look at and that's that."

"So, we go to a birthday party at Deleanor Hotel…" starts the detailed story of the evening I tell "CHD" - coffeehouse dude.

After, I'm happy to have made a fellow writer friend and write until the sheet is full and then stroll on the street back toward Dave's with a positive attitude about the smart creative people in LA. As I return, the couch is being hauled off to the dump by a trash truck.

"I guess I won't lay back down," I say.

I spend the rest of the day walking around investigating LA, meeting people and writing in a journal I bought with the money I saved on my free coffee connection. I feel the sidewalk move under me, as I record my travels. I'm fully immersed in California, and I've gone away from myself…whatever that even is anymore. All I can do is be here now.

Thoughts of the variety of urban California run through my head:

7-Mile Peninsula
People Pound
Down The Sauce
In San Francisco
Polarity, Plainly
Subcultural Sensations
Miles, Hours Above
A Giant Megalopolis
Of Lights And Smog
And Beauty, Tainted
Behemoth Sprawl LA
Los Angeles County

Where I'm just chilling when a smooth guy who looks remarkably similar to Jean-Michel Basquiat walks my way. He's decked out in a crisp white dress shirt, mint green pants and pink bracelet and silver pet jewelry from a store called Fifi and Romeo: silver necklaces that match a dog bone earring.

I sit down on a wall and say hello. He sits next to me and asks what I'm "working on so fervently." I tell him it's a book that he's in now.

 Best dresser ever and he's lived in Jamaica, Toronto, NYC and LA. Of Los Angeles he says he's "just passing through."

"How long have you been out here?" I ask.

He says, "Nine years."

We talk about my California experiences; his whirlwind visit to Atlanta; his favorite nightclub in LA; the Basquait show. Then I finally introduce myself.

He has the same first name as my eldest son, which stuns me!

We make tentative plans to meet again if there's time before I leave LA, and I get his phone number. He departs, saying he has "Thousands of good things he must do today. We should hang out again if possible."

I call Dave from a pay phone and he calls back and says for me to meet him at his house in an hour. I spend the hour-long walk back writing, and I make it to his place just as he's parking in front.

"D," I call out.

"Hey, Van." He says warmly. "You okay?"

Inside, we sit and he talks. I'm too manic and exhausted for a lecture, so I ask if I can take a shower now and listen to him talk later.

"Sure," Dave says.

I tell Dave about the cool Basquiat look-a-like I met, and when I mention his name I think of my eldest son and am forced to think of the damage I did to my marriage. I start to cry hard.

"This is too much," I tell Dave. "I just want to be back home working and have my family back."

"And what, work for some commercial real estate firm and commute from the 'burbs and act like you never even went out to LA?"

"No. But I'm having a bit of a tough time with art so far."

"Tough shit. You're an artist."

I walk back into Dave's bedroom and flop face down on his bed and sob. I feel unworthy of a bed and get down on the wood floor on my back and cry for at least an hour. I'm having a breakdown.

Dave walks into the room and says, "That's enough, Van. You're a little better. Come to work with me today so your date can meet you up there. Get it together in the shower, and then we need to leave."

"She's busy until after 8:00," I say, remembering our plans.

"You can write up there and just chill then."

In the Bronco, I'm feeling well scrubbed and on a tenuous up.

"That store right there was huge in my walk," I say. "Those figurines were symbolic of my journey to me."

"Your walk?" Dave says incredulously. "You are so fucked in the head. That wasn't going for a walk. Stop being an idiot. Why'd you leave and do that without the key."

"We discussed that last night."

"Because some coked up girl was mean to you. She actually wanted to hook up with you. What did she do?"

"Forget it."

"You sleep on the street. Some girl...what did she say?"

"Drop it. I slept on a couch." I chuckle as I say the word "couch."

"Not funny. You aren't a junkie so stop acting like one."

"I will. Stop bitching at me. It's too much right now."

"I'm worried about you again."

"Stop worrying about me. Perhaps you should think about your soulless conquests of loser women instead. I like this song."

"Who cares if you like this song, asshole," Dave says. He turns the radio off and says, "You have to start thinking right."

"Stop, Dave."

"No! You fucking listen to me! You have to stop being an idiot like this! You can't just go back to your old life, and you better make this new life work. Your priorities are not in check."

"Stop!" I yell. "Stop the vehicle."

I get out and again walk the same track I walked all day. I get my notebook out and start writing again.

Without direction, I wander and write what I see for several hours.

I eventually enter the store with the figurines and meet the Brit running the shop and interview him. His impression of the energy of LA cheers me up. Los Angeles varies based on perspective; it's full of life.

After, I call Dave and apologize. He sends someone to meet me, a girl from Bicco I hung around some my first week back in LA. She buys me a kosher hot dog and soothes me by telling me our little friendship has meant something to her. She just left a physically abusive relationship, and I made her believe that men could be good again.

We head back to Bicco, but Dave is not around. Her girlfriends finish work for the day, and I decide to accompany them to a Japanese restaurant up the block. Before we leave, a New Yorker thinking of moving to LA strikes up a conversation with me at Bicco's bar.

I say to him, "Rollercoaster full swing of emotions every day."

I record on paper the girl talk from the Japanese restaurant and seeing their pretty faces inspires me to again recall I have a date tonight.

I notice the young actor West from Bicco outside, and he comes in and walks over to the table. He smiles at the girls and says to me, "Dave wants to talk to you."

I walk back to Bicco, where Dave has just returned and is in his office. He tells me, "I had a major asthma attack and couldn't find my inhaler. I had to have my lungs pumped at the hospital. We are going back to my house to look for it. Go get in the Bronco. Take the keys."

I do and apologize, and we depart for his apartment. A huge SUV is blocking our exit onto Sunset. Dave rolls down his window and says to the driver, "That's okay."

"I'm sorry. What is?" she says. I recognize her from somewhere and she's gorgeous.

"If you can't drive. That's okay by me. Come see me at my restaurant right there when you get a chance. I have to run out now."

"I definitely will," she says, beaming at him.

To me as he rolls his window up: "That's Rebecca Romijn-Stamos."

We get back to Dave's house and find the inhaler on his bed under the filthy jeans of his that I wore.

"Dude," Dave says. "The funny thing about all of this drama is that I'm really going to miss having you around the day after you leave. I need to come see you in Atlanta soon. I miss my family there anyway."

I say, "Way to stay positive, Dave. I'm really sorry."

"That was as an example for you of how to act. Stay positive no matter what. Be confident on your date. I'll have food delivered for you here tonight. Call her from...my phone. Keep my phone for tonight. I need to focus at work the rest of the evening. Her number is in there."

BUDDHA'S 5-LINE:
(-Los Angeles)

The following day I'm in the living room, all rested and self-pleased after a nice evening with Katie. I pray and then call and apologize to my mom for yelling at her before I left, even though she somewhat deserved it.

I call and get my kids on the phone and tell them that I love them very much and that Daddy will be back home to Georgia soon. I talk to my wife too. The first real quality talk we've had since we signed for a divorce and she seems pleasant enough, considering. She let me talk to my kids at least, which is why I called, but it's good to hear her voice. I feel guilty that I went on a date, and then I remember we are legally separated now, so I quickly forgive myself.

I hang up and write for a few hours then make a collage by writing over the Basquiat cover of a free rag called LA Weekly. The end of my trip is near, and I'm commemorating the journey with some visual art. I'm positively stimulated and grateful for the experience.

I see Dave's large Buddha smiling at me and realize he's been with me during my time back in LA. I've slept and written under his pleasant gaze. I was raised sort of ambiguously Christian but grew up with a healthy respect for eastern religions, relayed to me from hippie parents and my studies of various religions in college.

I adorn the Buddha with flower petals left over from my date and place the notebook I've been writing in under him. I grab the apartment key that Dave and I've shared and place it on the notebook. I notice the key has a "5" on it. Since the notebook cover is lined like the notebook paper inside it, I adjust the "5" to look as if it's written on a line.

I think of "The Five" - riding Highway 5 in big open California, the number five Georgia jersey I had on when I realized this was a book, and growing up the oldest of five children. I start to cry thinking of the weight of my entire life and then start laughing, thinking of my wild summer.

Rollercoaster. One Miller High Life bottled beer remains in Dave's refrigerator from my date. I pop it open. For weeks, I've eyed the bottom of a bottle of expensive tequila on the kitchen counter. I pour the tequila in a coffee cup and say, "To the book."

I swallow and it burns with nearly the intensity of life, until I wash it down with the delicious cold beer saying, "I could've used a lime."

I check the clock and smile. I grab the guest skateboard Dave has let me borrow as I depart for my scheduled final hangout with my Mexican-American pal Alex. Meeting him at the coffeehouse where I remembered what I love about the invention the world calls California.

As I roll, the wheel sounds and breeze in my hair remind me of my childhood spent under the blessed American sun. Bright sun is shining on me, and the breeze blows me clean. I feel truly present in my life.

Dave enters the apartment that evening saying, "Let's paint the book cover tonight."

Then he sees my collage on his painter's pedestal and says, "Looks like you maybe already did. Well, let's just hang out and then watch the first half of the Tokyo Bowl and then head out to an X Games after-party. I know all those guys well from when I was in the Nike ads."

I say, "I want to meet Mirra. I'm a fan. He's always winning and has good Chi."

"He won tonight. I was just texting those guys. They were going back to Malibu with a hundred girls, like ten guys. We can go and ride jet skis with them later. How great are their lives?"

"Right"

"How great to be one of them. They live awesome lives, bro."

"I'm enjoying my life now. We are gonna be huge, remember."

"I'm just, ready."

"Me too, D, me too."

"Here's what we do before the game. You do your laundry, then I'm going to do a healing session for you if you want."

"I think you and this book already have. I'm...saved."

"I'll take you on a little journey, then the game, street Michael Vick versus my top gun, Peyton Manning, then Malibu, perfect last night."

"The bu, the bu, this is good."

We look at Alex Grey's art book together, at his metaphysical art.

"You need to do laundry." Dave says.

"I'm having too much fun for that," I say.

"Seriously do you have any clean clothes."

"These sweats I'm wearing and this Bicco shirt."

"I gave you all that shit."

"I know, I know. Which reminds me, I saved my last fly-wear shirt for you. Feel free to cut the sleeves off like you always do, big guns."

"I love it. Dude, do your laundry now."

"I'm gonna be huge."

"With clean laundry."

I gather my laundry. Weiss is looking at his pretty self in the bathroom's mirror and sees me sorting dirty clothes in the reflection and turns to me and smiles, because I'm finally listening to him.

"You reminded me of your grandma, Dave, classically Jewish."

"I know, right. I don't care how huge you're going to be, have clean clothes first."

"I have to remember to put grandmas in the book. Wolf mentioned he loved his grandma, and Nanny was my favorite during her lifetime."

"She was awesome, Van. Great huevos rancheros."
I leave for the laundry room and hear the door click locked before I make it all the way down the hall. I guess Dave needs some alone time.

I start my clothes and then get spooked leaving the laundry room basement. The hair on my neck stands up on end as I turn the light off. I walk briskly up the hall to Dave's door.

The door is still locked...knock, knock, knock.

Dave opens the door and says, "Why did you lock the door?"

"I didn't," I say. "You locked it."

"Why would I? You have the key."

"It's over there on my notebook. I walk through walls now." I say.

Dave says, that's the name of your book: I Walk through Walls.

We both smile and he hugs me. We have a seat on the couch and Dave says, "Let's get high one more time. I have some Northern Lights."

We smoke. Then I say, "Weird how that door locked. You did that."

"I didn't," Dave says. "That door takes the key on both sides."

"I told you the key's right there on the notebook. That was weird; I heard it lock. Then I got scared leaving the basement and practically ran back to the apartment."

"It's already time to advance your laundry, by the way."

"I'm not going down there alone again."

"I'll go with you. Not because you're scared, just because I don't want to miss anything."

Dave turns the door handle lock, making sure it's unlocked, I assume. We walk to the laundry room and put my clothes in the dryer.

When we walk back up and reach the door, we realize Dave has locked us both out. He locked the handle on accident.

"Is this part of the healing session, Dave?" I ask.

"Not funny." He says.

Dave is locked out with me in the same neighborhood where I slept on the couch, the area where I wandered and wrote and skated and thought of my life.

I say to him, "Now you're really in my book."

We walk outside the building and approach the open but barred window. Dave says, "I can remove these bars."

He tries and fails. We walk toward the Bronco, Dave saying, "Dude, I can pick that front door lock."

We get a few objects out of the Bronco to help in Dave's effort to break in, and walk back, and he tries to pick the lock and fails.

"We need a metal hanger," Dave says.

We walk back toward the garage where the Bronco is parked and see a female model-type on her front stoop and ask her for a hanger.

She returns with plastic and wooden hangers, saying they are the only types she has. We don't accept them and walk back to the apartment.

It's getting late and the Tokyo Bowl has started,

so we watch some of the game through the window. Dave compares himself to Peyton Manning and blabs about growing up the only Colts fan he knew. He liked them because his dad was from Maryland.

I lay down on the sidewalk and start to laugh and Dave says, "This isn't funny. I want to go to Malibu and get laid. Where is that key?"

"On the notebook, on the table, under the Buddha."

"We could have used one of those plastic hangers and a rope to grab the key, and we turned her down. I have no idea of her name or which apartment is hers."

Time passes. We decide to call a locksmith and do. Over an hour later he arrives. We make it into Dave's apartment too late for Malibu.

Dave says he is going to sleep and walks back to his bedroom. I flop down on the couch. I'm skeptical that Dave didn't originally lock the door, though the door handle locking was clearly unintentional.

I check the notebook and the key is still there, the "5" appearing as if written on a line.

I sit back on the couch, and the Buddha's playful grin comes into my line of vision.

"You did this," I say as chills run up and down my arms.

I lay myself down and start laughing and then look up to see the Buddha once again, and I'm comforted by his smile.

I close my eyes and almost instantly fall soundly asleep.

G.S.G. HYMNAL:
(-Los Angeles/-California Desert)

I wake up smiling the next morning, feeling enchanted, enlivened, almost even enlightened. I feel God's presence in me and am overwhelmed by my recent life experiences.

I write aloud the "G.S.G. Hymnal:"

I have been to the river and swam
I have been to the mountain and seen
Oh Lord, take me home
I have been to the valley and cried
Oh Lord, take me home
Oh Lord, carry me home
Oh Lord, take me home

Dave enters the room to my singing and asks if I'm okay.

I say, "Great. Best I've been since before I got out here."

We load up the Bronco with my stuff and drive to the bus station and Dave buys me a ticket. I hand him a worn fly-wear T-shirt.

Dave and I bid each other a warm farewell, and I enter the bus and depart for Las Vegas. Alone again, heading out to the great American desert, under a blazing California sun.

On a bus full of people headed through the California desert to Nevada, I find myself. These grievances, epiphanies...these Golden State grievances and epiphanies keep coming to me. The more that I travel, the more they flash to me. What I really love and what I don't like about California, America and the world. What my life is about and what I want my life to be. God has a plan for me. California has turned up my senses. My eyes are open again; they are opening.

It suddenly begins to rain hard.

And The VAN says, "God Bless, California. ...God Bless America."

Crying in the desert in the pouring rain as we near the state line, I feel blessed to have had such a good trip. I realize I'll take with me lessons learned this summer and create my new life. I'm saying my goodbyes to California: "Goodbye and thank you."

I pray and then sing aloud my "GSG Hymnal" of this California road trip, with its new last verse:

I have been to the river and swam
I have been to the mountain and seen
Oh Lord, take me home
I have been to the valley and cried
I have been to the desert and prayed
Oh Lord, take me home
Oh Lord, carry me home
Oh Lord, take me home

I'm crying again now, tears of joy. And I see the state line and pass over it sublimely thankful for my abundantly blessed life.

THE END...

Nevada Genius:
(-Nevada Desert)

(DAVE SAID LEAVE THIS A BLANK CHAPTER)

Acknowledgements:

Richard Silverstone, Justin Boria, Tom Bailey, Chuck Sambuchino, David Weiss, Robbie Lowie, William Floyd, Christine Santiago, Riley Blanton, Shawe Darwiche, Jacqueline Gurliaccio Vance, Tommy Morris, Ross Cohen, Paul Lutz, Ty Dartez, Dana Wildsmith, Dr. Thomas Lessl, Glenn Kurtz, Chip MacGregor, Brian Leary, Ryan Gravel, Chris Damico, Brendan Jackson, Brendan LaSalle, Mike Byrne, Keith Gardner, Michael Santini, Rick Lord III, Carol Gould, Warren Jackson, Andy Lee, Duane Kulers, Bart Young, Alexander Simmons, Scott Brown, Richard Laras, Rick Newton, Steven Jackson, Charles Bethea, Harriette Austin, Taylor Jordan, Alejandro Victor, Neil Hodgens, Nancy Love, Barbara Poelle, my stepmom Dale, Michael Robison, Joe Wenderoth, Tim Walsh, Kwanza Hall, Scott Buttorff, Matt Eldridge, Jennie Johnson, Damon Krebs, Spence Travis, Rick Esposito, Thayer Johnson, Wade Bradford, Dale Harris, Katie McDonald, Chef Rob Vance and Kat Vance, Chef Jason Hill, Chef Brandon Carter and family, Robert Goodman, Chris Alberts, Jeff Wallace, RickMo, Scammy, Boggs, Meredith, Patrick, Beth, Southard, Dr. Arthur Myles Williams, Amber of Jucifer, Clem, Michael Stipe, Cisco Adler, Lisa D'Amato, Charles Whitaker, Larry Gray, Kyle Bryant, No-L, Adam Friedstein, Matthew Peterson, C.J. Leonard, Will, Donnellshamell, Thadeus, Sama Doh, John B. Goode, Ron FOCUS Manager, Cocktails, InfraRED, Infinite, Jacob Bullock, Kimberly, the Keiths, the Jays, Jack, Andrea, Tyler, Glenn, Brett Bowen, Little Baby Dino, Dino, Saba, Paulo, Java Lords, Urban Grind, Baraonda, Vanessa Hobbs, Song Kim, Hollie Loblack, Bryan Kessler, Bill Hallman, Wendy Binns, Ted Cutler, Morgan CODA, James Booth, Stewart House, Daniel Riggins, Ian Fides,, Mike of KJ, Aimee Mann, David Byrne, Conan O'Brien, Dr. Veronica Duncan, Tom Cheshire, Matt DeBenedictis, Gene Kansas, Kimiko Nakamura, Kendrick Daye, Collin Kelley, Brian Charles Egan, HENSE, PaperFrank, Frank of A Cappella Books, Hidden Lantern Bookstore in Rosemary Beach, FL, Eric at Criminal Records, Book Soup, Distant Lands, Paradise Found, Alley Cat, the Atlanta Writers' Club, Writer's Digest, Jaime Lin Weinstein, Tova Gelfond Rosenberg, Decatur Book Festival, Tuk Smith, Jim Clinard, Andy King and Ra.

Plus, a most sincere thanks is here given to each of my family members for your love and help. With many an extra special thank you to my mom Nina, stepdad Mo and loving sister Anna for many years in kind support of my fledgling art career.

A super special thank you to my lovely wife Jami Buck-Vance for some editing of rewrites and her thoughtful contributions and mostly for our sweet eternal love: I love you, Jami!

All glory to God for awakening my true passion for life.

God Bless America!

Bonus Chapter:

Alternate Beginning (Epilogue) - Not Going (-Greater Metro Atlanta)

Before all this I was sad, mad and alone. I was at my parents' house in the Atlanta suburbs, Marietta, Georgia, where my youngest brother had recently moved home from college. He was gone for the weekend.

I was in his room listening to Aimee Mann's Magnolia soundtrack on a cheap stereo, speaking along with the music when I could get the words out between bouts of crying.

"It's not what you thought. Because it's not going to stop. Until you wise up. No, it's not going to stop. Till you wise up. No, it's not going to stop. So just give up...

"Fuck! I may have to get through that song one more time," I said aloud. Feel the pain, I thought. All I felt was pure remorseful pain. "The Van is cloaked in darkness."

"It hurts so bad. It fucking hurts, Aimee!" I said aloud to the artist.

You're never alone long at my mom's house. My sister heard my lamentations and entered the room asking, "Are you okay, Van?"

"No. I'm not," I said. "I will be eventually, I guess. I need to get out of here."

"You are going to California today," she said, trying to sound cheery for my benefit.

"I know, I know. She makes you cry even when you aren't sad," I said, tipping my head toward the music.

"I know she does, Van. That's why she is so great."

Then I told her: "And...I just signed my divorce papers. She made me sign before I left by...threatening me with legal fees if I didn't. I signed today."

"That sucks. How about a hug? I love you. I love you. Go ahead and cry. You are gonna be okay."

"Thanks, Sis," I said after the hug.

"I'm getting divorced, too, and I'm not too thrilled," she said. "I want to be divorced, but it's just...hard."

"Imagine how you would feel if it was all your fault, Sis."

270

"That must be hard," she said. "I'm sorry. I'm going to give you a minute, but I'm right out here in the living room if you need me."

"Thanks. You're the best sister ever. I'm glad you're back. I'm glad you're okay. I prayed for you to come back to us, and I thank God for bringing you back everyday."

"I figured you did, Van," she said. "I'm okay. Good to be back."

"And you're really back now," I told her proudly – I'm proud that she recovered from a full-blown meth addiction.

"I know," she said smiling, trying to reassure me further. "Right in the living room...and really back."

She left the room and I prayed in my head: Thank you for listening to me and saving her from her crystal meth-amphetamine deathtrap, God. She's a good woman and a mother, and not everyone makes it back from hard drug addiction.

Addiction and death had been around me lately, I thought to myself. Drugs took two of my best friends over a six-month span. In between, another neighbor had also killed herself, only she had been more intentional: carbon monoxide poisoning from her car. She was a dear family friend. The sleeping pills she had tried over a year earlier had only sent her to the hospital. The next time, she did it right. All her estate planning was immaculate, and the task was completed. I was out in LA last summer when I got the news of her death, only a month before my second Wes would go.

My first buddy named Wes to go was long gone by then, dead for months.

And I realized that I'd potentially been near dying, not just near death but my own death. I'd gone crazy on cocaine and more than a few times felt my heart beating faster than a drum roll. If I was unconsciously trying to kill myself, I'd been spared like my sister. We'd been cursed with drug addiction but blessed with survival.

I thought about all of that almost as if it were not me that it happened to. Not my family, almost, not me, almost. It was me that fucked up and it was my family and it was my friends. Those two friends are dead. They aren't coming back, and they were parents.

I was heartbroken and scared.

I prayed to God in thanks for sparing my family and me and wept for about ten minutes. And then I changed things up again and gained composure and played the song, "Goin' Back to Cali" by Notorious BIG, while I finished packing.

I play that song every year before I visit California.

I always do Cali now. I was doing only NY for years and loving that. Now I'm on California, especially San Diego and Los Angeles lately, the past few years, and I remembered bumping that song in my car two, or was it three years ago on my way to the airport when I still had a license?

"Bye, pain cave." I said while glancing around my brother's room. "Brave-new-world...brave-new-world."

I was almost finished packing when I heard: "You are not going to make it!" It was my obnoxious mom yelling into the room.

Fuck her, I thought. She played a part in my relationship getting so messed up, so fuck her. I'd just checked on her thirty minutes before, and she'd been sitting on the couch with a blanket over her head. That is so fucking bizarre to do that. And she does it everyday as part of her self-interested five steps daily self-help relaxation rituals. Go to your damn room or something. Take a drug or something if you need to relax that fucking bad out in the living room.

Then I remembered it was her house. I just wanted her to have some sense of fucking normalcy since she wants to tell everyone else how to live.

"Calm down," I said to myself and to her through the wall, knowing she could be lingering and listening while she straightened something.

I wished I had some weed and more time to relax myself, and I had to remind myself to breathe. I was hung over after drinking too much tequila and beer at a party the night before and trying to start a fight with a huge dude. It was the second time in three days I tried to fight. JP would probably have kicked my ass, but that second dude was a straight up alligator wrestler.

"I have anger issues," I said matter-of-factly.

Maybe I should put a blanket over my head and go sit on the fucking couch and ask people to please be quiet since I am resting. My parents suck. She can be worse than my dad is...almost.

"Negative. It's me," I mumbled. "I'm totally negative right now."

Get me out of this hole. I hate the fucking suburbs.

"Hey, Bo," I said as I sauntered into sight of my stepfather, in his home office.

My step-dude is totally chill and didn't even freak out about me owing him all that money for that cell phone bill. I'll pay everyone back.

"Hey, Van. You leaving today?" he asked.

"Yeah. Now, see you in a month, or two," I said at first monotone. I intentionally sweetened my voice a little on the "two."

Then I said, "Take care, Bo," as nicely as I could. He'd been great, and I wanted him to know that I really appreciated him.

"Have a good trip," he said. His eyes were smiling, while he gave me a nice grin. His eyes talk more than he ever says much.

I finally pulled away with a final walk to and OCD-like, glance-back-of-a-look into the room, at the crummy stereo.

I walked toward the living room, thinking I have nowhere to live. I have no stereo. I have no room. I'm not prepared at all for being single.

"Sis, thanks again for being there for me," I said while entering the living room. She jumped up off the couch with the sweetest almost maternal face and gave me another small hug. I could sense that she wanted me to come back whole.

She is whole. She's almost whole again.

Then my mom entered the living room saying, "You are going to miss the plane, and I don't care if you do."

"Thanks a lot, Mom," I said in an agitated voice. "Maybe you should give me a ride to the airport instead of the MARTA station."

"That is so unfair to me," she said. "I'm not going to do that."

We walked outside and got in the car. I was resigned to ride in complete silence. She wasn't.

In the car she continued, "You are not going to make it, and you are on your own. You can just deal with the

273

airline, and see if they care. You have been piddling around all morning while I have been patiently waiting for you and..."

I interrupted in a terse voice: "Nancy, I have been getting ready for a trip while you've been doing yoga and breathing exercises and sitting on the couch with a blanket over your head and other relaxation techniques!" I did not mention my emotional breakdown to her. She would not care.

"Van, I was ready," she retorted. "I have been ready the whole time waiting for you."

"Mom, a blanket over the head is a universal sign for do not disturb me."

"This isn't about me," she said. "I don't think this is about me."

Then I gave her a dose of her usual medicine, saying, "It must be mother because you are still talking about it. Just drive, quickly, please."

I figured that would settle it, but instead she totally went off: "You are getting your nails touched up by your sister when you should be hurrying, and I was ready an hour ago and..."

"Shut the Fuck Up, Mom!" I yelled. "I'd rather walk to California!"

I knew right after I said it that I had been way too mean, but at least she stopped her chirping. We rode in complete silence after that all the way to the train station, well except for her breathing techniques. I resisted the urge to tell her how much that shit annoys me and was silently thankful for the ride.

As she pulled up to the train station entrance, I got the last ten dollars she still owed me for doing pressure washing for her. She already had it out of her purse and in her hand, so I did not have to say anything while I took it from her and exited the car. Pragmatic parenting is all she understands.

I shut her door just a little too hard to let her know that I was still pissed. She'd volunteered to give me a ride and then just had to make it suck for me.

"So unfair to me," I mumbled spitefully disgusted in a near facsimile of her voice, after she drove away without gesture.

Such "hippie bullshit" I said loudly, doing an impression of Johnny Rotten from the band, Sex Pistols. Well, actually it was more an impression of the actor that portrayed Rotten in the movie, Sid and Nancy.

"Boring Hippie Bullshit," I said.

Then in my normal voice: "That's all it is." Thanks for the help, Mom, you unaware, selfish idiot.

I made a scoffing sound then sung that Sex Pistols problem song, loudly, eventually realizing I was the real problem, as usual. I chastised myself in my head. At least she'd cared enough to get me here.

I decided I was so selfish and rotten that my punk name was Sid Selfish or Van-Van Rotten or Van Vicious... or Vicious Van Rotten.

Definitely: Vicious Van Rotten. Sounded like punk royalty to my angry ears. I had been a huge fan of the Pistols for years, but I could really identify with punk rock more than ever at that very moment.

I caught the train to the airport. For most of the train trip I worried about making my flight. Mom had made me all worried, as usual.

I made it to the airport and hustled up to security and passed through quickly.

After, I thought again about what I was wearing that day. I knew wearing pressed and creased khakis and a dark plaid golf shirt had been the way to go, since I was in a hurry. They always search me when I dress how I usually dress, casual but with so much flavor and color.

I wondered: Do the terrorists have fashion sense these days? Or is it just the drug smugglers that know how to dress down with flair?

I still had over thirty minutes to wait, so I bought a Fast Company magazine with Montgomery Burns of the television show "The Simpson's" on the cover.

"You have all the boorish manners of a Yaley," I said aloud to myself outside my gate, doing an impression of Mr. Burns, embarrassed about how I acted today, for the past few days, this year, throughout my childhood, which has extended to age 34 and 10 months.

Then I went off in tangential thought again: It has always intrigued me that Yale graduates founded the University of Georgia. I wonder if that is where we got our game day manners? I'm occasionally one of the worst behaved adults in the country. That was probably one of Mr. Burns' best lines ever. Only a Harvard snob could think that a Yale snob is truly boorish. Conan and those other Harvard pricks that wrote for The Simpsons are rather clever, though.

"All the boorish manners," I repeated again to myself. Vicious Van Rotten couldn't have phrased that better. At least I was leaving for California, I thought, trying to cheer myself as I breathed in a gulp of the artificially antiseptic air of the ATL airport.

I'd land in SFO soon enough.

Further on the story:
"Get Inside...The VAN": GOLDEN STATE MISADVENTURES
is Van's memoir and true to him as a character. Though this
story is based very closely on my personal California travel
experiences, many of the people and places in this book
have fictitious names and some have fictionalized identifying
characteristics. I am real.

Author's primary website: www.hanvance.com

Publisher: www.silverstonepress.com

"God Bless, California. ... God Bless America." Van
Circa summer 2005